Unraveled

KATIE BROWN

Unraveled

A CLIMBER'S JOURNEY THROUGH DARKNESS AND BACK

MOUNTAINEERS
BOOKS

MOUNTAINEERS BOOKS is dedicated to the exploration, preservation, and enjoyment of outdoor and wilderness areas.

1001 SW Klickitat Way, Suite 201, Seattle, WA 98134
800-553-4453, www.mountaineersbooks.org

Printed in South Korea
Distributed in the United Kingdom by Cordee, www.cordee.co.uk

25 24 23 22   1 2 3 4 5

Contributing editor: Chris Weidner
Copyeditor: Laura Lancaster
Design, layout, and cover illustration: Jen Grable
All photographs by the author unless credited otherwise

Library of Congress Cataloging-in-Publication Data
Names: Brown, Katie, author.
Title: Unraveled : a climber's journey through darkness and back / Katie Brown.
Description: Seattle, WA : Mountaineers Books, [2022] | Summary: "Renowned rock climber Katie Brown shares the story of her meteoric success in the 90s, including US and international wins, while she privately struggled with an eating disorder and worked to overcome an upbringing governed by strict, ever-changing irrational rules"—Provided by publisher.
Identifiers: LCCN 2022014784 (print) | LCCN 2022014785 (ebook) | ISBN 9781680515466 (paperback) | ISBN 9781680515473 (epub)
Subjects: LCSH: Brown, Katie. | Mountaineers—Biography. | Rock climbing. | Eating disorders in women.
Classification: LCC GV199.92.B82 A3 2022 (print) | LCC GV199.92.B82 (ebook) | DDC 796.522092 [B]—dc23/eng/20220408
LC record available at https://lccn.loc.gov/2022014784
LC ebook record available at https://lccn.loc.gov/2022014785

Mountaineers Books titles may be purchased for corporate, educational, or other promotional sales, and our authors are available for a wide range of events. For information on special discounts or booking an author, contact our customer service at 800-553-4453 or mbooks@mountaineersbooks.org.

Printed on FSC®-certified materials

ISBN (paperback): 978-1-68051-546-6
ISBN (ebook): 978-1-68051-547-3

An independent nonprofit publisher since 1960

TO MY DAUGHTER

I know I said that you couldn't read this book. Right now, it's not a story that you should have to hold. But I hope that someday, when you are much older, you do.

I love all the parts of you, every nook and cranny that makes you uniquely you.

CONTENTS

A NOTE TO THE READER

In this book, god is intentionally not capitalized. If there is a god, it is not the one I grew up believing in. Additionally, weight in number form is never mentioned. Disclosing any number on a scale can be incredibly triggering and may lead some people to avoid seeking treatment.

Some names in this story have been changed, and certain events have been moved about in the timeline to preserve privacy. Everything written here is true to the best of my knowledge, memory, and the years of journals and letters I am lucky enough to have. I strove to be as factual and accurate as possible in telling this story; any errors are mine alone.

Sometimes, in the forest of the unknown, when it feels like darkness is coming to swallow you whole, there is no spotter, rope, or crash pad to catch you when you fall. You have only yourself to turn to. But sometimes that is all you need. If you are reading this book, you are still here—keep going. This story is for you.

PROLOGUE

The scenery changed from flat, grassy fields to jagged, broken rock formations. Clutching the steering wheel tightly, I drove around a bend as the canyon narrowed. Occasionally, a house dotted the edge of the road. How fitting that my family had ended up living here, amid walls of unclimbable rock.

I was going too fast, pushing the accelerator and pulling out into the next straightaway, the speedometer shooting upward. I felt sure in my judgment of how to operate within my ability. That awareness had kept me safe my whole life, whether speeding through the canyon or climbing hundreds of feet above the ground. But everything else I was unsure of.

My car's engine rumbled, mimicking the panic in my belly. At age twenty, I had won every national climbing competition I had ever entered, including a World Cup title and several international events. I'd become the first woman to climb 5.14 on my first try, graced the pages of *Rolling Stone* and the *New York Times*, and appeared on national television. In spite of my accomplishments, I was terrified. I was going to talk to my mom. About everything. I was more afraid of this single conversation than I had ever been of any climb or competition.

My new therapist had said that talking to my mom might help me find a way through the darkness I lived with. That if I confronted her, maybe a weight would be lifted.

"But I'm scared of how she will react," I'd said. "You don't know my mom. Sometimes, well, she's really hard to talk to."

"You are not responsible for her reaction," the therapist responded soothingly. "You can only control your actions, not someone else's response. Letting go and forgiving is about what you do—not what they do."

"Ok," I replied, still unsure.

"For you to be able to move on, I think you need to share with her how you feel. Then you won't be carrying around this heavy load anymore. And you might be surprised at how she responds. She's your mom, after all, and only wants the best for you."

You mean she wishes she were me, I'd thought, before I could stop myself.

Nevertheless, there I was, driving up the canyon. I imagined a moment where I told her how I felt, and she apologized and told me it was ok. Maybe I'd feel something I'd never felt around a parent, something I imagined other children felt around their parents. Comfort. Safety.

For a moment, I felt hopeful. Excited even.

I pulled into the driveway of a house set so close to the road that the whine of passing traffic and joyriding motorcyclists provided constant background noise. The house was small and military green, with a flat front and asymmetrical peaked roof. Jagged concrete steps led up to a wire grate in front of the door. It tipped back and forth, clattering, as I stepped up to go inside.

From the entrance, I could see past the wood stove, into the kitchen. There used to be a wall blocking the view, but long ago my mom had taken a sledgehammer to the drywall, peeling it away to the studs to open the space and let in more light. Of course, the remodel had never been finished. She was waiting on my dad to complete it, and sometimes, I think it was the waiting that had driven her to madness.

"Mom!" I called into the backyard. She was pulling weeds, maniacally making a trail that would loop around the steep, unusable hillside. "Can I talk to you?"

She used a rope rigged with knots to descend the hill. We stepped into the house and settled in the kitchen, making tea with too much vanilla creamer, until it was sickly sweet. I wavered, unsure how to start, but finally blurted out what I had come to say.

"So, I don't know if I told you, but I started seeing this therapist. She had this idea that I should talk to you about some stuff that's been bugging me."

Her eyes narrowed, her expression already defensive.

"Is she a Christian?"

"Huh? Yeah. Yeah, I found a Christian counselor." I took a deep breath and dove in again, before I could chicken out. "Anyway, so you know how I had an eating disorder."

"You didn't have an eating disorder—you had Crohn's disease."

I took a step back. Although I had expected this response, it still shocked me. Already, confusion began to sprout in my mind.

"No Mom, I did. . . . I mean, I think I did."

The truth that I had been so sure of only moments ago was slipping away. *Was I crazy? Did I make that up? But no, no, I definitely had an eating disorder.* If nothing else, I was sure of that one thing.

"Anyway," I continued, shaking my head as though trying to dislodge water clogged in my ears, "sometimes I feel frustrated with how lost I feel right now. I get stuck on these moments growing up when there were opportunities I could have taken, but you know, I wasn't allowed to . . ."

"So you think I ruined your life?" She cut me off, setting down her tea abruptly. It sloshed over the rim and onto the laminated counter. I looked at the fridge behind her, avoiding her eyes. Sometimes what I saw in them—well, to me, it felt like hate.

I had known this whole "confronting my mom" thing was a bad idea. The therapist had been wrong. Why didn't I *ever* listen to my gut? It was as if my gut was broken in more ways than one. My heart started to flutter. I needed to get out of this situation.

"No, no, Mom. Of course I don't think you ruined my life. I know that I've had a great life, that I should be thankful. That's not what I'm trying to say." Already I could feel my voice wavering, tears building behind my eyes. The doubt flooded me now, pressed me down.

"I gave up everything for you. What opportunities? If you didn't have opportunities, it was because you wouldn't even talk to people. I had to do everything. We did everything according to how you wanted it."

As I continued to question my version of reality, other familiar feelings rose to the surface. That I must be wrong. That maybe what she said was true. We *had* always visited climbing areas that I wanted to go to. *I* had decided what I ate. Sometimes I'd even felt like I was the parent. So why did it still feel like she was the one in control all the time?

Panic and helplessness took over as my chest constricted and I grew more confused. Soon, I knew, I would do anything, even hurt myself, to eradicate that feeling.

"Yeah, I know . . ." I stuttered. I tried again. "It's just that sometimes, there were things I feel like I could have done to learn how to get better as a climber, except I would have had to do them without you . . ." I could feel myself losing steam as I thought about the silent, selfish teen I had been. I kept my gaze averted.

She cut me off again. Her voice was louder. "I went with you to protect your purity from evil."

I could feel the tide of self-hatred washing over me. *Maybe it is all my fault. Maybe she's right.* I was so selfish. *Why doesn't it ever feel ok?* I wanted to rip out my heart, say I was sorry over and over, even if I didn't know why, just to make it stop. But it was too late.

I zeroed in on the fridge and disconnected, not wanting to hear what I knew was coming. There was a picture of me on the door, an old advertisement from The North Face taken on a sport route in Rifle, Colorado, when I was eighteen—one of my first trips without my mom. I hadn't climbed the route the day of the photo shoot, so in a way, the advertisement was a lie. Maybe my mom was right. I couldn't seem to figure out how to live with her *or* without her.

Holding up the ad were a couple of hand-painted magnets, things I had made as a kid. My mom made a lot of crafts with us when my brother and I were young. She must have loved me, must love me. I mean, my dad never did things with me. At least she did. A lot of kids probably didn't have that. Nothing made sense. I snapped back to what she was saying.

". . . and look what happened when I didn't go with you? I should have forced you to talk to people. You think I ruined your life? I gave up everything for you. *You are such a selfish bitch!*" She slapped me, whipping my face to the side.

I had heard those words—*selfish bitch*—so many times. Something in me cracked. I screamed and grabbed her thick dark hair by the roots, pulling her scalp. The hurt exploded out of my chest. "STOOOOP!" I screamed.

She looked shocked and stumbled to the side. My brother was the one who usually fought back, not me, so she was caught off guard. Realizing that I had started something physical, I suddenly froze with terror. When my grip slackened, my mom grabbed my hair. I mentally drifted away even as our hands clawed at each other. We screamed, slapped, pulled hair, and hit one another.

Finally, we pushed each other away, chests heaving from exertion and adrenaline. My skin stung and my scalp tingled. I had strands of her hair stuck between my sweaty fingers, and my whole body was shaking with sobs. I backed up, away from her, bumping into the fridge. Sometime during our tussle, we had rotated in the kitchen.

"I'm sorry," I said hoarsely.

I went to my old bedroom and closed the door tightly. Huddled in the corner, I rocked myself while I cried, stroking one hand against the soft skin on the inside of my other arm, a self-soothing trick I first started using when I was very young.

Later, I would write a note, asking for her forgiveness. That's how it usually went: me apologizing, even if I didn't know what I had done—anything to make it ok. But that night, as I lay on the floor, I also said goodbye to the mother who existed in my imagination.

I never went back to that therapist.

———

Almost two decades later, I stand in the bathroom and stare down at the silvery, puckered lines fanning out from my belly button—a reminder of carrying my baby girl. Below this bundle of skin, still slightly loose for my frame, is the small swell of my lower abdomen that no amount of exercise will shrink. My body reminds me of my mother's. While hers bears the marks of two babies stretching and moving, my abdomen bears a small, thin scar where my daughter was pulled from me.

I am thankful for that scar. It sets me apart. In my mind, my mother's stretch marks are deeper, thicker, the swell of her abdomen slightly more obtuse. I feel I am winning the unspoken contest she and I have been in since the day I was born—a contest I wish I could escape.

In some ways, she and I are the same, and that thought terrifies me, particularly now that I am raising a girl of my own. I had hoped for a boy, but out she came, precious, perfect, and tiny. Now it is my job to break the cycle—a heavy responsibility that weighs on me every day.

I glance up at my face in the mirror, yellow light casting dark shadows on my thinning, aging skin. Years of trying to make sense of ancestral pain has left its mark.

I remember sitting on a toilet in another bathroom, a long time ago, my naked mother looking down, dismayed, at the same marks and swell of belly. There is a visceral scent that pulls me back to that place. It speaks of a relationship without boundaries, where the line between parent and child blurs. One personality will nearly obliterate the other, until time and age—two forces that cannot be manipulated or silenced—force their distinction. Sometimes, when my body reminds me of her, I struggle to maintain my composure. Each time I am overwhelmed with disgust for myself—as though by scent alone I am doomed to become her.

CHAPTER 1
KETCHUP

I was born in Denver, Colorado, at the tail end of 1980. My dad had gotten a VA home loan, and subsequently bought into a new development on the outskirts of the city, where houses were more affordable and provided more space for two kids. It made his commute to his job as an accountant longer, but it was worth it to my parents.

Many days, he would get home at dinnertime to see my mom riding her ten-speed bicycle toward the house from the opposite direction, my toddler brother in a seat behind her and me strapped to her back. My mom had grown up skiing, canoeing, and ice skating—even a bit of mountaineering. She had been working at an electric plant when she met my dad, having recently dropped out of college to spend her time skiing and slalom racing. Being athletic and outdoors was sacred to my mom, and I will always be thankful for the many physical skills she taught us when we were young.

My brother, Scott, was two when I was born. People would often ask my mom how he reacted to suddenly having a sibling. She'd reply with some version of, "It was fine for him!" I wasn't that cute as a baby anyway, she would tell people, and Scott was so friendly that he got all the attention, while I hid behind my mom's legs.

It's true that Scott was outgoing and eager to please. He loved the things my mom did, like backpacking and skiing. When he was diagnosed with exercise-induced asthma at a young age, my mom decided the best solution was to exercise it out of him. By the time he was seven, Scott was running 5Ks, totally decked out in a sweatband

and knee-high striped socks, a cherubic smile on his face as he posed for pictures.

I, on the other hand, was a colicky, fussy baby who grew into an introverted kid with an intense need to be my own person. I didn't like the same things my mom and brother did, hated it when anyone copied me or when adults spoke to me like I was a little kid, and refused to be polite to strangers just because I was told to. Certain fabrics were unbearable to wear, the worst being stiff jeans or Sunday-morning tights that inevitably drooped uncomfortably in the crotch. I had to have my sleeve tucked into my mitten *just so*, and I refused to ride my bike without training wheels until my parents secretly raised them and then waited several weeks to tell me.

Loud noises—like the vacuum, a rain jacket that swished when you walked, a noisy restaurant, or a fight between my mom and brother—left me feeling overwhelmed and consumed by panic. My aunt once took me out to a fancy restaurant for my birthday. I wanted to go, but when we got there, the noise was too intense, too much to process. At the time, I didn't have the words to describe my feelings, and the sudden change in my demeanor confused my aunt.

From a young age, I was deeply fascinated by books. Reading became how I escaped from noises, sensations, arguments, or anything else that felt too overwhelming. I remember a Bible that sat on a low shelf in our house. I was allowed to circle all the words that I recognized, and I circled "the" and "and" for pages upon pages.

We also had a tall bookcase in our house, set next to the back door, and my mom kept many children's books on the bottom two shelves. My brother remembers a time when, at around two years old, I toddled toward those bookshelves and pulled out book after book. I was told "no" firmly and set down elsewhere. As soon as my mom turned away, however, I headed straight back toward the books, dumping them on the floor again in a quest to find the perfect one. My silent acquiescence, followed by my silent rebellion, sent her over the edge. In a rage, she threw me over her knee. It wasn't the first or the last time, but this time she didn't stop spanking me.

It went on and on. I cried and screamed, until finally my brother stepped in on my behalf.

"You know that look," Scott recalled years later. "We've all seen it. You look in her eyes and you can tell that she's just gone."

Later, my mom thanked my brother for making her stop.

Mostly, though, it was belts or paddles used for spanking. I have a clear memory of the closet where the belts hung. The worst threat was my dad's thick, black leather belt, cracked on the edges and bearing a heavy brass buckle. I also remember the drawer where the paddles were kept. Bought at the grocery store, they were the kind with the red rubber ball stapled to a stretchy string. The ball, string, and staple were removed, and the remaining thin, wooden paddle was placed in the drawer next to my parents' bed. When a paddle cracked or broke, a new one would replace it.

I remember lying over my mom's knees on that bed—the same bed with the brown patchwork bedspread I would crawl under when I had a nightmare—quaking with fear, staring into her bathroom, and waiting for the punishment to begin. But the actual spanking part is gone, buried in the recesses of my mind.

When I was four, my IQ was tested. During the test, the examiner asked me a series of word associations.

"Bicycle," she said.

"Something to ride on," I responded.

"Ears."

"I have two."

"Hat."

"Put it on your head."

"Letter."

"Stamp," I said. And on and on.

And then the examiner said, "Knife."

"Something to stab people."

I don't know why I said that. Perhaps the darkness that I would feel later was already brewing. Nature versus nurture, the age-old question.

One day in my third-grade music class we sat in a circle, crisscross applesauce, knees touching, singing a song and clapping in rhythm. The girl next to me bounced her knee up and down in time with the beat, bumping into me each time. The rhythmic thumping against my body was too much.

"Please stop," I told her.

She bounced her knee up and down again, staring straight at me in defiance. *Thump, thump, thump.* I wanted to scoot over, but my other knee was already pushed into the kid next to me.

"Stop knocking into my knee," I said again.

She stared straight ahead and kept going. I pushed her knee off of mine and tried to scoot back. She moved closer and kept going. So I punched her.

I was, of course, sent to the principal's office straightaway. While I sat in a big chair with wooden arms and itchy fabric, someone called my mom. I was terrified, with a capital *T*, of what she would do when she found out, but when the sound of her voice floated out of the school office phone, I could hear her laughing. It could be difficult in our house to predict what would, or would not, lead to punishment.

My mom would often tell people that my brother's arrival had been like getting a cake, and I had been the icing on top. It had taken her a long time to get pregnant, so having not just one but two kids was something of a miracle for her. She had prayed for a girl because she had such a close relationship with her mom, whom she lost to Alzheimer's before I was born, and she longed to have that close relationship with her own daughter. Later, she would tell me that I was not just a daughter, but a friend—sometimes her only friend.

There were times when I felt that, too. One of my favorite memories with my mom is of us sitting on the back porch, on one of the rare occasions that she and I were home alone, watching hot-air balloons float by and eating carrot sticks with ranch, and cherry-pie filling straight out of the can.

"I lost my mom and even my mother-in-law," she would tell me, "but I gained so much more in having you."

Still, I always felt like I wasn't *quite* what my mom wanted me to be. I was too girly, not outdoorsy enough, too sensitive, too shy. I asked my brother once what he thought my mom's impression of me had been when I was little—before climbing. "Honestly?" he said. "A disappointment. You were just really girly, and that stuff was bad."

Scott had figured out early that the rules in our home were always changing and rarely made sense, but if you could frame your requests through the lens of an "outdoor adventure," then you could get away with just about anything. To him, it was a game. And games by design were meant to be won. He tried over and over to explain it to me, but, clinging to my ever-stubborn sense of self, I never did wrap my head around it.

One year he asked for a Columbia jacket that cost four hundred dollars—an absurd amount of money for our financially strapped family. I wanted a pink peacoat that was considerably less expensive and would make me feel like Samantha, the American Girl doll.

My brother got the coat he asked for, but I did not get the peacoat. I was devastated. Scott was baffled. "Why didn't you just ask for something more outdoorsy?" he asked me. But an outdoor coat wasn't what I wanted. It was too noisy, not soft enough, and I couldn't ask for something just because it was what my mom wanted me to want. To her, the pink coat would be useless, and probably evil somehow—as though people who wore peacoats were more likely to veer down the path of satan than people who wore Columbia jackets.

A lot of my childhood memories revolve around what was considered "good" or "bad"—what was allowed versus what was not. When I was still very young, my family moved to a house that my grandfather had built in a subdivision in Parker, Colorado. My earliest memories are of that house, and many of them revolve around our Baptist church and its teachings.

We had attended Christian churches as far back as I could recall, so the Sunday ritual of going to services felt as normal as breathing. There was the mad rush to get everyone ready in time, which for me meant putting on those dreaded, itchy tights. Then Scott and I would sit quietly while a pastor droned on until it was time for us to leave for children's church. Falling asleep or fidgeting excessively would result in threats of being taken out to the car for a spanking. In my memories, the services lasted for hours (though in reality it was probably only a half hour), the monotony broken only when the ushers passed around small glasses of grape juice and thin, paper-like wafers for Communion—the celebration of the blood and body of Christ, taken by those who had been born again, baptized, and washed clean from their sins by his salvation and sacrifice.

In the summer, I went to a camp called Id-Ra-Ha-Je, which stands for "I'd Rather Have Jesus." Every day we attended chapel, and one day the pastor put out a call for all those who wished to become "born-again" Christians. We were all born sinners, he said, and only by inviting Christ to live in our hearts could we become washed clean again and make it to heaven someday. He quoted John 3:16: "For God so loved the world that he gave His only begotten Son, that whosoever believeth in Him should not perish, but have everlasting life."

In a rush of emotion, I made my way to the front of the chapel with a slew of other campers and said a prayer, inviting Jesus to come live in my heart, to wash me clean of all my sins. That night, as I lay in my bunk in the cabin where I slept, I felt good. In a world where most of what I liked seemed to be somehow evil, where I often felt like a square peg in a round hole, I suddenly fit. I wasn't alone anymore if Jesus lived in my heart. I was born a sinner, inherently flawed, but now I was washed clean as freshly fallen snow.

A couple days later, the pastor made another call from the pulpit of the chapel, inviting anyone who had fallen off the narrow path we were called to walk to come forward and rededicate themselves to Christ. I joined in this as well, and my counselor later told me that I was the only camper to both "get saved" and rededicate their life to Christ all in the same week. I was nothing if not an overachiever.

Under the tutelage of our evangelical-leaning church and popular conservative radio programs like *Focus on the Family,* my
mom started introducing a lot of strict rules, especially for topics
like purity and discipline. Barbie dolls were bad, and I mustn't play
with them. Those curves would lead to wayward thoughts. "Secular"
music and television were also evil and would lead us astray. My
grandfather bought us a TV despite my parents' concerns, saying
that we were being deprived, and occasionally Scott and I would
get to watch *Mr. Rogers, Sesame Street,* or *MathNet* after school. But
that was it. If my mom went out, she would put her hand on the TV
after returning and check to see if it was warm. Fear of punishment
kept me from breaking the rules, but my brother was undeterred by
spankings and lengthy time-outs. He wasn't afraid to stuff a book
in his pants before a spanking.

Books were good, especially if they were Christian. I could often
be found lying on the floor of the living room, the carpet so old and
dry that it was the color of limestone dirt, reading about Mandy, a
good Christian girl who solved Nancy Drew–style mysteries. I would
disappear into her world, totally checked out from the comings and
goings of the house. My fifth- and sixth-grade teacher, Mr. Morgan,
fostered my love of reading, introducing me to stories like *A Wrinkle
in Time, The Secret Garden, Watership Down,* and *A Tree Grows in
Brooklyn.* Reading, it turned out, was one way for me to circumvent
the strict rules in our home, as books were often less closely monitored than other aspects of our lives.

Dancing, on the other hand, led straight to sex—especially school
dances, which were expressly forbidden. So were movie theaters,
roller rinks, and any other place of youthful congregation where
kids weren't closely monitored. Ballet was allowed, but other dance
styles considered too provocative were not.

———————

Every winter I would get croup, usually for weeks on end. Through
trial and error we found that hot, humid air was the best way to keep
my chest from getting too tight, my breathing too constricted. We
built tents over my bed and put several hot air humidifiers inside

them so I could breathe. The pictures on my bedroom walls eventually warped from the frequency of this treatment.

Sometimes my mom rubbed Vicks VapoRub on my chest, and I'd run up and hug my brother, stinking of menthol, just to torment him. Other times I would lie on a pillow on my side and my mom would cup her hands and softly paddle against my rib cage, manually breaking up the mucus in my lungs. Strangely enough, I remember croup with fondness. It was during those times that I felt the most nurtured, the most cared for.

Holidays were a funny time in our house. Halloween, satan's holiday, was a veritable Pandora's box of evil. My parents didn't react as extremely as our neighbors down the street, who would turn all their lights off and hide in the basement to avoid the kids asking for candy, but Scott and I definitely weren't allowed to participate. One year, my brother asked our mom if he could trick or treat. Shocked, she pushed him into a fence, shaking him and screaming, "Satan, get out of my child!"

It was sometimes hard to predict what would be considered bad. You may one day unknowingly break rules you never knew existed, such as watching a movie at a friend's house or forgetting to also wipe down the counter when told to wash the dishes. As my brother got older, he fought back aggressively. My mom and brother would scream and hit and throw things at each other during brawls. I remember a kitchen stool once being hurtled through the living room. Another time, a hairbrush thrown at someone's head flew down the hall and struck my brother's door at such a high velocity that it became embedded there. For as long as we owned that house, jagged edges from the splintered, hollow core stuck out at all angles.

Christmas and Easter, of course, were important holidays, but they centered around the birth of Christ and his resurrection from the dead. I can't remember ever believing in Santa or the Easter bunny. As such, we always knew that presents came from our parents. One year, my brother and I found our presents hidden in the closet, so as punishment, they were taken away.

Nonetheless, we had several holiday traditions that I remember fondly. Every year we made summer sausage and fudge to gift to people in our neighborhood or church. My mom had always been artistic, and we would spend hours making Christmas ornaments or gift bags out of old wallpaper. And every Christmas Eve we would attend the candlelight service at church. My Aunt Erica, who Scott and I dubbed the "cool aunt," would sew or buy me a special Christmas dress. Those dresses were beautiful and a highlight of my year. I enjoyed the magic of the candlelight service. We'd sit in our darkened church, singing carols, each person holding a small candle, the wax slowly dripping down onto a paper holder. I'd look across the room at all the candles swaying in the darkness and feel the magic of Christmas as I sang along.

Sometimes after church we'd go to McDonald's for lunch. As a kid, I put ketchup on everything, from eggs to mashed potatoes to steak to broccoli. Consequently, I always needed more ketchup than what came with my Happy Meal. Invariably, I was told to go get it myself. But there was something about going up to the McDonald's counter, that I wasn't tall enough to see over, surrounded by a lot of big people, that felt like an insurmountable challenge.

"Just go to the front of the line and ask the cashier," my mom would say.

I couldn't imagine cutting in front of a long line of people, or how I would get the cashier's attention once I got there. I was sure the cashier wouldn't be able to see or even hear me. To top it off, everyone I had to cut in front of would be offended and angry at me for not waiting my turn.

It always turned into an argument, while I sat frozen and in tears, too terrified to comply. Eventually, in frustration, my brother would be told to go get the ketchup, and then he would get angry. "In my defense," he told me years later, "I was ten years old. My entire life I'd been conditioned to believe that you being shy meant that you were *bad*. So why would I want to do it? I was enabling you to do something bad—that's what they were telling me."

When I was eight I decided that I wanted to try gymnastics, so my mom registered me for a class. By the time we arrived on the first day, the class had already started. I looked through the large glass windows at all the kids, sitting in a perfect circle with toes touching. In unison, they stretched to one side in the straddle position. *If I go in late*, I thought, *the whole class would have to get up and move to make space for me. Everyone will look at me.* Again, the challenge felt overwhelming and impossible.

My mom grew frustrated. "I paid for this class. You either go in now," she told me, "or you don't do gymnastics." My insides felt like they were vibrating with anxiety. This was my one shot. How many times had I done this by now? I cried until snot ran down my nose, fear warring with desire inside me. But no matter how badly I wanted to try gymnastics, the terror of going into that class late was too much. And so I never did gymnastics.

Although many of my childhood memories are long gone, this moment has stuck with me. At eight years old, I learned that sometimes you only get one chance. If you are not strong enough, brave enough, or outgoing enough, you will never get another chance. Failure, especially repeated failures, are not an option. There are no do-overs.

From a young age I felt that who I was, the shyness in me, was not a character *trait* but a character *flaw*. In my mom's eyes, her children were a reflection of her, and I felt that I didn't fit her image. My shyness embarrassed her, but I felt powerless to change it. I was ashamed of this part of my personality. Rather than pushing me to become more outgoing, however, the idea that I was profoundly, inherently flawed pushed me deeper into myself, further away from my family and into the world of my imagination.

CHAPTER 2

HOW IT STARTED

As soon as I saw the rust-colored wall, shooting straight toward the ceiling in the center of the room, paneled with a variety of shapes and textures, I wanted to try it. Multicolored holds bolted to its surface looked like a yellow brick road, snaking its way to Oz, beckoning me to follow its path.

My mom wavered. "Are you sure you're going to do it? You can't bow out on me this time."

I was sure this wouldn't be like the gymnastics incident a few years earlier. There was no circle of kids that I'd be interrupting. No start time that we were late for. I was a newly minted twelve-year-old, and nothing scary was standing in my way. A twenty-something REI employee tied me in and belayed me. After I reached the top, he started lowering me back down.

"Do most people go up that easily?" my mom asked him.

"Nope," he replied.

A few years prior, my parents had transferred my brother to a private Christian school in downtown Denver, after my mom became concerned about the bad influences in public school. After they were let out for the day, Scott and a friend, Peter, would often go to a nearby climbing gym called Thrill Seekers. It was Peter who gave me my first pair of climbing shoes, an old-school high-top pair, which I wore to school in sixth grade because they matched my outfit. I remember walking to the bus stop, dressed in my red, blue, and yellow jester-style leggings and marveling at my awesome new shoes, blue with a hot-green and pink circle on either side.

After that day at REI, I climbed a handful of times in Colorado gyms and once outside at nearby Castlewood Canyon, a state park strewn with hold-studded boulders and short cliffs. I came home from that adventure to find a tick lodged in my skin, which brought on a hysterical, panicked meltdown. I swore I would never climb outdoors again.

Not long after that, my dad's company transferred him to Kentucky. The South was uncharted territory for all of us, far from my mom's beloved mountains, but my dad told us he would have better hours and a more stable position.

My dad had always worked long hours—maybe to escape or because it was expected. Being a father means different things to different people, and to him I suppose it meant providing financially. He'd had a rough childhood, and had started working to help support his family when he was in the seventh grade. This was followed by the Vietnam draft and the marks it left behind. Sometimes, though, my brother and I wondered if maybe staying away was just easier for him than being at home. Either way, he was gone more than he wasn't.

I have only a handful of memories of my dad from when I was young. I remember once holding my dad's hand to go get donuts, his palm leathery with callouses and stained with motor oil from tinkering with cars. I also remember him trying to do my ponytail once, when my mom was away on a mission trip to Africa and he was, uncharacteristically, left in charge. My ponytail that day was lopsided and pulled at my scalp in strange places.

Typically, though, my "family" felt like my mom, my brother, and me, with my dad on the periphery—there but not there. Many years later, when I asked why he never came to any of my competitions, my dad responded that he felt his presence might be bad luck.

———————————

Just a couple days before the start of seventh grade for me, and ninth for my brother, my family arrived in a small town in Kentucky called Paris. We rented an old, white farmhouse while looking for a house to buy. Scott and I were noticeably different at our school. Kids would stop me in the hallway and ask if moose roamed the streets in Colorado. Meanwhile, I marveled at how Southern girls carried purses.

Once, sitting on the bleachers in the gym, another student said, "Oh my god, your legs are so hairy! That's disgusting." I was mortified. In Colorado, nobody had ever paid attention to my hairy legs. I went home and asked my mom if I could shave my legs, telling her that I had been teased at school for it. "Not until you start your period," she said. I didn't understand the parallel between shaving legs and periods, but I knew not to push her.

Later, my brother pulled me aside. "Katie," he said. "Just shave your legs. There are razors in the bathroom. It's not like Mom can put the hair back on once it's gone."

I had never before considered this option as I was a consummate rule follower, but several weeks later, I was sitting in the kitchen, running my hands up and down my calves, marveling at how smooth my skin was, while my mom talked on the phone. She glanced over at me and then said into the mouthpiece, "I've got to go." I don't remember if I got in trouble or not, but my brother was right. She couldn't put the hair back on, and that was the end of the leg-shaving rule.

Soon after we arrived, my mom started looking for new outdoor pursuits. The Red River Gorge, a world-famous crag of red, sculpted sandstone and the locus of hard, East Coast sport climbing, turned out to be about an hour away. There was also a climbing gym in nearby Lexington. While she and Scott were gone, I rode my bike in circles around a horse barn that sat unused on the property we rented. I rode around and around for hours, lost in my imagination, until I could do the whole thing with no hands, eventually completing a figure eight through and around the structure. My biking routine got lonely, though, and my mom and brother would return from climbing, gushing about how fun it was. Soon, despite my earlier protestations regarding ticks and other bugs, I started tagging along.

At first, my mom, Scott, and I would take turns climbing the steep, pocketed walls of the Red. My round, blue glasses kept bumping my arms when it was my turn, so I switched to wearing contacts. I spent hours in the eye doctor's office that first day, determined to get the contacts in by myself so that I could climb without impediment.

Eventually, my fifteen-year-old brother wanted to climb with his peers rather than his mom and sister, so then it was just my mom and me swapping belays on the weekends, climbing alongside peers we had gotten to know at the climbing gym. I quickly learned how to lead climb so that I could hang a rope from the anchor, allowing my mom a toprope, and I methodically worked my way through each grade at the Red—first climbing loads of 5.9s, then 5.10s, 5.11s, and so on.

I liked the challenge of climbing, the intricacies of the movement and the way I could find tiny things that would work for me but not for anyone else. If I twisted my body and tucked my hips into the wall just right, I felt almost weightless. My mind, normally so occupied with my imagination and thoughts, could finally focus on one simple, yet complex, thing.

It wasn't often that I enjoyed something that fit within the confines of my mother's rules. Climbing, however, was not only allowed, but celebrated, and it felt as natural to me as reading books. In fact, all outdoor pursuits were encouraged, even though going out to a movie or listening to music with friends were not. The irony of this was that, for my brother, climbing introduced him to partying and substance abuse far younger than anyone should be. Scott learned early on that if he said he was going climbing or mountaineering, he could get away with anything. It was easy for him, at just fourteen or fifteen, to say he was going climbing, and then find himself at a college party instead.

When we still lived in Colorado, Scott and a friend bought a length of rope that was sold by the foot at REI and tied webbing and carabiners together for quickdraws. Too young for a driver's license, they hitchhiked to Eldorado Canyon to climb. Once there, they handed over asthma medicine as collateral for someone's guidebook and spent the day climbing with questionable gear and little to no experience. This kind of adventure was applauded, but it also left both Scott and me adrift in the world, with a skewed idea of how to operate in it, unsure of what was right and what was wrong, what was safe and what was not.

Our new gym in Kentucky, Climb Time, had a 45-degree bouldering wall where the more serious climbers gathered. I would mostly
sit on the bench, too shy to jump in, and watch as the guys made
up problems, then took turns trying them. When my brother asked
why I came if I wasn't even going to climb, I just shrugged, not sure
how to explain that I was learning by observing. Certain climbers,
like sport climbing pioneer Jeff Moll, or David Hume, one of North
America's best young climbers in the 1990s, were beautiful to watch,
and I would try to imitate their fluid movements when I got the courage to take a turn. I wanted to climb like them. It never crossed my
mind that, at just five feet tall, I was a foot shorter, or that being
a girl made a difference. At the time, I didn't differentiate myself
from them. I was just another climber—maybe a quieter version
with long hair, but essentially one of the guys. Looking back now,
attempting the same problems as those climbers meant that I must
have been stronger than I realized.

Eventually, Ellen Hume, David's mom, suggested to my mom
that I enter one of the junior competitions. My family had plans to
travel back to Colorado for a summer vacation, so we found a junior
regional competition in Colorado Springs that the Hume family was
also attending.

At the time, junior climbing comps were still somewhat novel,
attracting a hodgepodge of teenagers with as many skill levels as
there were gyms across the United States. In the 1990s, they were
usually buzzing with many competitors, spectators, judges, and
belayers—a loud, somewhat informal affair. Anyone could enter, and
each contestant climbed the same route, or sometimes routes, tally-
ing up points on a scorecard. A competitor's high point—the farthest
point up the wall they reached before falling—denoted point value,
and climbers with the most points advanced to the next round. Competitions generally consisted of a preliminary round, a semifinal
round, and a finals round. By the finals, there were only a handful of
climbers left, and each one tried to get as high as possible on a route
that none of the competitors had previously tried or seen. Whoever
got the highest won.

Most climbing competitions were, and still are, designed so that each climber is onsighting—climbing a route that they haven't tried before, and of which they have no previous knowledge. Competitors weren't allowed to watch each other climb and spent most of the comp in isolation, a separate room or taped-off area of the gym. The isolation room was usually adjacent to the competition wall, though, so climbers could sometimes gauge their competitors' progress by the cheers of the crowd.

When it was their turn, each climber was ushered out to sit in a chair facing away from the route until a buzzer sounded. They then had a set period of time to make it to the top of the wall. Time wasn't meant to be a factor in difficulty competitions, but each climber was given a time limit so that there was a steady flow of competitors.

At that first junior regional competition in Colorado Springs, we were divided by gender and age, with me falling into the fourteen-to-fifteen-year-old girls category. There were several climbers from different categories going up different routes at the same time, so each route had a parent volunteer acting as the judge and recording how far each competitor got.

There were so many more young climbers than in Kentucky, both girls and boys. At fourteen, I didn't know that I should conserve my energy while climbing, and when it was my turn, I fell off both the preliminary route and the semifinal route. But still, I made it higher than most, and ended up in second place going into the finals. The Red River Gorge, with its long, endurance-focused routes, had inadvertently prepared me well.

We climbed the final route by ranking, so I was second to last. I made it up the steep but narrow headwall, then fell attempting to pull out onto a horizontal roof at the top of the wall. The last climber, however, fell low on the route, which meant that I had climbed the highest and had won my age division. No one was more surprised than I was.

Afterward, some fellow competitors and their dad invited my family to go with them to see a movie. It's not that I had never been to a movie theater, but this kind of movie was a whole other ballgame. So when my mom said yes, it was a shock. As we sat in the dark theater, watching *Pulp Fiction* play on the screen, I wondered what the *hell* was happening. Suddenly *this* was ok? Becoming a part of climbing culture seemed to mean that the rules were changing, again.

Winning the competition in Colorado Springs qualified me to compete at Junior Nationals, held at the Solid Rock Gym in San Diego. While I have absolutely no memory of it, I have watched the video footage. In it, the camera pans to a series of white plastic chairs facing away from the climbing wall. It's 1995, long before fancy floor mats and colorful, aesthetically undulating climbing walls became the norm. Instead, the wall is vertical, tan, and gritty. The floor is covered in gravel, the kind that leaves your climbing shoes white with dust. Fourteen-year-old me sits down in a plastic chair that tips precariously on the gravel. I'm not yet tied into the rope, nor are my shoes on. My ponytail is still tucked into the back of my shirt, which looks as though I have just hastily thrown it on. A judge faces me, holding a clipboard to score my climb. As I tie my knot, the loudspeaker announces that there are "twenty-five seconds to start time." I don't pause or look around. The man behind the camera says, "Uh-oh, twenty-five seconds until climb. She's gotta get her shoes on. That's a bad spot to be, isn't it."

The only giveaway that I've even heard the announcement is when my climbing shoe slips out of my fingers and lands in the gravel. I snatch the shoe up and put it on.

"Climbers ready, climbers begin," says the announcer. I lean back in my chair to slip on my second shoe. My face looks slack and composed.

"Well, she hasn't panicked yet," says the man behind the camera.

"Is that your daughter?" someone off screen asks.

"No, oh no," he laughs nervously. "We just met her today."

I'm still lacing my shoes. In the background, my mother, a volunteer judge, holds a clipboard as she watches another climber.

Finally, I stand up to face the wall, and the judge shows me the route. The competitor on the route next to me is most of the way up by now. I casually, almost obtusely, study the route before climbing, as if I am reveling in being so far behind, such a long shot—the girl who didn't even have her shoes on when the clock started.

The first route is a short, slightly overhanging toprope on a gray wall about thirty feet tall. I climb easily to within a few moves of the top, where a distinct crux section gives me pause. I try a few different body positions, going up and down, debating which hand to move first. There's no rush. I eventually go with my right hand, then pull the remaining few moves to the top.

Next up is a steep lead route with a roof about halfway up. The moves don't seem too challenging as I climb the wall, past sponsor banners promoting PowerBar, Five Ten, Bison, and others. I clip the anchor, revealing no emotion.

The hardest route comes last: a rightward traverse off the deck, followed by a steep wall leading past two roofs to a headwall finale. The first two competitors fall low, at the first and second bolts. Five more young women attempt the route, each gaining ground on the last, yet all falling well short of the anchor. Then it's my turn. Despite climbing for only two years, I pass the spots without hesitation where the others had struggled and failed. As I watch my fourteen-year-old self easily top out the finals route, still largely unanimated, I can't help but wonder what I was thinking, what I was feeling.

After Junior Nationals, we heard about an adult national competition being held in San Francisco. Up until that point, juniors rarely competed in adult competitions, so there was no official age limit. Several of us, including David Hume, Chris Sharma, Tommy Caldwell, and Beth Rodden, decided to give it a try. The situation was somewhat unprecedented. Our band of teenagers not only did well against the climbers in San Francisco, most of whom were in their twenties and thirties, but stood on the podium, with Chris handily winning the entire competition.

It was in San Francisco that I first met Robyn Erbesfield-Raboutou, the reigning world champion, in what would be one of her last competitions before retiring. She struck me as thoughtful and knowledgeable, confident and brave, and I wondered if I could be as good as she was someday.

Junior Nationals had earned me and my new friends invitations to Junior Worlds in Laval, France, and soon I was off on my first international trip, with my mom chaperoning and coordinating the USA Juniors team. It was a big group, with kids of varying ages, and several parents. We were each given a team jacket, a heavy, turquoise-and-black parka that came down to my knees. I could have easily passed for a ten-year-old. I climbed my way to a win in Laval, but looking back at photos and videos, I can see that I had already begun to grow thinner.

About a year prior, I had decided that sugar was bad. It happened at about the same time that we moved to Kentucky, when climbing was taking precedence in my life, and I was beginning to compete. I don't remember what precipitated the decision, but I know I had started to feel that my life was out of control, and focusing on what I ate gave me a sense of calm. I started looking at labels on food to learn how many grams of sugar were in each item, and then slowly eliminating as many grams as possible. Feeling so organized and in control was comforting and solid.

For me, getting thinner was never about climbing harder. In fact, initially I didn't even correlate controlling what I ate with getting thinner. I've always operated more on emotion than strategy. Although climbing and food would eventually become so wrapped up in one another that I couldn't separate them, in the beginning it was more about a feeling of calm, success, tidiness I got from knowing that I had total control and organization over this one thing that I had decided was off-limits.

After I decided that sugar was bad, I shifted to fat, zeroing in on those grams. Soon, everything I ate was fat-free this and fat-free that. Eventually, carbohydrates became bad. Within a few months, I didn't even need the labels anymore. I could tell you exactly how many calories were in everything I ate.

After Junior Worlds, most of the competitors and parents went home, but several of us went to Robyn's house near Laval to climb. My mom came as a chaperone. It was a training camp of sorts, and the first semiformal climbing instruction I had ever received. I was thrilled, enamored of all that Robyn seemed to know, by the energy and attention she seemed to want to impart, and by the potential for progress I felt simmering inside me. I felt ready to explode under her skilled tutelage.

At Robyn's we would climb for hours, seemingly indefatigable. I had already dropped quite a bit of my natural weight, but my energy was sky-high. One of the tricky things about an eating disorder like anorexia is that, at first, you feel light and unstoppable. Plus, I had developed a habit of consuming a lot of fiber, which kept my body empty, emphasizing that amazing feeling. My mom usually had a laxative tea around the house, and in France she bought me a fiber cereal that looked like twigs.

At one point, noticing that things were a bit off, Robyn tried to talk to my mom about how I was eating. She was the only person—that I'm aware of—who ever attempted to confront my mom about my developing eating disorder. My mom later told me that Robyn was possessed by the devil, that the whole place was surrounded by evil. We were being attacked by satan at Robyn's house. Any possibility of staying to climb in France or ever going back to Robyn's to train was effectively eliminated.

CHAPTER 3
WRITING IT DOWN

In the story *Anne of Green Gables*, a lonely orphan girl, "Anne with an E," has a special "window friend" named Katie. And while Katie is simply Anne's reflection, her presence offers comfort and companionship, someone to talk to when all the adults in Anne's life respond negatively to her personality.

I have always admired Anne. No matter what adversity she faced, she kept a firm hold on her sense of self, refusing to change or stop speaking her mind. Like Anne, I had many imaginary friends growing up, and they gave me a whole world of companionship as a child. As I got older, my journal took the place of those "window friends."

I started journaling on February 16, 1996. Although still fifteen, I was traveling more and more for climbing competitions, having succeeded in adult national events as soon as I began entering them. The cash prizes helped cover my travel costs, and junior competitions had quickly fallen by the wayside.

I don't really remember whose idea it was to jump into that level of competition, but I do remember being ok with it at the time. On the other hand, I also had no idea how to plan strategically to become a competitive adult climber at the national level. My world was moment by moment, with no thought of the future. I missed nearly three months of ninth grade while my mom and I went from climbing gym to climbing gym, plunging me into a career I was wholly ill-equipped for. Almost overnight, my life condensed into climbing, my mom, and god. The best I could do was hold on and try not to get thrown overboard.

One Sunday in Chattanooga, Tennessee, we found ourselves looking for a church. We no longer attended our local Baptist church regularly, and climbing always took precedence when we were out of state. But sometimes, if my rest day coincided with a Sunday, we would try to go to a morning church service.

As we drove toward Precept Ministries, a Christian conference center and camp where my mom had studied, she said she wanted me to meet someone. We followed a long drive up to a farm-style building at the top of a small hill, not expecting anyone to be home. Carol, however, greeted us at the door, a flicker of annoyance at our surprise arrival casting a shadow over her eyes. Just as quickly, it disappeared, and she invited us in for tea.

The house was dark and cluttered with plush items, enveloping me in its warm interior, like the hugs I was unable to give or unwilling to receive.

"You've always been a cold person," my mom had told me more than once. "You never liked affection or being hugged." I had long accepted this as truth. After all, I was resistant to any kind of human touch, particularly from my mom, and had barely any memories of giving or receiving affection. Yet a deep part of me yearned for a hug, a soft place where I could feel cared for, to be wrapped in comforting arms that held me close, where I could lay my head on someone's chest and sob. I didn't understand or like this part of myself, so, like many other aspects of my personality, I tucked it away quietly and stood rigid, untouched and unavailable.

My mom greeted Carol, her megawatt smile in full force as she presented me, her prized possession. Fresh off my win at Junior Worlds, I was gold. I stood quietly as Carol gazed at me, her eyes laser focused.

My mom bristled. I could feel her moods like a palpable presence. Too much attention had shifted away from her, so I retreated further into myself and hoped we wouldn't stay long.

Carol sat us down and poured tea for us. She handed mine over in a delicate china cup, set atop a matching saucer. It was white, with a gold rim, striations in the china, and covered with tiny pink flowers.

"How are you feeling?" Carol asked me, pointedly. "I sense that you feel lost, empty. Do you feel that way? What do you wish for yourself?"

I wanted to answer, to spill my guts, but my mouth refused to speak. I was pulled, inexorably, toward anyone who expressed care and concern for me. Whether Carol's concern was real or not, in that moment I felt seen. Still, no words came out. My tongue refused to move and my mind was fuzzy with the confusion between what I *wanted* to say and what I felt like I *should* say and whether either of those things were the *right* thing to say.

My mom, accustomed to answering for me, started to respond, but Carol quieted her. She seemed unfazed by my silence, something my mom hated about my personality.

Then Carol began to tell me about myself. "You are standing under a tree," she said, "covering yourself with it, hiding from the world. You are watching others, wishing to join, but feeling different, alone, unable to participate."

Yes! My tortured fifteen-year-old heart screamed. *Yes!*

"Your eyes hold sadness and pain but also empathy. You are afraid that your innermost desires will not come to pass. A premonition that what could be will somehow be lost, that things will fall apart almost before they can begin."

Tears ran down my cheeks at her words. My mom was stiff at my side.

"But let me tell you," she said. "You will live to see the end times. You will be part of god's army. He has a purpose for you, a big one, or he would not have put you in this place. You have a special, tender heart, and this will be your coming out. Your mom will only have three, maybe four years left with you."

I remember my mind snagging on this bit. *Why?*

"Do you want to stay here and talk more?" Carol asked me. I understood it was an invitation for me alone.

"We're supposed to meet someone to climb," my mom quickly offered. She kept her annoyance in check.

Everything Carol said sounded crazy, but at the same time I desperately wanted to believe there was a reason that I was the way I was, that I was in so much pain, that things were happening that felt out of my control—I wanted to know that there was hope. I wanted to stay with Carol, to leave everything about my life far behind. But instead, I left to go climbing with my mom.

I had never really thought about whether I wanted to climb or compete. I wasn't—I'm still not—sure if I liked it or not. I think I did, in the beginning, but after I started winning, it quickly took on a life of its own. It hadn't even occurred to me to think about what I wanted. I was too busy trying to guess what I was *supposed* to want.

On our way out the door, Carol gave me a journal covered with watercolor flowers, the teacup I had been drinking out of, and a book called *Hinds' Feet on High Places*.

My mom ignored me on the drive out. My entire life had just shifted, but she'd already erased the conversation from her mind. *I feel like she's jealous*, I thought. Wishing we could talk about it, I poured my heart out into my journal that night.

For more than ten years, I journaled nearly every day. I already considered myself a born-again Christian, but after I met Carol, god became my solace, my refuge, my judge, and my confidante—an invisible, silent force that I would try every day to please and understand, much in the same way I tried to please and understand my mother. Every day I read the Bible and then poured my heart into my journal, trying to make sense of my life, trying to be as "Christian" as possible.

Hook, line, and sinker, as they say.

My newfound, intense relationship with god became a fresh source of contention with my mom.

"I feel like I'm losing you," she told me.

To who, god? I wondered. *She's jealous of god now?* It felt like she needed to experience everything I was experiencing, until I wasn't sure who I was, what I wanted, or what was right. I couldn't tell where I ended and she started, or vice versa.

"I have to put god before her," I wrote in my journal. *"I know I need to be there for her, but this is something I need. Mom wants to be a part and understand, but she can't. Is that being selfish?"*

The conversation with Carol had made me feel special, unique, like my existence had a purpose. Usually I felt like I was getting everything wrong, but Carol had given me something to strive for, a reason to be a better person. Along with the Bible, I read the book she gave me every day. It seemed to be saying that I just needed to suffer through adversity and be "Acceptance-with-Joy."

Hinds' Feet on High Places, written by Hannah Hurnard in 1955, is an allegorical novel about a girl named Much Afraid who must learn how to live a Christian life. Over and over she discovers that there are no obstacles in her life that god cannot overcome. Much Afraid preaches that the only way to reach her personal "high place" is by "learning to accept, day by day, the actual conditions and tests permitted by god, by a continually repeated laying down of her own will and acceptance of his as it is presented to us in the form of the people with whom we have to live and work, and in the things which happen to us."

The problem was that I didn't see this book as fiction, nor was it presented to me as such. When I tried to adopt Much Afraid's way of thinking, I understood it to mean that I shouldn't try to change my increasingly less-than-ideal circumstances. Rather, I should sit back and accept it as the will of some higher being. Instead of taking agency in my life, I fully accepted the teaching that my struggles were nothing more than a trial, one willed by god, that I must endure in order to be "good enough" in his eyes.

One such test happened that spring. My English class had been studying *Romeo and Juliet,* and for a field trip, we were going to see the play.

"I would like to go," my mom said when I gave her the permission slip. "Ask your teacher if I can go."

Field trips had been a sticking point between us as far back as I could remember. Classmates would always tell me how awesome my mom was after field trips. She was active, engaged, like one of the kids. But I wanted to go on this field trip without my mom as a chaperone to see what it was like.

"It's not that I don't trust you. It's that this trip is something I'm interested in, too," she said over and over, her expression implying that this should explain everything.

"It's not that I don't want you around," I replied, trying to explain my position in a way that wouldn't put her defenses up. "It's just that I'd like to do one by myself. Plus, I'm not comfortable asking the teacher if you can come every time. It feels embarrassing."

Eventually, I won the argument and attended the play alone. When I got home, however, my mom was angry. Many hurtful words and tears later, I found myself begging for her forgiveness.

"Please," I said, crying jaggedly. "I'm sorry. I won't go alone again. Please forgive me!"

As usual, my journal was my safe place to vent. *"I need to pray for mom, it seems like she's really struggling with something. It's almost like she's wanting to experience and have what I have, and I don't understand. It almost makes me not want whatever it is that I have."*

Later, my mom gave me a note.

Katie,

I forgive you, but that does not take my pain and make it go away. Just as you want forgiveness, not for going or not going to the play, but because no matter what the cost you wanted to go alone and you want me to forgive you for not wanting me anywhere close and for not even asking your teacher if I could also see the play. I forgive you for wanting the play, the trip, everything, all to yourself.

Why? You didn't need my forgiveness because I mattered not in the least, you had your mind made up. Why is it so important that I forgive you? Maybe your own guilt? For what, is the question.

I forgive, like I have many times in the past and will again. But it will not take the pain away.

Love, Mom

My heart thudded in my chest, feeling at first like it was skipping beats, then slowing to nothing. I wanted to rip it out, just to make the hurt and confusion go away. Was I wrong for wanting to go to a play without my mom? I had wanted a little independence to see who I might be, or who I might become, in the company of my peers. Other kids' parents seemed to be ok with this.

I flipped the letter over, and there was more. The cursive scrawling had gotten bigger, loopier, as though her thoughts were coming at a more frenzied pace.

I've forgiven much more than that one thing but I hurt from every one and that does not go away. In France, it was constant spiritual warfare against the devil and his evil. As will Tucson be and has always been there, wherever you go. Prayer is a constant at those times and I do go, not because of you being drawn in but because of your purity and innocence that god is so dearly keeping within you for his purpose. My purpose is to see that it is maintained through being totally entwined to your and my (our) Lord, for your protection. So that when you go out on your own you will be equipped for every good work.

So, how did you fare today at the play? Did you rejoice in Him, or the opposite?

The letter finally ended, leaving me battered and empty, convinced that there would be evil wherever I went. What did that make me? Evil, too.

I wished I had never heard of *Romeo and Juliet*.

In March my mom and I headed to Nationals, held at a gym called Rocks and Ropes in Tucson, Arizona. Having not yet competed in many adult competitions, I was profoundly nervous. I had been unable to sleep the night before—a pattern that would repeat itself in future competitions. At the time, though, I was paranoid about my exhaustion, thinking that the fatigue would prevent me from climbing well.

A seemingly insurmountable number of competitors crowded into the isolation space. *There is no way I could possibly beat all of these people,* I thought.

My mom regularly told me to "climb not unto you, but unto god. Don't let them see Katie, let them see god. Have the attitude of a competitor, which is not to focus on doing well, but on doing your best as unto the lord. People need the love of Christ and need to see the difference in you. Concentrate on god and he will allow you to accomplish that which you are called to be. Finish this comp with the love and joy of the lord on your face."

The competition wall was tall and gray, built in the panel style popular in the late nineties and peppered with small roofs. I didn't do well in the semifinals, falling off the route lower than many competitors, but it was enough to squeak into the finals.

In the finals, competitors were allowed to pick the song that would play through the speakers while they climbed. I watched as each person handed a CD to a staff member. I didn't own any CDs. Since I wasn't allowed to listen to anything but Christian music, I wasn't familiar with any popular artists. Maybe Paula Abdul. I had heard her once at a birthday party a long time ago, and the lyrics, about being caught in a "hit and run," were so different from my world that the song was seared into my mind.

"Just play whatever," I told the staff member, uncomfortable. "I don't have music."

I looked around, feeling a deep divide between myself and my fellow competitors, and again thought how unfathomable it was that I could win against a group of such strong, grown women. Somehow that gave me solace, as though the impossibility of being "the best" took all the pressure off competing. I relaxed.

Since I was low in the rankings heading into the finals, I was called out of isolation early. Music blared from the speakers as I started climbing, some nineties rock song that I had never heard. It didn't matter. I was already gone—lost—as the climbing took over my mind and body. I felt nothing, not the pump in my forearms nor the fatigue in my muscles. I heard nothing, not the grating music or claps and cheers from the crowd as I moved past the previous competitor's high point.

I would be hard pressed to tell you any individual move of any climb that I have ever done onsight. Onsighting was a world where I felt completely, wholly at home. It's just see how far you can get before you fall, and give it your all. No do-overs.

I moved on pure instinct, something deep and primal inside me activating, my intuition finally able to bubble up to the surface and take over. Each move made perfect sense, as if the routesetters made the routes just for me. I felt an unspoken connection to them through the routes that they created.

I clipped the anchors—the sign that I had successfully finished the climb—and with that soft *click* of the carabiner, I came back to reality. The crowd cheered. My forearms suddenly throbbed. I had seen other competitors wave and smile as they were lowered, but as I hung from the end of the rope, I was once again back in my frozen body, filled with an unnamable shame. I averted my gaze as I was lowered. *I must seem like such a spoiled bitch*, I thought.

CHAPTER 4

EATING

Since I had missed so much of ninth grade, we decided that I should homeschool for my sophomore year.

"You can't tell anyone. It has to stay a secret," my mom told me.

I wasn't sure why she insisted on secrecy, but I was also accustomed to explanations that didn't quite ring true, but that I needed to accept nonetheless. As I walked the halls of my high school, I wondered how I was supposed to just disappear off the face of the earth at the end of the year.

"You won't have any friends," my brother said.

"I don't have any friends anymore anyway," I told him.

I used to have a small group of friends, but I started to pull away from them as my life grew more focused on competitions and controlling my food intake. When I was at school, I barely spoke to anyone. Over the next several months, I grew ever thinner, my attitude changing, becoming more morose, my silence deepening as what would be my last year in public school grew closer to the end. My world started to seem very small, as though I was living with blinders on.

I began to see enemies around every corner. I was convinced that my band teacher hated me because I was always traveling. I was convinced that my French-English teacher hated me too. A former straight-A student, I now had to read passages in my textbooks five or six times to understand them. I would be up until eleven each night after climbing, unable to focus on homework. In class I would fall asleep while the teacher droned on, the words incomprehensible to my foggy brain. When I was awake I was jittery, my leg bouncing up and down, and unable to focus.

It was better when I was outside, moving and distracted. Sometimes my forearms were so sore from climbing the day before that I could barely hold a pencil. That part I liked. Being sore made me feel like I had accomplished something, earned the right to sit there in school, sedentary and resting. But my grades slipped to Bs, which felt catastrophic.

There was a homeschooling group in Lexington, taught by a psychologist, for kids who couldn't attend traditional school. I thought that maybe I'd be able to meet people there who had weird lives like mine. Secretly, I also hoped that the psychologist would notice my "little problem with food," as I thought of it, and help me.

"I have to overcome this thing with food," I wrote in my journal, *"before it messes up my body."* But I didn't know how. I didn't really even want to. *"I'm trying to get better. . . . Actually, why do I write that? It's a lie. I'm not really trying. I feel like I have to hide."*

I wore long johns to school to stay warm, and, as the healthy fat disappeared from my face, wrinkles appeared in my cheeks when I smiled. At night, when I lay on my side, I had to put a pillow between my legs to protect the bones of my knees from knocking painfully together. I looked so old, and yet, paradoxically, impossibly young, as any sign of puberty came screeching to a halt.

My food restrictions had gone from odd to straight-up weird. One day I mixed up lettuce, pickles, tuna, and an assortment of raw vegetables in a bowl for lunch. When I opened my dish at the cafeteria table, kids started staring.

"WHAT are you eating?" someone said.

"Oh my god, what is that smell?" Someone else said as they leaned away. "It smells like fish."

I stared at them as pure, unadulterated panic—that I wouldn't be able to eat the food I had so carefully planned for, that I had earned, waiting through hours of hunger—filled me. Now I'd have to put away my stinky, gross lunch that I'd obsessed about all morning. My sit bones grated painfully on the hard lunchroom bench. The thick wool sweater that I'd borrowed from my mom's closet suddenly felt itchy around my neck, constricting my throat.

"Leave me alone!" I screamed. *"It's just food!"* Heads swiveled in my direction. The silent climber girl had spoken. Panting and mortified, I packed up my lunch and left the cafeteria. I headed outside to eat alone, hunched against the spring air that felt like an icy wind on my thin shoulders.

That night I awoke to the sound of my bedroom door swinging open, slamming against the wall. My light blinked on and I sat bolt upright in bed, terror coursing through me.

"YOU ARE KILLING YOURSELF!" My mom screamed at me, her hair crazed. I looked at my clock. It was a quarter to three.

"You're killing yourself!" She screamed again. "Look at you! I wish I could get as skinny as you so you could see how shitty you look! I am eating for you, and LOOK. AT. ME. Look at what you are doing to me."

I looked, and saw what I always saw. Sparkling blue eyes, dark hair. My mom was beautiful, petite but strong. But when she looked in the mirror, she must have been comparing herself to me—the food she ate out of worry for me, the weight she carried that I didn't, the opportunities she had lost through marriage and parenthood that I now seemed to be squandering in my desperate, starving attempt to become invisible.

She had written me a note the previous day, so in a way I knew this was coming. We often corresponded via notes, perhaps a byproduct of my maniacal journaling. I also shied away from any kind of verbal confrontation, so sometimes it was easier for us to communicate in writing than in words. I understood that she was worried, but screaming at me only made it worse.

What I wanted to say was, *I know. I feel myself dying, but I'm powerless to stop. I'm so exhausted from this thing that is controlling me that sometimes I don't know how to keep going. I don't want it. I want to be strong for climbing. I look at people who can eat normally and I'm so, so jealous. But screaming at me does not help. Not one bit.*

Instead, I said nothing and followed her to the kitchen, where I made a bowl of frozen yogurt and sprinkled pecans on top for extra calories. I swallowed spoonful after spoonful even though it made me feel so full that I wished I could die, and then I crawled back into bed, clutching my stomach, and waited for the sun to rise.

Several days later, I tagged along with my brother to climb at the Red. It was a rare opportunity to climb without my mom, who planned to meet us later. Scott, now seventeen, had saved up his money and bought a red Jeep that was falling apart. He had to pump the brakes to get them to work at all, sometimes slowly coasting into the car in front of him and landing with a soft tap on their bumper. If I was riding with him, we'd both hold our breaths to see if they noticed that we'd just run into them.

On that particular day, Scott picked up a friend in Lexington and they blasted a No Doubt album as the wind buffeted us through the Jeep's open windows. It was music we weren't supposed to be listening to, and I didn't know where he had gotten the contraband, but I loved listening to Gwen Stefani sing about being "just" a girl.

As we drove, we whipped past horse farms, white fences, grass so green it looked blue, and pillared houses that eventually gave way to rolling, treed hills. After we turned off the highway, the houses became ramshackle, with peeling paint and sagging roofs—the land that time forgot. Cars sat in front of the houses, grass growing up around them. Sofas leaned at odd angles, abandoned, with springs popping out, and pieces of long-forgotten farm equipment lay rusting on their sides. We passed a small, cedar-shingled cabin on the left that was barely wider than its white front door. Sometimes a person sat out on a small porch, smoking a cigarette or drinking a soda. When the door was open, we could see straight through the house, one door dividing the space into two rooms, and all the way out the back door, as though someone had cut a regular house in half.

Our first stop was Military Wall, where the exquisitely patterned sandstone featured countless holds—edges, pinches, pockets, jugs—and therefore some of the best moderate routes. Beginner climbers would test their mettle here, while the advanced crew used it as a warm-up. On that day it felt crowded, which gave me pause. My brother, already annoyed by the "little sister" vibe, told me, "You should have just waited for Mom then." But I hadn't wanted to wait for her. I liked being with someone other than my mom sometimes. Another thing that made me feel guilty. It seemed that no matter what I did or didn't do, I felt guilty. It was an inescapable, suffocating feeling.

Eventually, my mom arrived, and she and I headed to Left Flank, a conspicuous south-facing wall of compact rock that was decorated with ridges and grooves reminiscent of tree bark. Again I wanted to leave without quite understanding why, but instead I got on a route that I had been wanting to try, *Table of Colors*. Situated in an overhanging alcove peppered with large boulders, the climb was an area test piece—a must-do 5.13 for anyone capable of linking so many hard moves in a row. It was the hardest route I'd ever tried, but sometimes, I would look up at a climb and just know that I could do it, regardless of the grade. This was one of those routes.

I went up but fell at the crux, screaming in terror as I slammed into the wall. Frustrated with myself for falling, I got back on the route, letting my anger surge to the surface, taking the place of my fear. I tried again but couldn't figure out the moves—they felt awkward and out-of-balance. The route starts on a sheer, slight overhang fifteen feet left of a smooth corner and ascends via tiny, sloping pockets sometimes big enough for only two fingertips. The toughest moves are near the bottom, where climbers must link small holds to execute huge reaches.

"Take," I said, my voice whiny and petulant. I screamed again, drawing stares from climbers nearby, feeling on the edge of hysteria. I loathed myself when I failed, and sometimes gave in to outbursts. I kicked the wall and punched my thighs, not caring who saw me. My mom lowered me wordlessly.

When I was back on the ground, she whispered "Your attitude is ruining the day for everyone around you."

I said nothing in response. My attitude had been ruining things for people my entire life.

Instead, I curled up on a rock in the sun and fell asleep. Perpetually bone tired, I could fall asleep anytime, anywhere. A half hour later, I was ready to try again. I felt foggy and disoriented as I tied my knot, a rewoven figure-eight, through my harness. My fingers went numb early on the climb, but since I had rehearsed the moves through the crux, I knew where to go. My mind slipped into that familiar place where I was no longer mentally present, but simply a physical body, moving instinctively on rock. I no longer noticed my fingers or where I was.

After the last reachy crux move, I snapped awake, surprising myself and forgetting where to go next. I almost fell off from the shock. I was normally mentally checked out until I clipped the anchor at the top.

"Lower," I said to my mom, a commanding edge to my voice.

My mom had recently gotten a job at a travel agency because my dad was worried about finances. When I asked him about money, he said, "God must be testing us, seeing how much we can withstand."

I thought it was my fault, that my climbing and competing was the cause of our financial stress. I felt the implication was that our mounting credit card bills were because of me. Traveling, sometimes multiple times a month, to competitions certainly cost more than the prize money I'd won, less than two thousand dollars at that point.

I never paid much attention to the business side of my climbing career, so I don't know the details of it. My mom and I shared a bank account, email account, and phone number. She often answered emails for me and almost always answered my fan messages. She frequently opened my mail and deposited checks for me. She or my dad booked our travel and accommodations.

But still, my shoulders felt heavy with the weight of it. I decided not to enter any more competitions that didn't come with prize money. It would be less expensive for us if my mom didn't go with me every time, but I knew she would never allow it. Plus, when she was there, I got to choose what, where, and when I ate. Without her I would be guided by a different chaperone, who might insist on going to restaurants or who would provide meals that I would have no control over.

I was also afraid that, without her, I wouldn't be able to keep winning. At Junior Worlds in France, my mother had chaperoned some of the other competitors who arrived solo. I watched them struggle, trying to navigate the stress of competing without the support of their parents. I wondered if that was why I won, and they didn't.

In addition, I didn't know how to act around other people anymore. If I liked someone, my mom told me they were evil, that satan was using them to pull me in. She constantly warned me that the people we met through climbing didn't actually like me, that they couldn't be trusted, and only wanted things from me. After hearing that message over and over, I no longer trusted my own intuition regarding people. I couldn't open up to anyone. The only person I could trust was my mom. She had given up everything for me, after all. I owed her, and I needed to make her happy.

Although part of me wanted to get away from her, I also felt that I needed her. When we were together, I controlled everything about the day. I'd wake her up, make her breakfast, pack her bag, clean the house, plan where we were going to go, have a meltdown if it didn't work out or if I couldn't do the route I wanted to do. And yet at the same time, I felt impossibly out of control and helpless, as if I were being strangled and expected to perform at the same time.

Even to this day, as a forty-year-old adult, it's difficult to navigate. Was I selfish, or wasn't I? Was I in control, or was she? Perhaps I'll never know.

―――――――――――

My dad took me climbing only two or three times over the course of my teen years. On one of those occasions, we ran into Shelley Presson, a fellow competitor. She had spent significant time in France, considered the hub of hard sport climbing at the time. Stateside, she lived in Chattanooga, Tennessee, and worked for PMI/Petzl. I liked Shelley. She wore pretty colors and dangling earrings, did her hair, and even put on makeup to climb. And yet she still climbed hard. She was always nice to me and spoke to me as an equal, seemingly unruffled by my silence. But my mom had warned me of her "worldliness," how her mind was "unclean" and there was evil around her. "She's full of satan," my mom said. "You must be careful or you'll be pulled in." I watched Shelley differently after that, wondering what lasciviousness lay underneath the surface that I couldn't see or feel.

While we were climbing that day at the Red, somehow the subject of my dad's job came up. "You know," said Shelley, "PMI/Petzl is hiring an accountant." My head whipped around from tying my shoe to look at her. *NO!* I didn't want to move to Tennessee. My whole life, my career, my responsibility to the world and to god, were all in Kentucky.

"I'll have my boss call you," she told my dad. I silently prayed that she wouldn't, that she'd forget and nothing would come of it.

"He's convinced his company is going to fire him," my mom confided as we drove to the Red on another day, the spring bluegrass making me sneeze uncontrollably and my eyes swell up until I couldn't see. The pollen in the air would fade at the rhododendron-laden gorge, so I waited it out and kept a wet washcloth draped across my eyes.

I knew that my mom saw me as her best friend, and I would try to listen and comfort her, but the talks sometimes put me in a position I didn't belong in, leaving me unsettled. My mom would frequently talk to me about her feelings, including her relationship with my dad. She had a few church friends, and she'd tell me about them and what they were going through. Since I didn't have any friends of my own anymore, I would pray for her and her friends, writing their names in my journal.

"I know, Mom," I would tell her. "You shouldn't have to do it all." I felt angry at my dad for burdening her this way. I vowed to be there for her, to support her through her trials, to try to make life easier for her. I could clean the house, help with the cooking, go grocery shopping.

"I'll do better with food. I promise." I pulled out a banana and choked it down, trying to fight the panic rising inside me.

CHAPTER 5

A PERFECT
TRACK RECORD

Yet another competition was coming up, but I had a cold I couldn't seem to shake. I felt dizzy and lightheaded all the time, and in between the fatigue and breathlessness, I was frantic with worry. I didn't want to tell my mom, because she'd tell me to eat more. Everything had started to become about how much I ate.

My mom was growing increasingly agitated about trying to fit her job around my climbing schedule. She, my dad, and my brother frequently argued about who would take me climbing. I didn't have a driver's license yet, and I climbed Tuesdays and Thursdays after school at the gym, and Saturday and Sunday at the Red. That meant I needed four rides each week just for my training. I was paranoid, maniacal about climbing enough, panicky and agitated if it seemed like plans might fall through. My mom was feeling left out, and I was convinced that one missed climbing day would mean that I'd be out of shape for the next competition. We were nearing a breaking point. We could all feel it coming.

One evening an argument boiled over, and before I knew it, my mom was screaming. My parents had been arguing for a while, but my dad, like me, said nothing as she reached a fever pitch. It made me hate him.

My mom ripped the green plastic phone off the wall and hurled it across the dining area. I flinched, even though she threw it at no one in particular. It landed and splintered, emitting one last wheezing *brrrring* as it broke.

"I'm getting Alzheimer's!" Mom yelled, staring at the phone. "It's like something just snapped and I had no control." She hiccupped and said, "My mom had troubles with anger in the beginning."

"*It's like she's a little child,*" I wrote later. "*I wish Dad would try and understand. He does nothing while she takes it out on me and THEN he gets mad. She can't handle it. He needs to pretend she's a little kid, but he doesn't.*"

The competition in Pontiac, Michigan, was one of many Nationals competitions I traveled to in 1996. The gym was modern by mid-nineties standards, with an overhanging, curving climbing wall that was used for the finals. This time I was climbing last. When someone came around to collect my music, I said, "Nothing. I don't want to play any music."

"No music at all?"

"No, just quiet," I responded. My friend, the one other female teenage competitor, handed over her music, "Brown Eyed Girl." I secretly wondered what she liked about the song, since her eyes were blue.

After a long wait in isolation, I finally headed out to climb. It was too quiet with no music, and the several dozen spectators rustled uncomfortably. Inwardly I snickered. *Welcome to my world, the land of being uncomfortable.* I derived a feeling akin to pleasure from how awkward the whole thing was. These tiny acts of teenage rebellion were strange and often hurt me more than anyone else, but at fifteen I didn't have the self-awareness to understand my motivations. In this instance, however, the quiet didn't matter to me because I mentally checked out the second I began climbing.

I was starting to feel comfortable winning at the national level. It had become a foregone conclusion that I, in spite of all my self-doubt and questioning, could take stock in. Once I started climbing, I could just zone out and let my body do what it did best. I understood the route and the route understood me—clipping the anchor was as natural as breathing.

From the top of the podium, I leaned down to give the second- and third-place competitors a kiss on each cheek, French style. I was starting to get the hang of this competition thing, and for once, I felt good about winning.

But I chastised myself later for my imaginary sins, writing, *"The reason I'm miserable and having a hard time is because I'm being self-centered, thinking only about me and not focusing on god to take care of everything. I'm not letting his will be done. Plus, maybe I'm getting proud and 'full of myself' from winning so much. I need to be humble, let god take care of it, and then I will have peace."*

Because of the success that a handful of teens—such as Chris Sharma, Beth Rodden, Tommy Caldwell, David Hume, and I—were having in adult competitions, ESPN invited a few of us to participate in the 1996 X Games, held in Providence, Rhode Island. At the time, the X Games, a televised, international event, was as close to the Olympics as you could get in climbing. We were considered wild-card attendees because we didn't have established rankings within the American Sport Climbing Federation (ASCF), the governing body for climbing competitions at the time.

The Rhode Island air felt humid, but with a cool saltiness rather than the sticky humidity I was accustomed to in Kentucky. The competition wall was huge and gray, but it was also squatter than I had anticipated, with a long, horizontal roof in the middle. Since my strength as a climber came from my endurance, I worried that the steep, short wall would require big, powerful moves that would be hard for me.

It was my first competition held outdoors, so I figured it would be hot on the wall. Without anyone to guide or coach me, I'd made up my own training regimen, which included climbing in the sun at the Red—to get used to the heat—bouldering the next day at the gym, and then taking one day off before starting the split again. At the Red, I'd try to do as many routes as possible, finishing the day by climbing laps on my favorite warm-up route until I was so tired that my hands opened up on even the biggest holds. I decided to take three rest days before the biggest comp of my life so far, with no idea as to whether or not it would prepare me.

As I entered the isolation area behind the competition wall, I heard people speaking a number of different languages and saw well-known climbers from all over the world. Feeling incredibly intimidated, I found a corner where I could put my things, pulled out my Bible and journal, and curled up in my huge, red fleece jacket. I lay on my side, using my backpack for a pillow. As usual, I hadn't slept at all the night prior, and as my nerves bubbled up, I clenched my jaw to push them down and away, taking my mind somewhere else entirely.

Like many competitors, I had developed some superstitions. I always wore the same jewelry—a set of silver Kokopellis on my ears because I played the flute, and two necklaces, one with pewter letters spelling *CLIMB* and another with a cross between two feathers. I always ate rice and black beans for dinner the night before a competition. I had heard somewhere that it was a complete protein—whatever that meant. I also wore my watch when I climbed. Commentators often mentioned this oddity, saying that perhaps I wore it because I climbed so slowly that I needed to keep track of my time. That wasn't true. I only allowed myself to eat at certain times of the day, and my watch let me know when it was time to eat. Still, I enjoyed the mystery of it. Something about being a bit of an enigma appealed to me.

My performance in the preliminaries qualified me for the semifinals, and by the end of that round, I was in first place—my painfully slow style contrasting starkly with my competitors' quicker movements. I would climb last in the finals on the following day.

As we left the competition area after semifinals, several reporters wanted to interview me, but with my head pounding and my jaw aching from clenching, I couldn't get a word to come out. Watching the videos decades later, I see that I am wide-eyed and frantic when a reporter asks me a question. I glance at my mom, then at the sky, then at the floor. My teeth gnaw on my lip as I look around but don't respond, for nearly a minute, as though I haven't heard the reporter at all. Finally I mumble an answer so quietly that I can't even hear what I said. In a way, I feel that the person in that video is someone I've never met.

How I responded to interviews and reporters is one of my bigger regrets about my past, and one that I understand the least. It was more than shyness; sometimes, it felt as though my mouth was literally latched closed. It's impossible to explain, but I was terrified I would somehow say the wrong thing.

At one point, after a phone interview I did from home during which I mumbled and barely said anything to the person on the other end, my mom slammed down the phone.

"You are not allowed to answer the phone anymore if that's how you're going to respond!" she shrieked. "No one will EVER like you if you don't learn how to speak."

To this day, I feel a sense of dread when the phone rings, and more often than not I let it go to voicemail.

As a teenager, I found myself hoping that someone, maybe one of the reporters, would magically know what was in my heart and vocalize it for me. That they would ask the questions that I needed to answer. *How are you? Are you ok? Do you need help?*

But instead, the reporters always asked the same infuriating questions. They asked for my thoughts on competing, how I felt about my competitors, if I thought I would succeed, and whether I thought I was the best. Part of me wanted to laugh at them. Of course I didn't think I was the best. That was ridiculous. Did I look like this was working for me? I was the most flawed human imaginable—just ask god. Or my mom.

Couldn't they see that I had no idea what I was doing? That I didn't really care about the other competitors, or even winning? That I wasn't even sure why I was doing this? That I just wanted someone to see me? Consequently, whenever I did speak, my answers came out snappy and irritable. If someone asked me about my goals, I would say, "I don't know. I'm a teenager. I don't know what tomorrow will bring!" Or, if I was asked about my competitors, "I'm just climbing against the wall, not other competitors." Or when they asked what drew me to competitive climbing. "It just happened." Once someone from a French magazine asked, "What is your dream in climbing?" My answer was full of vitriol. "My dreams are mine alone and will remain dreams for me alone."

In those days, I liked being the invisible underdog, the one no one expected to do well. I had a hidden rage, buried deep inside, and it came rushing out in those early competitions. *I would show them,* I thought.

But I also never expected to have a perfect track record. I never expected much of anything. Life was less painful that way. At that X Games in Rhode Island, I was an undiscovered teenager, and I could let my obstinate, prove-you-wrong nature out on the wall. But by the end of 1996, the weight of knowing that everyone expected me to win threatened to drown me. By that point, the only thing that made sense were the routes—and even then only once I started climbing. I had no answers to satisfy reporters. I didn't have a competitor's mindset. To me, everything that was happening seemed like one giant accident.

On the final day of the X Games competition, the isolation area slowly emptied out as each competitor left for their turn to climb. Robyn Erbesfield-Raboutou had been one of the routesetters, which began with more than fifty moves out across a horizontal roof painted gray, with sculpted panels and modular holds. This section, which resembled a bulging belly, was dubbed "The Beast." Above, the wall overhung less steeply, but the holds were smaller, fewer, and spaced farther apart. This headwall was called "The Terminator."

Shelley Presson climbed first, fighting through to The Terminator. She looked strong and solid, until an unfortunate foot slip sent her off the route. Mia Axon, at thirty-seven years old, went next. Climbing slowly, and relying on her strong upper body, she reached Shelley's high point but teetered backward from an off-balance move.

Next up was gold-medal hopeful, Liv Sansoz, of France. Though taller than me, she had a similar skin-and-bones build, topped off with a short, boyish hairstyle. White climbing tape adorned her wrists—indicative of joint instability or possibly an injury. Near the current high point, Liv used a different, more difficult sequence, trying so hard that her body visibly vibrated. She somehow pulled through and matched the high point, then set up for a big, left-hand deadpoint—a committing move that requires a climber to catch a hold precisely when her body's momentum stops her from moving toward the wall yet before she starts to fall away. She went for it and made contact but couldn't quite grasp the hold. With a high-pitched scream, she sailed into space, barely taking the lead.

From a routesetter's perspective, the climb was a massive success, as each competitor slowly upped the ante, one move at a time. Laurence Guyon, of France, followed suit, latching the hold that spit off Liv, but falling seconds later, unable to make the next move.

From isolation, I listened to the cheering crowd as each subsequent climber reached a new high point. I pulled out my journal. *"Today I have to climb last,"* I wrote. *"I'm a little nervous but also confident I'll do god's will (that sounds conceited). Yesterday I was being really selfish and I asked for forgiveness, but it almost seems like I do it just because I'm hoping god will let me do good today. It's confusing."* I laid my head down, and before I knew it I was asleep.

Suddenly, someone was shaking me awake. "Katie, it's your turn to climb."

I gasped, shooting up into a sitting position. "What? Have I missed my turn?"

"No, but it's your turn now."

Flustered and disheveled, I quickly took a sip of water, yanked on my harness, and grabbed my shoes. This wasn't how it was supposed to go, but I almost preferred having the odds stacked against me. By setting myself up for failure, I would never have to admit that, secretly, I did care—it was my private way of saying "fuck you" to the world.

I started climbing and, without a thought, floated through The Beast. My mind left my body. Soon, I arrived at the leftward traverse where Liv had nearly fallen. I crossed my right hand over my left and lurched for a small knob, my fingers latching on the second they made contact. Unknowingly, I passed Laurence's high point. When

I was nearly level with the anchor, the sun hit my eyes. I paused to look around, scanning for holds. Finally, my right hand popped out rightward.

Thunk. The hollow clunk of my hand hitting the final jug woke me up, and in a rush I was back in the world. *No way*—I did it. The crowd below me erupted in cheers.

As I was lowered to the ground, I managed to give a tiny wave to the crowd, crossing my climbing shoes at the ankle. I smiled a little. I felt happy, elated even—a dangerous feeling that rendered me vulnerable.

On the ground, Robyn rushed up and gave me a big hug. I almost leaned into it a little, a rush of feeling rising to the surface, before I quickly stuffed it down, pulling away from the embrace. My mom was watching and would not like it if I was giving someone else attention, especially Robyn. Viewers might think it was Robyn, and not my mom, who had played a role in my success. I was always on alert for what might anger my mom.

In a lot of ways, I wished Robyn *was* my mom, or at the very least, my coach. With Robyn, I saw the potential for mentorship and support. I felt optimistic around her, infused with energy—and good about myself, like I had earned my accomplishments, and could earn a million more. My sense of loss over not having Robyn as my mentor was so strong that it took my breath away if I thought about it too much.

My mom felt threatened by Robyn and disliked her more than almost anyone else we met through climbing. I tried to adopt my mom's view of Robyn, because that was easier than wanting something I couldn't have. I put her on a pedestal, but was also angry when she didn't save me. Instead of being angry at my mom, which was far too scary, I sometimes took it out on Robyn.

People crowded around us, thrusting microphones in my face, holding out papers for autographs. I was stunned. *Am I a celebrity now?* Signing my name made me feel foolish but also somehow proud and conceited. Why would a grown adult want an autograph from messed-up me?

The X Games was also where I first met Lynn Hill. A few years earlier, Lynn had become the first person to free climb The Nose of El Capitan in Yosemite. It had been attempted by many of the best male climbers of the day, to no avail. Incredibly, she returned the following year to free climb it again in less than twenty-four hours. She gave The Nose a rating of 5.13b/c, but it has since been uprated to 5.14a. Lynn seemed like a mythical creature to me, possessing a talent so unlike any other that I could barely talk to her. So when she said on TV that "Katie Brown is the best female sport climber in the history of the sport," I thought the comp organizers had told her to read the line from a teleprompter. Since then, we have become friends, and Lynn is one of the most thoughtful, generous people I know. No matter how long it has been since we've talked, she always welcomes me with open arms. That first compliment from her is one of the most important I've ever received.

On the flight home from the X Games, I felt calm and happy, like a world was about to open up to me, like maybe it would bring me the freedom and independence I so desperately craved. My mom felt otherwise.

Not long after we got back, I was invited to attend the Outdoor Retailer trade show. This biannual event, I discovered, was an industry tradition, and the place where sponsored athletes came to negotiate contracts, appear at their sponsors' booths, sign posters for fans, or teach clinics. While we were there, I asked if I could go to a party with a climbing friend.

"Nobody wants me around!" my mom screamed. "I want out of climbing! Nobody ever wants me around; they're just out for themselves. And for what, to discard you when they're done? I'm so tired of everyone wanting you and hating me!" The way she looked at me almost felt like hate. "I'm just going to leave. I want nothing to do with it. You go to the party without me, see where it gets you. Nobody cares about me anyway. I should just leave."

The idea terrified me. She was my mom, and ultimately, I still needed her.

"Mom feels like she's gonna get left in the dust," I wrote. *"While I feel like spreading my wings, it's almost like she's clutching at the apron strings instead of me."*

"What are you writing about?" my mom asked, suspicious. Sometimes she read my journal and got angry about what I had written, so at times I wrote what I knew she would want to read, or else downplayed certain events or feelings, fearful of her rage.

"Nothing," I said. "Just writing down my devotional from this morning."

Back at home, I sat on a chair underneath the kitchen phone—the same one my mom threw—and held a letter in my hand, a letter from a boy. In the letter, he said that he liked me. I liked him, too.

He was also a climber, and we often competed and climbed together, but we were never around each other without my mom. *What would that be like to have a boyfriend like a normal teenager? To have friends?*

I wanted to clutch the letter to my chest and scream, "Yes! Yes, I'll be your girlfriend!" But inside I knew it wouldn't be allowed.

At the summer camp I had attended back in Colorado, Id-Ra-Ha-Je, girls were instructed to change their clothes if their shorts weren't long enough. Shorts could be a "stumbling block" for the boys. In chapel we were told that girls were like delicate flowers. "Each time you hold hands with a boy or have impure thoughts about a boy, you lose a petal," they told us. "You must keep your thoughts and bodies pure for marriage, and only for marriage."

In fifth grade, my parents refused to let me participate in my school's sex education class. Instead, I sat in the hallway, alone, while my classmates learned about their bodies, safe sex, and who knows what else. I was the lone religious girl, and I tucked my head in shame and embarrassment as kids passed by me en route to the bathrooms. Later, my mom handed me a book she'd checked out from the library about sex. I don't think I looked at it once. I carried it around in my backpack for a week, terrified that someone would see it and laugh at me. The idea of my body being anything other than a tool for Christ was so taboo that I couldn't even bring myself to consider what might be in the book.

So I had no choice but to say no to the boy who liked me, who wanted me to be his girlfriend. I couldn't have my mom say no, or worse, have her decide that we couldn't be around him at all because of it. She would tell me that he was a sinner, evil. She'd tell me that I shouldn't be yoked to an unbeliever. That he couldn't be trusted. So it was better not to ask. What *I* wanted didn't really matter. What mattered was doing the "right" thing. I had to shut my feelings down before they could even start. I sat and stared at the letter for a few minutes, savoring each word that made me feel valuable and desired, wishing I could escape into one of my imaginary stories from childhood where happy endings existed. I tucked away the note from that boy, and I still have it to this day.

Sometimes I wonder what made me believe all the things I was taught. If I had thought independently, rebelled, or stood up for myself, perhaps I would have gotten to experience innocent teenage infatuation. Perhaps I wouldn't have starved myself just to have control over something.

CHAPTER 6

ROCK MASTERS

In the summer of 1996, my mom and I boarded a flight for Italy, where I was scheduled to attend the Rock Masters competition in Arco, the crème de la crème of worldwide climbing comps. My X Games victory secured me a last-minute invitation; only the top climbers from around the world were invited, so it was quite an honor. At fifteen, I'd be the youngest competitor there. Robyn had won in Arco two years before, and Lynn had a record five wins.

Shortly into our flight, we made an emergency landing in Pittsburgh because something had hit the windshield of the plane. We were delayed, and didn't get to New York to catch a new flight to Italy until the next day. I tried not to, but I counted on my hand how long it had been since I'd climbed. Three days. I started to panic, convinced that I was going to get out of shape. In addition, my arms, and sometimes my legs, were starting to bother me with a strange tingling, almost numb feeling. In hindsight, those few days off may have been just what I needed to squeak by on my limited resources.

Eventually, my mom and I arrived in Milan and found the train station. Our luggage was massive, packed with way too much stuff, and everything was smaller in Europe. Other passengers turned to watch as we struggled to squeeze our bags down the narrow aisles.

Someone from La Sportiva, one of the sponsors I signed with after my win at the X Games, was apparently supposed to pick us up in Trento, but when we arrived we could not get through to them. It was the middle of the night, and a kind German couple who spoke

English took pity and showed us to a nearby hotel. The woman checking us in wore a lacy, red, low-cut bustier and sat behind a wall of glass.

"We stayed in a brothel," my mom would later say in an interview. "But we were safe because we were mother and daughter. That is a sacred relationship, so no one bothered us."

Our room was up a tiny, steep set of stairs, and we had no choice but to shove our luggage up the narrow space, literally squeezing the bags in between the walls. I swore that next time I would travel with less stuff. In the hotel room, I lost it, sobbing that I was out of shape, and doing pull-ups compulsively on the door jamb.

The next morning, we finally found a ride to Arco, a beautiful town on the edge of a placid lake. The limestone climbing area rises seemingly at an angle on the far end of the town, past winding and ever-narrowing cobblestone streets. There are more limestone cliffs on the opposite side of Arco, as though watching over the passersby on the streets below.

We didn't have a car, but discovered that in Arco we didn't really need one. Nearly everything was within walking or bicycling distance. The roads were dotted with small vineyards, and it was easy to pluck an apple or a bunch of grapes on the way to our destination. Even the climbing area was just a quick bicycle ride up a hill on the edge of town.

If it was hard for me to talk to people in the States, it was twice as hard in a country where I didn't speak the language. My mom and I argued after nearly every encounter. "No one will ever like you if you don't learn how to talk," she'd tell me. I knew she was right, but it just felt so impossible.

The night before the competition, I dreamt that I was climbing with several people. Everyone around me was talking about how skinny I was. Someone was worried about me. "Are you ok?" she asked me. "I can see that you need help. Let me help you grow strong again." In my dream she gave me a hug. But instead of feeling comforting, the pressure felt intensely painful against my frail bones.

When I awoke from the dream, I was filled with the deepest sadness I had ever felt. I lay in the dark, crying into my pillow.

The competition started with a work route. This redpoint format—
where climbers practice and rehearse until they are able to get to
the top of a route without falling—was unique to this event. Each
competitor got one practice session on the work route, to learn
the holds and moves and rehearse its sequences, before trying it in
competition. The second route was a more traditional onsight route,
which meant we had to climb the route successfully on our first try,
without any prior knowledge of it.

We were each given thirty minutes to practice the work route,
which was designed to be significantly harder than the onsight
route. My assigned time slot was at half past seven in the morning, so my mom and I got up at half past five to go warm up at the
local crag. Whenever possible, I preferred to be outside on real rock.
Also, something about the quiet solitude of climbing by headlamp
appealed to me. Up there on the limestone, I was the only person in
the world. My mom catered to my whims as a competitor, and for
this I am grateful.

The sun was up by the time we arrived for the work route, though
morning dew still coated the grass. The competition wall was the
tallest artificial wall I'd ever seen. It was staged outside, near the
center of town, with a large grassy area where spectators could
spread blankets or lounge in chairs to watch.

In the early days of Arco, the competition was held on the limestone cliffs that now loomed in the background. To avoid a competitor having prior knowledge of a route, and therefore an unfair
advantage, the organizers chipped and chiseled new holds into
otherwise featureless rock. As climbing culture progressed, however, this was deemed unethical, and the competition shifted to the
now-famous artificial wall.

The competition wall was three walls really, with varying degrees
of overhang, that were connected before the final headwall, more
than eighty feet off the ground. I wasn't sure how to "work" a route,
so I spent my thirty-minute time slot just climbing it, asking my
belayer to hold me in a particular spot whenever I felt tired or
wanted to rehearse a challenging sequence. I tried to remember the

moves, something I didn't normally do while climbing, and it felt draining to be so present. Many of the moves were long spans, but one in particular stymied me. I tried it several times but couldn't seem to do it. Finally, with my allotted time running out, I pulled past it and finished the route. I was in tears on the way down.

J. B. Tribout, the routesetter and one of the top sport climbers from the mideighties to the midnineties, stood at the bottom. "Don't cry," he said in his thick French accent, giving me an awkward pat on the back. "You did good." He was clearly uncomfortable consoling an overwhelmed fifteen-year-old child who had been suddenly thrust into the world of international competitive climbing.

While the next competitor started practicing the route, I sat to the side and cried for a few minutes. My mind started to replay the move over and over again, and I imagined all the ways that I hadn't tried when I was up there with tunnel vision, too focused on my supposed failure to see the other options. That, coupled with watching other competitors' strategies, gave me hope. I grabbed a page from my journal and tried to draw a map of the route, noting each move and each corresponding foot placement. I wrote, *"I think I might get it on redpoint, I just won't let go, that's all!"*

The following day was a rest day. I wanted to see Robyn or Lynn, but my mom refused, which I found confusing. If my mom wanted me to do well in competition, why didn't she want me to learn from better climbers? When we were at the trade show, I'd attended a training camp hosted by Robyn, and I had loved it. I ended up climbing with the men most of the time, since their climbs were more challenging, and at the end of the day she had helped me design a long, hard boulder problem. I knew I was on the precipice of being able to get *really* strong.

When Robyn encouraged me to eat to fuel my body, I complied. Her advice, and the way she phrased it, made me feel that it was safe to eat. But now all that potential was slipping through my fingers. I didn't like the feeling of wanting things. Wanting things meant dealing with the inevitability of loss, and I needed to shut that down before its tidal wave consumed me. It was safer to not want anything, to be more dead than alive.

"I don't need them anyway," I wrote. *"I only need god."*

Later that day, in our hotel, I was filled with a horrible, foreboding feeling. It had been building for weeks, but in that moment it felt like everything was going to come crashing down. I felt that I should not have hope, because anything I hoped for would be taken away.

Perhaps it was a premonition that my body had officially begun the slow process of dying. Perhaps it was just starvation-induced anxiety. Either way, I lay down on my bed and cried. My mom ignored me, clearly frustrated over my moods. She'd been growing increasingly angry over my refusal to eat more than the tiniest bit. That, combined with her feelings around her own weight and diet, meant that her patience was growing thin. I knew she wanted me to be happy about our life together, but I just couldn't get there. *This*, whatever it was, wasn't working for me. I could not perform in a vacuum. Still, I desperately wished she would comfort me instead of ignoring me.

Sometimes I wonder if it was the eating disorder, more than anything else, that caused our relationship to fall apart. At the time, I thought that made me to blame. As many times as I told myself that I needed to eat to stay strong for climbing, I then chose not to eat. The fear of what would happen if I ate mattered more than anything else in the world.

My mom's efforts to help me get better—by screaming at me, forcing me to eat, making me promise to eat five times a day—were misdirected. When she got in my face, screaming obscenities about what I had or had not eaten, how she'd given up everything for me, how she ate for me, how god was going to take away my talent, and how I was so selfish—in those moments what I felt was not that I needed to get better. I felt power over her. She'd look me over, from top to bottom, assessing, comparing, and I'd feel like I was winning. At fifteen I felt completely powerless, but this was one thing she couldn't take from me. She couldn't win, couldn't make me eat.

On the first day of the competition, I managed to complete the onsight route along with five other competitors. If more than one of us finished the work route, there would be a superfinal to determine the winner. I felt buoyed up, despite my dark thoughts from the day prior.

The next day I felt prepared for the work route. I had decided that I just wouldn't let go, and, when I started to climb, I found I could make it so. I had an intense determination and fire inside of me, and that came out in Arco.

Sometimes at the Red my brother would fall while clipping the anchor of a climb, his forearms too "pumped," or fatigued from lactate buildup, to complete that last, final move. This baffled me. *Why*, I would wonder, *would you possibly fall off when all you have left is clipping the chains? Just decide not to!*

Back then, I often felt like a silent doormat, being run over by everything. But when I climbed, I allowed myself to feel, to need, to want, and it all exploded out of me in a fierce, there's-no-fucking-way-I'm-letting-go mindset. Nothing could control me up there—nothing. It was just me.

The French climber Liv Sansoz also successfully completed the work route, and so we continued on to a superfinal—another onsight route—at the end of what had become a very long day. I barely eked out more moves than she did before falling off. We were both exhausted. I had never been more evenly matched with a competitor.

As I stood on the podium next to Liv, I saw the tears running down her cheeks and knew she was battling some of the same demons I was. I felt something in her, mirrored in me. Or vice versa, I wasn't sure. Her sadness was palpable, and I felt as though I was standing in her place, crying her tears. Instead of feeling happy about winning, I felt almost devastated, believing Liv should have won. I thought, *I don't care enough, don't deserve this, haven't earned it and wasn't even sure that I wanted it.* And it was so clear that she did.

Later, I wrote in my journal, *"I felt bad. I almost wanted her to win. But I also didn't want to fall intentionally just so she could, and then I ended up going higher. I wish I could explain it better, but it broke my heart to see her cry. She should have won. But I also can't not do my best for someone else's sake. It's confusing."*

The competition paid 10 million lira (the equivalent of about 6700 US dollars at the time) in cash to the winner. The stack of bills was the most money I had ever seen. My mom told me that we should spend some of it on things that don't lose value like gold and silver. Her first stop was a jewelry store to replace the wedding ring she'd recently lost when she left it in our car while it was at the shop for an oil change. I also purchased a couple small pieces of jewelry.

My mom then told me that we should put the rest of the money into our shoes, slipping stacks of bills under the insoles, and carrying the money through customs without declaring it. She said that if we did that, we wouldn't have to pay taxes on the income.

By the end of 1996, I had won more than a dozen national and international competitions—in effect, storming the world of competitive climbing. (At fifteen years old, I was not allowed to compete in World Cup events, which had a minimum age of sixteen.) Even my climbing peer, Chris Sharma, arguably the most naturally gifted climber that the world has ever seen, didn't have the same winning streak. To the outside world, I was unstoppable.

I've thought a lot about young athletes who are considered phenoms in their sport. Many suffered the same fate as I did: a quick rise, followed by a swift fall. Despite that, I would be remiss if I didn't own that what happened in 1996 was significant. My success sharply contrasted with the archetype of a champion climber—older, more experienced—it was one of the first whiffs of a changing tide toward youth climbing. More than one climber has since told me that I was the reason they retired from competitive climbing.

Discord within the American Sport Climbing Federation (ASCF) about whether to create an age limit for adult competitions led to the formation of the Junior Competition Climbing Association (JCCA) in January 1997, which aimed to elevate youth climbers and youth competitions around the country. It was an immediate success. Teenagers swiftly changed the landscape of competitive climbing, and I was an important part of that shift. In 2020, the oldest competitor in the Olympics sport climbing competition was twenty-two years old.

The late mountaineer and author David Roberts often told me, "You *must* explain how you got so good." I still can't. And in 1996, despite my undeniable success, I did not see myself as "so good." What I felt at the time was mostly loss and guilt. When I look back at what I did achieve, it feels like another person, another life that I don't feel much connection to. I look at photos and videos of that girl and I'm surprised to see that I really was actually quite good.

So how did I get there? And where did that girl go? I look at her face in those early competitions and I see a grimace of fierce, undeniable determination. Something in me made it possible to endure pain, to wage war with each wall placed in front of me, to do battle against each route as though it were life or death. In life, other people controlled and dictated my identity, but when I climbed, I refused to relinquish control.

CHAPTER 7

IN ISOLATION

In late 1996, my family moved from Paris, Kentucky, to Lafayette, Georgia. My dad had gotten the job with PMI/Petzl in nearby Chattanooga. My hopes for that homeschool group, with the psychologist who might have noticed my eating problem, were gone.

Our new home was a short drive away from several small outdoor climbing areas in Tennessee and Alabama, but it was at least two hours away from the nearest climbing gym. When I heard the news of the impending move, I said to my dad, "I will DIE if we move." In my mind, a climber without a climbing gym was akin to an Olympic gymnast with only the school jungle gym to train on.

At age sixteen, I felt I had a responsibility to keep climbing, to keep winning, to keep earning money. After the X Games, I had signed several big, new sponsors—La Sportiva, PMI/Petzl, Clif Bar, Oakley, and others—and was now earning money from my sponsorships. I would soon be working with an agent, who could help me bring in even more money. Carrying those responsibilities for my family would be too much, too hard, without the climbing gym and the Red River Gorge. I felt so much expectation, and yet also profoundly abandoned. It was as though my parents wanted me to do this thing, while at the same time they were paradoxically making it impossible.

Moving also meant that my school plans would need to change, and my brother, who had recently turned eighteen, would lose out on in-state tuition for the college he planned to attend in Kentucky. Scott decided that, rather than stay in Kentucky, he would move back to Colorado to establish residency and go to school out there. Weirdly, my parents no longer seemed to have much of an opinion about what he did. It was as though a switch had flipped in their eyes. One day he was seventeen and under their care, obligated to follow their rules. The next day, he was an adult, adrift and unguided. They never said anything about his decisions ever again.

As for me, we decided I would now homeschool via video and correspondence courses. With my schedule, there was no way I could attend a traditional high school. So I moved to Georgia and started climbing alone and schooling alone, all while competing in front of huge international audiences. I felt a thousand years old.

I'm an early riser. I feel the most energetic and optimistic in the morning. As the day wanes, I start to lose motivation and a sense of foreboding sets in, a strange disquiet creeping up my spine as the sun sets. For this reason, I always wanted to climb early. My mom, however, entered a depressive period of her own after our move to Georgia. Always on the go, she suddenly struggled to get out of bed in the morning, even when I needed her to take me climbing. As the time ticked by, later and later, I would grow anxious. If we waited too long to get out to the local cragging areas, I would grow tired and lethargic, making the training more torturous.

While I waited for her to get up, I would pack my climbing bag, pack her climbing bag, get her water filled and snacks packed, and make her breakfast. Then, to warm up my body for climbing, I would clean the house, getting down on my hands and knees and scrubbing the floor.

Eventually, she would rise. I would hover, trying to hurry her along unnoticeably. Invariably, by the time we made it to the car—if we made it to the car without an argument—I would be so drained from trying to manage my anxiety and stay patient that I would lose all energy and motivation. Climbing started to feel *heavy*, different than it once had. I felt I was losing the person I had been the year before.

To cope, I started running more. The endorphins soothed me as I listened to my feet fall on the wet leaves while my breath created a rhythmic drumbeat. It was the only time I felt peaceful, at ease in my body and free from all my adult responsibilities.

Since we did most everything together, my mom and I frequently ran together. One morning, though, I headed out for a run before she got up. When I returned she was seething, her blue eyes flashing.

"Why didn't you wait for me?"

Oh no, I should have thought about it first. I hadn't though, had thought only about myself. Startled by her anger, I said nothing.

"All you do is think about yourself!" she screamed. "You never think about anyone else. I wanted to go running too, but instead of thinking about someone else, you just do whatever it is you want to do! You are so selfish!"

The innocent decision to go for a run now felt fraught with danger. I should have known better, should have asked if she wanted to. Instead of putting her needs before mine, I thought only about myself. The only solution was to always be on guard, to do my best to predict what might upset her.

"I'm really sorry, Mom," I cried. "Please forgive me." I was pretty sure we weren't going to make it out climbing that day. If we did, I'd make sure to belay her, or put up topropes for her, as much as I could, to make up for my selfishness.

Later I wrote:

> My quiet time was about showing our Christian faith. I sure blew it. If only I had given a little and waited, if only I had bent a little. It's just a small thing, but I feel so bad about it and Mom's really upset. I asked for forgiveness but it doesn't seem to make any difference. If only I could rewind time. I hope she forgives me. I feel so bad. Why didn't I just wait for her. Why? I'm so stupid. I really showed what a great Christian I am.

On another day, I got it right and my mom and I ran together, the sound of our footsteps dampened by the thick layer of musty leaves that coated the trail. The landscape in the Southeast is heavily treed, the air rich with moisture and plant life. I glanced over at my mom. She was decked out head to toe in gear from my newest sponsor, The North Face.

I had an agent and several new sponsors by then, and I was worried about performing for them. *"What if I get all these big sponsors and then I start doing bad?"* I wrote in my journal. One company that I had been introduced to recently was called Franklin Climbing Equipment. They were headquartered in Bend, Oregon, and had invited me to visit their local climbing area, Smith Rock. Smith was the birthplace of American sport climbing—it was there that local pioneer Alan Watts had bolted and climbed *Watts Tots* (5.12b) in 1983. A crackless face, unprotectable without bolts, it's widely considered America's first true sport route. Over the years, some of the most well-known classic hard routes had been established at Smith Rock. I desperately wanted to go, and broached the subject with my mom as we ran. Sometimes it felt easier to talk when I was running, my fear of saying the wrong thing dissipating with each footstep.

"I don't trust those people," my mom said. "They only want things from you. If they won't allow me to go, then you can't go. They just want to push me out and take you. It's not because I don't trust you," she clarified, using the words I had heard so many times before. "It's that it's something I'd like to do too, and I need to be there to protect your purity."

As I listened to her response, one I'd known had been coming before I'd even asked, I looked from my mom to what I was wearing. I had on a fleece of hers, while she was wearing my new gear. Why was I *always* wearing my mom's clothing? The North Face was my sponsor, after all.

"Mom," I said carefully. "Can I have some of The North Face stuff back?"

The conversation quickly escalated into a full-blown fight—words and hands flying. In the end, I lamented in my journal about how foolish I felt for letting things devolve into a petty and childish fight over some stupid material goods, something that shouldn't even matter in the grand scheme of things. I shouldn't want so much, need so much.

Years later, in my early twenties, I wrote an essay about how magical it was to run with my mom, and how she was my best friend. I suppose that part was true. She was my best friend. Yet I don't know why I wrote that essay, a bold-faced lie. I suppose I wasn't yet ready to confront the true nature of our relationship, and what I wrote was something that, at the time, I needed to believe.

In 1997, I entered the Phoenix Bouldering Contest, one of the few outdoor competitions that I took part in. It was held at Queen Creek, Arizona, a vast area east of Phoenix, packed with towers and boulders of volcanic tuff, a highly featured rock similar to the welded tuff found at Smith Rock. In this contest, each climber would run between boulders, trying to amass as many points on their scorecard as possible. Strategy was key. Some competitors went for sheer quantity of climbs, while others devoted themselves to just a few very hard boulder problems with high score counts. Each boulder problem had a judge who marked your score after a successful climb, and many of the higher boulder problems had topropes set up for safety.

Because of how short the climbs are, bouldering requires more power than route climbing, and power was never my strength. So although I bouldered for fun, I generally shied away from bouldering competitions. Because this contest was held outside, however, with a looser format than traditional competitions, I thought it sounded fun.

That year, the temperature in Phoenix dropped to record lows. The organizers considered canceling the competition, but in the end went ahead with it. My emaciated frame could not handle the cold, and I shivered uncontrollably between climbs. My teeth chattered incessantly and my toes turned white. My hands and feet went numb. In a video from the competition, I'm on a boulder problem, and my friend Chris Sharma is standing at the base, trying to offer advice. I grunt in effort but pause long enough to yell down, "Shut up, Chris!"

Climbing was the one thing in my life that was all mine, and to this day I still fight the urge to lash out at anyone who dares to try to tell me how to climb. In the video from back then, I fall off the boulder and squeal in frustration, kicking the wall. Nobody seemed to know quite what to say after my outburst. Chris said nothing and meandered off to climb elsewhere.

Needless to say, halfway through the competition, I was not doing well. I fell off each boulder problem, screaming bloody murder on the way down, not trusting the stranger who was assigned to spot me below. Finally, Robyn grabbed my shoulders and gave me a little shake.

"Those people will not let you fall," she said emphatically. "You. Can. Do. This. Your feet will not even touch the ground. They *will* catch you."

Somehow her words shook me out of my terror. I found renewed confidence and strength, and the tide turned for me. I ended up winning the contest and setting a record for the competition.

Throughout the day, however, I had spent a lot of my mental strength carefully doling out serving sizes from a jar of macadamia nuts. The nuts tasted buttery and rich, like the most decadent thing I could imagine, and eventually, in my hypothermic state, I could no longer control myself. I ended up eating the entire jar, which sent my stomach into painful spasms as it tried to process the sudden caloric intake. My stomach, in fact, had been bothering me more and more as of late, and I had to make frequent trips to the bathroom each day. It was a portent of things to come.

As my fame grew, so did the quantity of fan mail. Since I generally declined to respond, my mom sometimes developed pen pal relationships with fans she decided were Christians.

She grew particularly close to someone I will call "Bob." He came to our house in Georgia frequently the first year we lived there, and he and my mom had long, deep conversations. Once, I heard him call her "Mom."

I felt a deep unease around the fans my mom developed relationships with, as though an invisible boundary had been breached. I shut down around them, turning cold and unresponsive. I'm sure it came across as aloofness, but it was a defense mechanism that sometimes, unfortunately, made me suspicious of male fans, of anyone that expressed interest in me without really knowing me, even as an adult.

At one point, my mom told Bob he could take photos of me in the backyard, ostensibly for marketing or head shots. I was wildly uncomfortable with the whole thing. I wondered why I wasn't supposed to trust anyone, not even my brother, who would supposedly lead me down the path of sinners, but I was supposed to trust this creepy twenty-something guy who wanted to take my picture. Just because he professed to be a Christian. For the photos, I put on a floor-length skirt and buttoned my shirt all the way to my neck. Another sweater of my mom's went on top, hanging down to mid-thigh. Totally ensconced in layers of clothing, I sat outside, silent, while he took my picture. Later, my mom became enraged when he only gave her a few images instead of the whole roll of film, as promised.

I'm not going to lie; I feel pretty uncomfortable writing about this time in my life. The story sounds like one long complaining tirade about my poor relationship with my mom, but if I am going to write an honest account of my life, this is the truth. It was climbing, yes, but behind closed doors, my mom and I argued almost every day, over eating, climbing, my desire to do things alone, sponsors, whether I said the right things—when I said anything at all—or any number of other things. There was no "I" in my life at that point. There was only "we."

My journal reveals that my world turned hermetic during the years we lived in Georgia. I had tunnel vision and little outside influence or socialization. My world was focused solely on god, my mom, food, and, lastly, climbing. My climbing career was at its peak, but it was a footnote. The strangulation of influence and experience was my life, and it brought on a darkness to which I hope never to return.

At the same time, my experience of this period was also a direct effect of anorexia. My brain was incapable of processing anything else. Would my mom have been less controlling if I had not also been dying before her eyes? Or would I have resisted the urge to die by starvation better if my mom had been less controlling? I don't know. But it would be unfair and inaccurate to pretend that one didn't exacerbate the other.

CHAPTER 8

MY THREE-RING CIRCUS

Earlier in 1997, my mom and I traveled to Las Vegas to spend a week with writer and mountaineer David Roberts. He was writing an article for *Women's Sports & Fitness*, a magazine that would go belly-up before the article was published. Years later, when I first considered writing my story, I tracked David down via social media to ask for advice because he'd said something that will stick with me forever.

"You're like an onion," he'd told me. "I keep trying to get to the core, but it seems that I just peel away layers only to find more."

He was one of only a very few who seemed to understand that there was more to my story than what lay on the surface. I liked being an onion.

One morning, we drove from the hotel where we were staying in Las Vegas to a climbing destination in Red Rock. At night the city was lit up, full of life and people and excitement, but in the early morning, Las Vegas looked dead and gray, with only a few stragglers exiting the casinos, hungover and broke. David looked at me.

"What do you think of Las Vegas?"

My gaze followed a casino as we passed it.

"Evil." I said.

———

At that time, I often felt like a bomb about to explode. I had heard that Lynn Hill and Scott Franklin were doing a teen training camp. I wanted to go, but since everyone seemed to be a threat in my mom's eyes, I knew I wouldn't be allowed.

"Mom keeps talking about all these people who are out to get us," I wrote in my journal. She had become obsessively paranoid. Not long before the Vegas trip, Shelley Presson had come to our house. She had been letting me use the gym she'd built in her home, since there was not a local climbing gym for me to train at. She'd even gone so far as to give us a key so we could get in whenever we wanted. But while at our house, Shelley expressed that she was feeling taken advantage of, as though we were only nice to her to use her gym.

"I think she's got her gym tapped," my mom told me after her visit. "We'll have to be careful what we say in there because she's listening to us. She seems to know an awful lot about us." Later, while climbing in Shelley's gym, I looked around. The idea that someone had bugged their climbing wall seemed pretty unrealistic. I was starting to doubt some of what my mom told me, but I still couldn't discern what was real and what wasn't, who to trust and who to be suspicious of.

I felt cold and tired every day. *"Almost scary,"* I wrote in my journal as a tiny voice, a long-smothered voice of intuition, whispered that my body was on the verge of disaster. *"I feel like my brain isn't working. The tendons in my arms hurt when I grab holds, not like anything I've ever experienced. I feel really weird, almost lightheaded. It scared me so I quit climbing for the day. I know it's because I'm too skinny. Why did I ever get myself into this mess?"*

We decided that I would climb my first multipitch route at Red Rock during the week we spent with David Roberts. In this style of climbing, the leader climbs to a stance, belays the follower up, then climbs even higher to another stance. It allows you to climb features that are longer than one rope length. I got to place gear for the first time, and learn the intricacies of slotting nuts in tapered cracks and cams in parallel-sided cracks, and how to place and remove gear anchors. Multipitch climbing was something I had been wanting to learn, but that morning, my mom and I had gotten into yet another fight, and I felt stretched to the limit.

We were always late. Running through airports to catch our flight, or missing flights entirely, was par for the course. In the years prior to climbing, I spent many afternoons sitting on the steps at school, long after pickup time, waiting for my mom to arrive. On that particular morning in Vegas, I had begged her to be early for a change.

"Please, can we go?" I said, feeling desperate.

"No," she insisted. "I'm not ready, and we don't have to leave yet."

"*Agggghhhhh!*" I screamed in frustration.

"*Stop taking it out on me!*" she yelled back. "You just don't want to admit that the reason you're angry is because you're stressed out about David Roberts and the fact that you haven't gotten to climb!"

That hadn't even crossed my mind. Now she's putting thoughts in my head. I just want to go.

That time, I was the one who reached out in anger, hitting *her.* Hitting, slapping, spanking—none of it was new to me. I just wasn't usually the one doing it. I'm not sure where my hand landed, because at that moment there was a rap at the door, and we both quickly tucked our fight away. David was here, and it was time to leave.

On the climb, I quickly grew frustrated over how long it took me to figure out where and how each piece of gear fit. On easy terrain I felt a pull to just keep moving. I was irrationally irritated that I had to stop and fiddle with nuts and cams when I wanted to keep moving.

I had wanted this, but now I didn't want it anymore. *Nothing is ever good enough for snooty old me.* My feelings of self-hatred and helplessness, heavy and dense, felt like they were coming out of every pore and frazzled nerve. I ended up throwing a tantrum—one of many I had during that trip—in front of everyone. The emotions were overwhelming, too overwhelming. I didn't know how to manage them.

That night I was physically and emotionally destroyed—so drained that I felt like I could hardly stand. I just wanted to lie down and close my eyes.

"You haven't been eating again," my mom said.

Not this. Not now, I thought. I didn't have any energy or reserves left to talk about this again. But my mom didn't want to talk about my eating habits.

"Mom wanted to talk about some things that were bothering her," I wrote the next day. *"Boy was that hard. I was so tired I really didn't want to listen. She could tell because she got upset and said that I didn't care about her. But in the end she got to talk, almost like a small child. But I guess I do the same thing sometimes."*

Sometimes on road trips, I did feel close to my mom. Occasionally on rest days we would buy a matinee movie ticket, then when the movie was over, we'd sneak into another movie that was about to start. Sometimes we would watch three or four movies in one day. She'd long since discarded her earlier rules about "evil" movies and TV. On other rest days we would go to bead shops, where I would collect supplies to make necklaces to give away to peers, my silent love language.

Several months before Las Vegas, we had been having one of our "good" trips when we stopped in Waco, Texas, to meet up with a TV crew from Nickelodeon. The approach to the climbing area where the shoot would take place, Reimers Ranch, was totally flat. There wasn't a rock in sight, but as I walked, a small limestone fissure appeared along the ground, growing larger and deeper, until I found myself scrambling down inside it. The rock was dripping and otherworldly, hidden in the crust of the earth, the routes steep and unique.

I hadn't wanted to do the interview, but my mom had, so she told me to pray about it. Praying, however, had begun to feel difficult. I was feeling really angry at god—well, more accurately, angry at everything. The isolation of my life in Georgia had sent me into a deep, profound depression. I agonized over each and every decision and what it meant. If I went climbing and it rained, did that mean I had sinned and god was punishing me? If I didn't climb and it was a beautiful day, did *that* mean I had sinned? Would I get out of shape if I skipped a day? No matter what I did, I was haunted by guilt. I couldn't figure out why everything that I *wanted* felt wrong, while everything I thought I *should do* felt exhausting. I couldn't find the balance between god and climbing. Sometimes I'd feel afraid that I was putting climbing before god, which I wasn't supposed to do. But then I'd think that god wanted me to climb. Most of the time I didn't even enjoy climbing, but I felt like I was sinning if I wasn't outside climbing. I even felt like I was sinning if I was in the gym instead of outside. The inside of my head was a three-ring circus.

I went to my mom for advice the day before the photo shoot at Reimers Ranch and she told me, "You just have to do your best. You can't do it yourself. You can't be self-activated. You have to rely on god's power to do what you cannot do. All you can do is what you can. It's all about your attitude. You must have an attitude as unto the Lord, rather than one of discontent. Call out to god and give it to him and he will mount you with wings of eagles." Her advice was often wrapped in religious jargon like this, phrases pulled from Bible verses, and other miscellaneous anecdotes from things she had heard or read.

Feeling good about her response, I tried to tell her how I had been feeling about my eating problem. "I feel full all the time, but I also want to eat all the time. I don't know the balance of that either. I just hate it," I said. "All I think about is food. I hate myself and I'm sick of it. I'm disgusting and in sin but I can't do anything about it. Sometimes," I said, afraid to keep talking, "I feel like I can't go on."

"Every time you eat, take a bite of food and say, I praise god. I eat unto the glory of god," she replied. She didn't get mad, but she didn't hear me, either.

Feeling relieved to get some of what I had been feeling off my chest, I grinned and goofed off a little with the camera crew the next day. The interview with Nickelodeon went surprisingly well, and we all went out to eat at a restaurant after. Normally, restaurants terrified me because I couldn't see a label to count the calories, but that night I ate my whole dinner and still felt really good.

On the way home from the restaurant, though, my mom pulled into a parking lot and slammed on the brakes. She turned to me and yelled, "You aren't eating enough!"

Whenever I felt like I was doing a little better with food, she'd start worrying, and I'd get defensive. But when I was really struggling, she didn't seem to notice. It was almost as though the worrying had more to do with her than me. Or maybe I was just rationalizing so that I didn't have to get better. Either way, the hurt I felt at that moment sliced me deeper than a knife ever could. I felt blindsided and wanted to punch her, punch myself, punch anything. I had to be good enough for her, but not too good, or she would be jealous. People would want me and not her, which was dangerous. No matter what I did or didn't do, it wasn't enough.

"Fine!" I screamed back, my body shaking, tears streaming down my cheeks. "Give me the food! *I'll eat it all!*" I took all the food from our climbing packs and stuffed it in my mouth while we drove home, eating and eating and eating. My stomach felt like it was ripping open.

When we got back to our hotel room, I lay down on the tile bathroom floor, clutched my stomach, and sobbed. My mom was livid.

"You are so mean!" she screamed. "Why? Do you hate me? *You think I never do anything right!* I do everything for you! What else do you want from me? You just can't ever be grateful," she yelled while I laid on the floor.

All I felt was hate, radiating out of me in every direction and reflecting inward as well.

I closed the door and tried to stuff my fingers down my throat, but I couldn't do it. I have never thrown up easily and couldn't stand the feeling of my calloused fingers scratching the back of my throat. *That* kind of eating disorder would never be for me.

CHAPTER 9

TO KEEP THE HEART FROM STOPPING

After we moved to Georgia, my homeschooling happened through video and correspondence courses. My French class videos looked as though someone in the mideighties had held up a camcorder during a live class. I would often fall asleep during them. Math and science were correspondence courses. I got lesson booklets in the mail for each new section, then took a test at the end and mailed back my results. These subjects were difficult for me, and without anyone to ask for help, I spent many a day slumped over the table crying, frustrated and dejected. A couple of times my dad tried to help me late at night, after he got home from work, but I was exhausted and on the verge of tears before we even began.

I discovered that the answers to the tests were at the back of the book, and since I didn't have much adult supervision on "school days," it was easy to cheat on math tests. Even with the answers right there, I still barely made it through the first chapter of the chemistry book. English was the only subject that I could just sail through.

Finally, we all realized that homeschooling wasn't working, so my parents decided to create a fake homeschool diploma from "Brentsville Academy," named after the street we had lived on back in Kentucky, so that I could attend community college. There, I could arrange to take in-person courses when I was home for longer stretches between competitions.

Sitting in our kitchen, my parents discussed what grades to give me. "Let's give her a C in chemistry," my mom said. "Since she's not good at science it will look more real. . . . And a lower grade in math." They typed it up and printed it out and voilà, I had graduated high school.

I was becoming even more isolated—and exhausted. I broached the subject of my fatigue with my mom, unsure of how to communicate how serious it felt. I understand now that when muscles have no glycogen, they are in a permanent anaerobic state. There is no glucose in the system to fuel them. Add in an anaerobic activity like climbing, and it's a recipe for extreme fatigue. Malnutrition also affected my sleep. My body was essentially afraid to sleep too deeply because it was trying to keep my heart from stopping.

My mom mentioned taking me to a doctor a couple of times, but each time, for one reason or another, that plan fell through. Finally, one of the appointments stuck. *"I'm going to a doctor on Monday,"* I wrote late at night, unable to sleep despite my fatigue, my handwriting careening off the line in the darkness. *"I almost want to see how skinny I can get before I go. Almost like I want him to see how bad it is. Sorta like I want bad news."* The fact of the matter was that when I looked in the mirror, I didn't think I looked all that skinny. I didn't think my weight was actually low enough yet for anyone to notice. I didn't think I was sick enough.

That weekend, as I starved myself in preparation for the doctor appointment, my mom and I went for a run. I felt like I couldn't breathe as we jogged together. My chest hurt with a ripping pain and I felt sick to my stomach, like I was going to throw up. When we got home, my heart sent spasms shooting through my body, like electric shocks. My pulse sped up, as though my soul was screaming, *No! Stay alive, stay alive!* My forehead grew damp with sweat, my hands shook, and my skin prickled all over with goosebumps. Wooziness flooded me and my vision closed in, nearly to darkness, before opening back up again. Normally after running I'd feel hungry, but now I only felt bloated and strangely full.

My entire arm went numb, which I thought was because we had been running in the cold. When I tried to peel an orange, my thumb collapsed in on itself rather than puncturing the rind. I shook my hand out, like I did when trying to shake lactic acid out of my forearm on a hard route, trying to get it to work again. Still, I couldn't peel the orange and I nearly cried from the desire for calories. Instead, I sliced the orange open with a knife and greedily sucked out the juice.

That evening, I slipped into my room and grabbed a piece of paper from my pile of unfinished schoolwork—another area where I was supposed to somehow be totally self-motivated. I didn't even bother finding my journal. I had to get the feelings out before I burst.

I should read the Bible, pray, do something. Why aren't I? I'm just sinning and I know it but I'm not doing anything about it. I want to talk to Mom but I can't because she'll just get mad. I want to scream, hit things, anything. I'm driving myself insane and I know god can help but I'm not doing anything about it. Why? STOP YOURSELF!!!!!!! I want my desire for climbing back. Did god take it away because I wasn't grateful for it? Mom is just mad but she is literally the ONLY person I have to turn to. If only I could tell her, but she'll just get angry. Why? What's wrong with me? I just want to eat, but when I do I can't stop, and that's gluttonous, which is also a sin. I'm afraid god will punish me. Does he do that? Where's god? Have I let satan in, like mom says? Make it stop! I'm going crazy. Am I? What is this? Where's my mom? Why am I so messed up? My whole being feels tormented with something I can't quite put a finger on. God help me! What is happening? Where are you?

Afterward, I lay in the dark, panting, unable to sleep, my body on hyperalert.

While my initial desire was for the doctor to notice that something was wrong with me, by the time we made it to my appointment, the tide had turned. I was now consumed by a debilitating fear that something horrible would happen if I ate even one calorie too many. I was scared the doctor would make me eat.

I wore long johns underneath thick, fleece-lined work pants, and hoped that no one would question my wardrobe since it was winter. By that point, I had to wear multiple layers to stay warm in even balmy weather. On top I wore a turtleneck and a heavy wool sweater of my mom's. Clunky approach shoes completed the outfit, which I left on when they weighed me.

Despite all that clothing, I was shocked by the number on the scale—I'd lost more weight. *I don't even weigh THAT much,* I thought after seeing the number, almost as a self-congratulation. *I bet my clothes alone weigh at least five pounds.* But the doctor said nothing.

I have no memory of the doctor performing a throat culture that day, but somehow I left with a prescription for amoxicillin for strep throat. The doctor told my mom about mono, which he said went around among kids my age and could start as strep. He also mentioned that I was severely hypoglycemic, saying that I should increase my protein intake and eat several small meals throughout the day to manage the symptoms. He casually mentioned seeing a nutritionist. He did not comment on my dangerously low weight.

A week later, my mom and I went to the Red in Kentucky. Normally we camped when we came up to train, but the antibiotic had made my stomach feel weird from the outset, and suddenly I had diarrhea so intense we were forced to check into a nearby hotel. My stomach was painfully distended, puffed out as though someone had blown up a balloon and shoved it down my shirt. My skin was hot and tight to the touch. I felt excruciatingly full, and yet also violently empty. In between bouts of diarrhea, I sat in bed, propped up by pillows, eating Dairy Queen and watching television. Although I didn't know it at the time, my body would never be the same.

After the weekend at the Red, my stomach continued to bother me. It would remain painfully ballooned out for years. The waistband of my climbing pants dug into my distended stomach until my mom thoughtfully let out the elastic on each pair to accommodate my bloated belly.

I spent weeks lying on my stomach in pain in my bedroom, poring through thick study guides for the ACTs and SATs. I had taken the ACT and SAT previously so that my homeschool diploma would look more "real" when I applied to colleges, but I felt that my first go at the SATs wasn't good enough, so I took them again. The second time was in Paris, France, shortly before the World Championships in Birmingham, England. My mom and I got up very early and drove around Paris, lost, for what seemed like hours, until we found the American School. We arrived late, but I still fell asleep waiting for the test to begin. When the proctor announced the start in both English and French, I snapped awake, bleary and disoriented. Nonetheless, my score was slightly higher than my first attempt, so I took it. It was good enough that it would appear, on paper at least, that I had been all the way through high school.

We had also built a climbing wall in our garage in Georgia, and I trained there in true isolation, doing laps on the wall, grabbing the same holds over and over. There was nothing scientific about my routine; I just climbed until I'd done what felt like enough. Sometimes I'd draw tick marks on a paper, counting the number of laps I'd completed, like an inmate counting days in prison. After the antibiotic, there were many days when, in pain, my muscles on fire, I couldn't muster the energy to make up boulder problems. Instead, I'd just clock a certain number of moves or even just hang on the wall for a certain number of minutes. The goal was arbitrary, but it was the best I had.

Some days my belly would be slightly less distended than others, but everything I ate now ran right through me, completely undigested and painful. Still, my mom and I argued over my eating on an almost daily basis.

My anorexia had become even more complicated because, in addition to the mental aspect, eating now exacerbated the unbearable physical pain I was in. Even if I wanted to eat more, most of the time I physically couldn't.

I would lie on the floor of my bedroom, ostensibly the best female climber in the world, curled in the fetal position; my homework—words swimming in front of my eyes like indecipherable hieroglyphics—spread out next to a can of Ensure with a straw sticking out. There were days when the pain in my gut was so unbearable that I could only consume liquids, and the straw made the Ensure more palatable somehow.

I pulled further and further into myself, and began to wonder again if god was punishing me for some unknown transgression. I didn't know how to figure out what god's will was. Even small decisions felt huge and potentially catastrophic if I made the wrong choice. I was finding it harder and harder to pray. It had started to feel like I was speaking into a toy telephone, with no one on the other end, not even an echo—just the smell of plastic and a Fisher Price logo staring back at me.

CHAPTER 10

GOD WILL PROVIDE

In 1997 I won my second X Games and Rock Masters, as well as a number of other national and international competitions. I honestly don't know which ones or how many because I wasn't paying attention. While I traveled across Europe and to other places around the world for competitions, I also climbed countless other routes, from the tall, overhanging limestone of the Virgin River Gorge in Arizona to the white seaside cliffs of Les Calanques in France. Some of the climbs were rated as hard as 5.13+, and I regularly reached the top on my second or third try. By then, if I didn't onsight every 5.13a or 5.13b I got on, I thought I sucked. I know this because I have pieces of scratch paper that list the routes I climbed. Alongside each list is another long set of numbers, tracking each and every calorie.

And yet, despite all of this data to the contrary, I thought I was terrible. Anorexia had shrunk my view of the world. I was starving and desperate, constantly on the lookout for danger.

As an adult, I can appreciate that where we lived in Georgia actually had quite a bit of quality outdoor climbing, like the sandstone band of Little River Canyon, Alabama, the bouldering in and around Chattanooga, and the famous Tennessee Wall. The Obed River Gorge was nearby, and the New River Gorge wasn't too far either. At the time, however, I couldn't see it. I felt stuck in Georgia and I missed the

Red so much that my mom and I often drove up to Kentucky for a weekend of climbing.

Before one such trip, I planned out my climbing schedule so that I'd be rested and strong when we got to the Red. On the morning we were to leave, my mom said, "Change of plans. I don't want you to have to get up early, with your stomach and all, so we're going to leave in the afternoon instead."

"I'll adjust," I wrote as I waited. But at some point I realized the delay was because she was waiting for something to come in the mail from one of my sponsors. It didn't arrive until very late, so we decided to leave the next day.

The next morning, she still wasn't ready. She bustled about the house, fixing and cleaning, needing to send an email, go to the store, make a phone call. I climbed indoors. It was harder to stay patient. *"She said she wanted to help with training, but it feels as though she's intentionally keeping me from it, using my stomach issues as an excuse."* I wasn't sure if I was making this up or not, if I was selfish or not, if I could believe her or not.

It was late the following day that we finally left. My anxiety over the derailed plans had skyrocketed, but I tried to remain calm and patient so as not to anger my mom. Nonetheless, my wants, my desires—what I thought of as my selfishness—were too strong and slipped out. My mom got angry, once again battering me with words as we pulled out of the driveway.

"You need an attitude adjustment," she said.

I sat in the passenger seat of our silver SUV and cried as we got onto the highway, pulling off my wire-framed glasses to wipe away the tears. I couldn't take it anymore. I had tried so hard to be patient for so long, and all of my trying didn't seem to matter at all. In a frenzy of deep emotion that I had no idea how to process, I bent my glasses in half in my hands, squeezing them as they folded at the nose bridge, the metal frames digging into my palm. I focused on the pain. If I squeezed hard enough maybe I could break the skin, make the other, bigger pain in my heart go away.

WHOMP. My mom's hand shot from the steering wheel over to my side of the car, the back of her fist connecting with my chest. I sat back in my seat, my breath rushing out in a whoosh. Clutching the spot where her fist had landed, and my now ruined glasses, I uttered a slightly strangled sound and pulled my knees up to my chest. I was crying more now, but the brief moment of violence had somehow expelled the toxic energy, and we both calmed down.

As was her pattern, my mom was somewhat contrite after her outburst, not apologizing exactly, but more ready to listen. The conversations we'd have after these violent episodes sometimes felt like they brought us closer, as though the anger had to come out before she could hear my perspective, before I could see her viewpoint and let go of my own wants.

That day I told her, "I feel like I can't be good enough. When I mess up or make a mistake it hurts really deep and sometimes I need someone to say, 'You're trying. It's ok to make a mistake.' But it feels like you always tell me what I'm doing wrong and that I need to fix it."

"It's not so much what you're doing," my mom said as she drove, "but what your attitude is like and how you accept what happens to you."

I looked over at her and then back down at the destroyed glasses in my hands. Somehow my mom's words made it seem like the whole thing was my fault, like I was the one who needed to change. But in the aftermath of her anger, she was more comforting than damning, more soothing than judgmental, and I decided that she was right. I needed to do better, be better. I shouldn't have ruined the glasses. I'd need to put in my contacts, since I couldn't see anything without them. And I'd pay for my new glasses, since it was my fault that I broke them. I reminded myself that I needed to accept things and be thankful for them, rather than always wanting things to be done my way.

I needed an attitude change. I should have been blessing god every day for the amazing things he'd allowed me to do, instead of complaining. I should have been moving ahead with god in faith, even if things weren't perfect. I should have been humble and satisfied. Also, god was always there for us. His care was constant, through thick and thin, and I should have been listening for his voice, telling me what to do next. I sat in the car as we drove, letting go, letting go, letting go. Straining to hear god's voice.

This was my attitude as I approached my second X Games, which were held in San Diego. We rented a house by the beach, and I walked along the wet sand, curling my toes in it. There had been an athlete's meeting the night prior, and for a moment, as the meeting got underway, I desperately didn't want to be there, didn't want to be anywhere near the competition. It was all I could do not to get up and run out of the room. I gripped the chair with white knuckles, clenching my jaw and jiggling one leg up and down maniacally as a wave of emotion urging me to flee ran through me.

I was not prepared for the competition, and yet everyone was expecting me to win. I was terrified. *Just focus on finishing,* I muttered to myself. *Just get through the comp.* That had become my mantra. Life in our house in Georgia had become so unbearable, so intensely lonely, that I felt like I was literally going insane. Each day I would tell myself to *just get through the day.* That was how I kept going.

It was during those moments that I leaned on my religion to lessen the stress. My favorite Bible verse was about god lifting me up with the wings of eagles, and reading it would soothe my panic, give me something to focus on.

Liv Sansoz was, as usual, my primary rival at the X Games. The 80-foot overhanging competition wall, gray and speckled with texture, featured two large roofs—the first at one-third height and another at three-quarters height. The second roof was about 10 feet long and, just below the lip, it was so steep it tilted beyond horizontal. Liv and I both successfully completed the preliminary route, but she lost points for clipping the anchor mere seconds past the twelve-minute time limit, which put me ahead of her in the semifinals. Again, we both onsighted the route, along with thirty-one-year-old Russian expat, Elena Ovtchinnikova—an elite competitor in both speed and sport climbing who began competing for the United States a year earlier.

The finals route weaved a circuitous line up the same wall as the other rounds. Near the top, a long leftward traverse at the lip of the second roof guarded the hardest moves, followed by a rightward traverse toward the finishing jug. Muriel Sarkany, of Belgium, and Liv both completed the route, which meant I had to do as well in order to win.

I don't remember the climbing, but the X Games recap footage shows me in my element on a steep wall, moving slowly, methodically, and without any apparent stress. Even the crux above the second lip appeared unchallenging as I worked my way through it. A final little pop to the finishing hold sealed my win and, as I was lowered down, I raised my arms in victory. Atop the podium, a wide, bright smile betrayed my shy, sixteen-year-old reticence.

I wrote in my journal that the route wasn't even close to being hard enough. Liv and I had both onsighted all three routes, but she had run out of time. I felt like I had won by default. *"I won the competition, but it wasn't because of me,"* I wrote. *"I didn't really feel like I had actually won, but I'm still incredibly grateful. I have never felt so much pressure in my life. I have never prayed so hard."*

After the X Games, I found out that my dad had booked us tickets for another major international competition in Serre Chevalier, France. Given the now chronic issues with my stomach, I wasn't sure if I was up for doing it. My mom must have made the decision, though, and as per usual, he followed her lead.

The timing for Serre Chevalier was complicated. For the past few years, my mom had taught at a Christian camp in Colorado called Horn Creek. Usually I went with her, but there was almost no way to climb at the camp, making it very difficult to adequately train for a difficult competition.

Prior to the X Games, I had said, "If I end up doing Serre Chevalier, I'm a little worried I won't be able to get in enough training because of Horn Creek."

"God will provide," my mom responded. "I can go with you to Colorado Springs to climb at the gym on my days off."

"Totally," I responded, then added slowly, "Wouldn't it be crazy if I, like, stayed in California after the X Games to train?"

She looked at me, scanning me up and down with her eyes as though searching for subterfuge. I already knew it was a no. Since she was committed to teaching at Horn Creek, she wouldn't have been able to stay in California with me.

"And climb with who? People who will lead you astray, pull you down the path of satan." I could feel the irritation coming off of her in waves.

"Well, some people said that I could—"

"You're supposed to help with the kids at Horn Creek," she said, cutting me off. I felt like she was about to boil over.

"Yeah, yeah, you're right. Never mind," I mumbled.

"It bugs me that she doesn't think I can withstand the pressures of the world. I'd like to prove to her that I can," I wrote later. *"She won't let me do anything that she's not there for. She seems to be more and more controlling. I mean, who can take better care of me than god? It makes me look forward to being eighteen."*

When I found out that I'd be attending Serre Chevalier, I felt a deep sense of panic. I wrote over and over in my journal that I didn't know how I was going to do it. That I was scared to death. That it was such a leap of faith.

Soon after, a fax arrived at my dad's office with details about the competition, and he brought it home after work. As I looked it over, my mom reading over my shoulder, I felt only fear. I was completely overwhelmed, in way over my head, with no way out.

"Can I please, please skip Horn Creek so I can train?" I begged my mom.

"No, we are committed to Horn Creek," she shot back. "*You* wanted to go."

"But that was before I knew I had to do Serre Chevalier."

"You are never content, never thankful," she responded. "I'm doing Horn Creek for you. So you can be around other Christian teenagers.

You just have to trust god. He will provide, as long as you have an attitude unto him. Just climb unto the glory of god, and it doesn't matter how you do."

But it doesn't work that way, I thought, realizing that now there was no choice. I just had to get through it. *And it does matter.*

CHAPTER 11

WATCHING THE STARS

Horn Creek sat at the base of the Sangre de Cristo Mountains near Westcliffe, Colorado. The sprawling, picturesque campus had a wide variety of activities, from a ropes course to swooping waterslides where black flies bit my ankles while I waited in line. The conference center resembled the log cabins where the campers slept. Some of the buildings had rock chimneys that I could boulder on, and I would traverse the buildings in an effort to maintain some of my climbing fitness during our two-week stay.

Eating at Horn Creek was always a challenge. Food was prepared banquet-style, rich with bread, fat, cheese, and oil. Nothing was packaged and it was impossible to control the number of calories I consumed. It was a veritable land mine for an anorexic, and I struggled at each meal. Added to this was the fact that certain foods seemed to exacerbate or alleviate my constant stomach pain. Sometimes I skipped meals entirely, preferring instead to boulder on the rock buildings, circling them in a traverse while everyone else was at breakfast or lunch. Other times, I would slip out of the meal early, hoping that no one would notice.

One good thing about Horn Creek was that I got to bunk with the other teenagers instead of my mom. I was rarely ever without her, aside from being in isolation at comps, and never around kids my age. I found myself observing the other campers almost as if they were rare, exotic animals. My own cloistered life felt so far removed from that of an ordinary teenager that it was hard for me to relate at all. Despite my odd, silent ways, the kids at Horn Creek were incredibly kind to me, and I felt both less shy and more energized around them. I was still an outsider, but I felt ok about it. Nobody treated me like the twelve-year-old I looked like.

One evening, all the teenagers went to a nearby rifle range. "Come on Katie," they hollered. I followed, running to catch up with them as they wove through the treed property of Horn Creek, laughing and joking the whole way. At the rifle range, everyone laid on their backs in the grass. I lay down on the edge of the group and looked at the stars, listening to the other teenagers talking and laughing. I marveled that it could be so fun to do such a simple thing. They seemed so relaxed and carefree, confident of their place in the world.

"And then," one of them regaled, "the entire soda exploded, basically in his face!"

Everyone laughed at the story. I grinned. It did sound funny, shaking up a soda to prank a friend in the middle of a movie theater. I had never been to a movie theater with just friends.

"You're sixteen, right Katie?" someone asked me. I wasn't sure who it was coming from.

"Um yeah," I responded.

"Do you have your license yet?"

"Um, no. Not yet." I wasn't sure how to explain that I spent half the year traveling to competitions, and that, since I was with my mom all the time, I didn't really need to know how to drive.

"Oh my gosh you have to get yours!" A girl said excitedly. "It's the best." She started telling a story about getting hilariously lost the day after getting her license.

I drifted off into my own thoughts, listening to them chatter. I wondered what that would be like, driving in a car that my parents had bought me as a gift, by myself, or with friends maybe. To go through life feeling like you belonged, rather than feeling like you were taking up space meant for someone else. But for now, I was content just being included at all, despite my obvious differences.

On another night, while most of the teenagers were around a bonfire, a few people decided to break off and head back to the bunk-
house. They invited me to go with them. I wrote about that moment
in my journal with a lot of exclamation points. I could not believe
that they'd invited me, that they liked me.

There was one boy that I liked in return. He was loud and cracked
a lot of jokes and I was drawn to the carefree ease and confidence
he projected. Secretly I wondered if I would be allowed to have a
boyfriend if he was a Christian. Then I looked down at my prepubes-
cent body with its swollen belly and felt ashamed. I couldn't fathom
anyone, ever, wanting me to be their girlfriend.

The next morning, my mom came to get me. She was wearing jeans
and a green Horn Creek sweatshirt, her dark brown hair shining in
the sunlight, mascara and concealer carefully applied. Her smile
was wide and she talked and laughed with another teacher as they
strolled down the path. When I saw her, the bottom dropped out. I'll
never forget that moment. I wanted to die. Right then, right there.
Just disappear into the folds of the earth and never come back.

The day before the bonfire, my mom had a day off teaching, so we
had gone to a gym in Colorado Springs. I had gut-wrenching diarrhea the entire day, but I didn't want to say anything to my mom
because I knew she would make me eat. Instead I just told her that
I didn't feel good, didn't want to climb. It led to an explosion of fury.
In the end, I climbed.

"She got so mad at me because she thought I was depressed again,"
I wrote. *"Nothing is ever good enough for me. It hurt me very deeply,
all the things she said. I can't even repeat them, there were too many
to even write. She just drove me into the dirt."*

Unlike most of our fights, we hadn't resolved this one. The hurt
from her words still lingered when I saw her the morning after the
bonfire, like a heavy cloak that I couldn't get rid of.

The only way I could process my feelings was to write them
down, but that time I couldn't bring myself to write out what she
had said to me. It was as if putting that on paper would make the
experience more real, when all I wanted to do was forget. I couldn't

accurately recall any of what was said, so I won't try. I just know that it was worse than usual.

Instead, I wrote:

> *I hate it when people are angry at me because I want to be liked and accepted. The reason I hate climbing is because I feel like people only like me because of my climbing. It hurt so deep when mom told me all those things I was doing wrong because I just wanted her to love me the way I was. I don't want to have to try and be good enough for her too. I also realized that I'm very cut off from any human affection. I don't even get hugs from mom very often. Some of this I didn't tell her though.*

I knew that part of the reason she didn't hug me was because I didn't let her. If she tried, I would stiffen and pull away. But still, I wanted someone to envelop me in a giant hug and tell me that it was all ok.

As an adult I learned that a lack of physical touch or affection as a child can have a profound effect on the ability to form bonds with other people later in life. The vagus nerve, a bundle that runs from the spinal cord to the abdomen, needs touch to develop fully. A lack of touch can prevent the glands that produce oxytocin—the hormone that helps us form bonds with other people—from developing properly, resulting in a decreased ability to be intimate or compassionate.

———

At Serre Chevalier, the loudspeakers played "A Whiter Shade of Pale" while I climbed, my mom muttering "good girl" from behind the lens of the video camera each time I moved past a tricky section. I tied with Liv for first, which sent us to a superfinal, held late at night. We were put on the men's route, a large spotlight highlighting our movement up the dark wall, where I was stymied by a huge rightward span between two handholds relatively low on the route.

I tried several body positions before deciding to just stab for the hold, even though I knew I couldn't reach it. I fell off where Liv—a bit taller than I am—had finagled herself into a horizontal position with her right hip against the wall. She had lurched and barely caught the hold. The crowd roared applause, and she continued another twenty feet before she finally pumped off. I ended up coming in second, but I had put in my all, so I felt good about the end result.

Back home from Serre Chevalier, I got a call from *Outside* magazine. They wanted to fly Chris Sharma and me to Yosemite National Park, the heart and soul of traditional climbing in America, for an article. I was so excited. I desperately wanted to climb in Yosemite, and with Chris, so I said yes without thinking. But I had forgotten one thing. To check with my mom.

After a recent competition, I'd had a long conversation with Chris. We had talked about the future, and what climbing meant to us, and about wanting to do a big wall someday. Sitting there with legs outstretched, cold concrete at my back, it had felt nice to share my experiences with someone who could actually relate. He knew what it was like to not really go to school, to feel the push and pull of being an athlete and a teenager. Talking to Chris had given me a feeling of connection and belonging. But *Outside*, and Chris and Yosemite, were all too good to be true, and I knew it. The opportunity was quickly squashed, with all the rage and suspicion I had become accustomed to. There would be no Yosemite trip.

My mom warned me, saying "You need to be careful spending so much time with Chris. You have to be careful what people think. They will start talking. Chris will be your trial that will take you down the path of sin."

Late that night with a pillow stuffed under my abdomen to relieve some of the pain and distention, I wrote about the impossible tightrope I had to walk. Be friendly and outgoing and talkative, or else no one would like me. But not too much, or else people would talk and my mom would feel abandoned. Be in the world, but not of it. Stay wary of anyone who only "wanted things from me" but still perform well and show Christ through my success. Succeed, but without anyone's help or tutelage. Be happy, don't be depressed, accept every obstacle that god threw in my path with grace and joy, without a single selfish teenage bone in my body. Most of all, be my mom's best friend and confidant, while telling reporters that she was my coach and teacher.

I wrote about how I couldn't wait to turn eighteen and leave home. I wrote imaginary tales about what my life would be like when I was free, finding escape in the stories I wrote. It seemed so peaceful compared to my present life, which felt like constant, exhausting effort. Chris and I had also been talking about climbing big walls, but I knew in my heart that my mom would never let that happen while I was still with her.

Sometimes I thought, maybe if I starve myself enough, if I get just sick enough, I would have to go stay in the hospital—and *then* someone would notice and help. Or maybe I could take just enough painkillers, not to die exactly, but to overdose so that I'd be taken to the hospital. And then I'd get to rest. After I had to turn down the trip to Yosemite, I sat down at the family computer to try and find out exactly how many painkillers I'd need to take for that to happen.

By August it was clear that my stomach issues were not getting better, so my parents scheduled a colonoscopy for me. We had been to see a doctor a couple of times since the antibiotics. Once, I was prescribed probiotics. On another visit, a different doctor again suggested that I see a nutritionist for my severe, recurring hypoglycemia.

I went to that nutritionist once. She never directly mentioned my weight, focusing instead on the hypoglycemia. She told me to keep a food diary to monitor my blood sugar. Telling an anorexic to keep a food diary is like telling an arsonist to play with fire.

My parents' behavior during this period also felt strange. My mom knew I was starving myself, but when confronted with doctors, the story changed dramatically. It felt like we were all dancing around the obvious thing, going to doctors here and there, looking for all kinds of medical reasons—some disease or malady—for my problems, rather than addressing the truth. I started to wonder if maybe there really was something wrong with me—a terrifying thought.

The day before the colonoscopy, we traveled from the Red to Georgia. I was supposed to drink a large jug of clear liquid prior to the appointment. Eight ounces every thirty minutes. What I didn't realize, though, was that the drink was designed to empty the digestive tract of everything—and quickly. My mom and I were forced to pull over at a grocery store. I drank eight ounces after eight ounces of what looked like water but was actually thick and disgustingly sweet. I gagged on it as I choked it down, my shrunken stomach stretching painfully with all the liquid. As it passed through my system, I made a mad dash to the grocery store bathroom. In and out I went for hours. In to use the restroom, then back out to drink eight more ounces, then back in. It was mortifying, but I was in so much discomfort that I had to compartmentalize everything else and just get through it. Eventually, long after darkness had fallen, my trips to the bathroom grew less frequent. I lay in the seat, exhausted and empty, as we drove home.

The medical report from the colonoscopy stated that, essentially, the lining of my intestines was gone. The blood vessels inside my colon were exposed, and there was a fair amount of bleeding. The scope itself even caused some spontaneous bleeding. The ileum, the last section of the small intestine, specifically, had numerous inflamed areas, which suggested ulceration, possibly ileocolitis. I was prescribed an anti-inflammatory called Asacol. That's it. Once again, no one mentioned my perilously low weight.

From that moment onward, though, my mom latched onto ileocolitis as the cause of all my problems. The medical report and the doctor had said that it was possible, but we didn't pursue it further to get a definitive diagnosis. I suppose ileocolitis was a much easier explanation to swallow than anorexia, and so that was the story she told everyone. End of discussion.

"You don't have an eating disorder, you have Crohn's disease," she'd tell me whenever I tried to broach the subject. She told me that I had Crohn's so many times in those years that eventually I wasn't sure what was true.

Sometimes, when the moment was right, I would ask why I hadn't been actually diagnosed with Crohn's, if that's what I had. "It's an insurance issue," she'd tell me. "They don't want to write it down because then you'd have a pre-existing condition." At the time, it made sense and I ended up telling people I had Crohn's disease myself. Sometimes I even found myself wondering if I had made up the eating disorder, despite it taking over my life behind closed doors.

Because the lining of my intestines was essentially gone, I was no longer digesting the little food that I was able to eat. At one point, when I was sixteen, my weight plummeted even further as my electrolytes were thrown out of whack and my blood sugar continued to dip. On some days, my whole body shook when I tried to climb. My muscles would burn and it felt as though the tendons in my arms were tearing. I felt indescribably tired all the time, hot and sweaty one second, my skin prickling with goosebumps, freezing the next. At night, unable to sleep, I'd stay up late, writing in my journal.

Eating solid food hurt too much, so for a while I lived on Ensure drinks and Ben & Jerry's ice cream, the only things that didn't feel like they were destroying my insides. Even now, when I get a stomachache, I head straight for the ice cream aisle. So thank you, Ben and Jerry—you saved my life.

And yet still, just a month after my colonoscopy, my body and mind falling apart, I went back to Italy and won my second Arco Rock Masters.

CHAPTER 12

BIRMINGHAM

In 1997, Christian Griffith invited me to climb in Europe with him and Tommy Caldwell. Christian was one of the best American sport climbers in the 1980s and early 1990s, and the owner of my first sponsor, a climbing company called Verve. Of course my mom said no, and I didn't press the issue. Instead, my mom, my brother, and I went on a family climbing trip to Europe, culminating in the World Championships in Birmingham, England, held in November, on the day I turned seventeen.

Birmingham was cold and gray when we arrived. My mom and I entered the large building where the competition would be held, passing Liv Sansoz on a stairwell. She and I were competing against one another on a regular basis at this point in our careers. Despite rarely feeling brave enough to talk to her, in some ways I felt like I knew her.

Muriel Sarkany, on the other hand, wasn't on my radar in the same way. She was my height, sturdier in build and calm in temperament, with thick, brown hair that she always pulled back in a low ponytail. By 1997, it wasn't only Liv and I vying for first place—now it was Liv, Muriel, and I.

Muriel didn't seem to hold any darkness, didn't seem tortured in the way I perceived Liv to be, or in the way that I was, so she was of less interest to me. Instead, I would watch Liv as she warmed up or talked to her fellow French competitors. I wanted to know what was going on in her mind. Part of me wished I could say to her, "I see your pain. Can you see mine, too?" But thoughts like those sounded crazy, even to me.

Sitting quietly in a corner, I watched Liv, Muriel, and the other competitors chat with team members and get massages from coaches. Watching was how I had learned to climb, but sometimes I wondered what it would be like to have a teammate, coach, or friend.

Despite feeling exhausted and unwell, I made it to the finals. Before the climb, the other finalists and I were ushered out of isolation to preview the route, two undulating, nearly 45-degree walls, sweeping up as though forming the sides of a square to meet at a giant, horizontal roof. From there, the wall continued up steeply, eventually turning the lip of the roof, before finishing with a short, overhanging headwall. Any climber that made it to the end of the route without falling would have to pull up a rope heavy with drag to clip the anchor.

In this style of competition, each climber had one chance at the wall. Fall, and you were done. This now-or-never mentality usually worked for me. But instead of tracing a path up the wall in my mind, memorizing holds, anticipating tough sections, and making a plan, my thoughts that day were a blur, preoccupied with how horrible and empty I felt.

The wall felt like a stage—World Cups were designed as a spectator sport. Spotlights illuminated the dark amphitheater, causing the route to glow and casting shadows all around. Rows of chairs and bleachers lined the cavernous space where spectators watched, craning their necks upward to view the tiny climber far above. Climbing was much more popular in Europe than in the US, with athletes traveling in teams sponsored by their township, sometimes with a team coach, and wearing team jackets in the colors of their flag. I was at least ten years younger than all but one or two other competitors and often the only American.

I was freezing. My body had long since lost the ability to stay warm, so I clutched my arms around my midsection, my legs jittering in an attempt to warm my core, my jaw clamped down tight to quell nervous teeth-chattering. My mom's oversized fleece was draped over me, my long hair in its usual ponytail, thinning at the temples so that small tufts stuck out at all angles.

We were allotted six minutes to view the intricacies of the finals route, to decide which hand to place on each hold to maximize effort, how to strategically place our feet on each nub, where to clip the rope, where to rest. One wrong move and I could find myself out of sequence, hands irreparably crossed, making it impossible to move to the next hold, thus ending my competitive run.

Some competitors held their arms in the air, moving from one hold to the next, pantomiming how they would later climb the route. Others used binoculars, trying to get a closer look. Many of them stood in small clusters, chatting to one another in various languages, as they tried to read the path that the routesetter had created. I refused to put my arms in the air to visualize my path up the wall. I had an intense need to make it as hard as possible for myself, to not take any advantage, to convince myself and everyone else that this meant nothing to me.

Liv and Muriel shared a language and would occasionally speak to one another, pointing at holds and peering through their binoculars. Beyond the customary kiss on the cheek from the podium, my interactions with her and Muriel were extremely limited. The few times I had spoken to Liv it had been halting and very awkward. I wondered what they thought of me, but it didn't matter. Even if we had shared a language, I would have been silent.

My stomach took a turn for the worse while we previewed the wall. A ripping sensation tore through my abdomen, sucking the breath out of me. I tried not to double over. *Not now. Oh god, not now.* Sweat beaded on my upper lip and I felt feverish and weak. I feared my legs would buckle at any second. My skin prickled as if a thousand tiny needles were bouncing all over my face and arms. It was my blood sugar plummeting—a feeling I knew all too well but didn't have a name for at the time.

I focused on the only thing that mattered—not shitting my pants, on a stage, in front of everyone. "Please hurry," I muttered to the clock under my breath. "Oh god, please help me."

God did not respond. Beg as I might for help, or for answers, there were none. Just empty space, and a mountain of unanswerable questions.

"Think about something else," I told myself. "Put your head somewhere else. You know how to do this." I made my mind into a tunnel, with a door at the end, and in there I tucked away my pain.

The wall loomed overhead. It looked alternately blue or gray in the spotlights, tan maybe. After one climb, I thought, it would be over, and I could leave. Just get through the day, don't think about it. Just get through the day, and then it will be over.

Finally, the six minutes were up and the competitors were ushered back into isolation. I headed straight to the bathroom and sat there, chills quaking my frame, my face turning white and clammy as I lost the contents of my body. The pills that I was taking for intestinal inflammation—two pills, three times a day—came straight out of me, whole, as did everything else I had eaten recently, which admittedly, wasn't much.

I'd told the doctor about how I wasn't digesting the pills, my face turning bright red.

"That's normal," he told me. "You're still getting the benefits of the medication."

As my distrust of doctors grew, I researched the medication online and learned that "you may sometimes see whole or partial tablets/capsules in your stool. If this occurs frequently, tell your doctor. You may not be absorbing enough of the medication."

Of course the doctor didn't listen, didn't help me, I thought as I sat, stranded on a toilet in England, my teenage brain drowning in self-pity. *Nobody sees, nobody ever helps me. Nobody. I am on my own.*

I clutched the handicap railing as I laid my forehead on it, cooling my feverish skin. I didn't think I could get off the toilet, but I also knew that I had to climb soon. I had to convince all those people watching to believe in god, through my performance on the wall.

Liv and Muriel both climbed before me, and I had heard the cheers from the crowd. I knew they did well, maybe even finished the route.

I felt the weight of that knowledge on my already tired body and mind. Sitting in the cold isolation room, watching each climber exit the finals, one by one, I begged god and my body to cooperate.

Finally, it was my turn to climb. As I was ushered out, I felt weak, dehydrated, and distracted. My stomach was unnaturally distended from my latest bout of intestinal duress, and my harness pressed on it, hurting but also supporting the stretched skin.

Sweat dried on my temples as I approached the spotlit climb. My hands felt clammy. I had no idea where the climb went—I wasn't really thinking about that at all. I was thinking about how bad my stomach hurt, how achingly tired I was. I tried to tell myself to get it together and focus, but my mind was foggy.

I stepped up to the start of the route. Reaching up on tiptoes, I grabbed the first hold with both hands, pulled my feet off the ground, and began clawing upward very slowly—my signature style. The timer had started; the crowd was watching. Before long, my muscles began to burn, creaking and quivering with each hold. Each move was painful, like something inside me was tearing. Normally on competition climbs I could focus so intently that everything else would disappear. It made sense to me, and I could find the path of least resistance. But this time, I couldn't detach.

I was present in the moment, but I couldn't tune into my body, leave my mind behind, or *feel* the way the movement of the route should go. Instead, I heard the rustle of spectators behind me. I felt the texture of the hold I was gripping, the slip of the rope as it slid through my fingers to clip into the cold metal of the quickdraw. I heard the sound of faraway music playing from tinny loudspeakers, a bright, cheery tune about perseverance that grated on me, utterly dissonant to my state of mind. I felt my forearms swell as they filled with lactic acid from gripping tiny holds, sensed the fatigue in my fingers as they lost strength.

On the overhanging 45-degree wall, I gripped an edge with my right hand, barely large enough for a single finger pad, then pulled with all my might, stepping my left foot high and reaching as far as my frame would allow. I braced my right arm in a lock-off until my left hand slipped over a small, bulbous hold called a sloper, not in-cut but rounded and awkward for my small hand. From there I twisted my right hip into the wall, pivoting my body and pushing with my left arm, to reach out to the side and catch another small hold. The moves felt longer than normal, each pull to the next hold burning my insides as my muscles struggled for oxygen, energy, and electrolytes.

Finally, I reached a hold that I could get three pads of my fingers over, and I sagged onto it, tucking my hips tight into the wall, my feet sharing a small edge beneath me, knees jutting out in a strange, vertical crouch. I relaxed my shoulders and arms as much as possible, letting my body hang from its frame to rest my starving muscles. I swung one arm down toward the ground, giving it a couple of solid shakes from the elbow, returning blood flow to my extremities and attempting to relieve my fatigued forearms. Once I had recovered a bit, I switched hands on the hold, giving the other arm a shake. I looked above and behind me at the path where the route went as it turned from 45 degrees to a horizontal roof.

I edged out from my perch and glanced at the clock. Time isn't supposed to be a factor for difficulty climbing, but I was climbing agonizingly slowly. Even with twelve minutes on the clock, there was still a risk that I would run out of time. Not as much time had passed as I expected, which was strange for me. I just wanted to get this over with.

On the roof, my calves and hip flexors strained as I used every ounce of leg strength I had to pull into the wall and relieve the stress on my arms. My long ponytail dangled straight down as I pulled up rope for another clip. Already the rope drag felt heavy from all the changing angles, and the weight of it twisted the figure-eight knot tied to my harness to the side.

I reached right to an undercling in the roof. The crowd applauded and a new song came on: "A Night to Remember," by Shalamar. Suddenly I realized that I had been distracted, thinking about all sorts of things rather than focusing on climbing, and I'd gotten ahead of myself. I had the wrong hand on a hold, and was in the crux section of the roof with no rest in sight. My heart stopped and my skin prickled with anxiety. Why hadn't I focused on what I was doing instead of thinking about my stomach, and pills, and food, and god?

I looked down through my feet at the horizontal terrain I had just crossed. Should I try and down climb, switch hands, and get in a better position for the next move, or would that cost too much energy? Distracted, my body lost its tension and my foot popped off its foothold. "Ooooooohh!" the audience groaned. I kicked my right foot above my head, searching for something to hook my heel over, but nothing stuck. I tried my left foot overhead instead, but again, my feet cut loose and my body hung limp. I swayed on the single handhold like a leaf in the breeze. A few seconds later I mustered the strength to get my feet back on the wall, but confusion fogged my mind—it was as if I had no idea how to move. I walked my feet out right but they cut loose once more. Dangling by my arms, I tried to lift my foot back to the roof—to no avail. After a few moments, I gave up, let go, and landed at the end of my rope, several feet down, in midair. A small squeal, then a puff of breath, came out of my mouth as I hung there.

The crowd gasped in shock, and I covered my face with my hands. I *always* finished the finals route, *always* clipped the chains, *always* won the competition.

I looked at my mom and saw her hands covering her mouth, not in jubilation as in the past, but in horror. The crowd was silent, stunned, and then gradually offered a brief smattering of the expected applause. As I was lowered down, dangling and spinning in space, my skinny arms and legs limp, I looked out at the people watching in the dark. The only thing I could think was, *now no one will believe in god.* Above all else, this was the one permeating thought. I had failed god.

———————————

I ended up in seventh place. I had never placed seventh before. I had barely even placed third before. Muriel won and Liv took second. I could feel the questioning eyes on me as I packed up my belongings from isolation. I felt as if everyone was saying, "We'll never believe in your god now. You've failed."

"What happened?" my mom asked me.

"Nothing," I responded. "I don't know. I'm tired."

But inside I was screaming, wishing someone would hug me, tell me that it was ok. But I didn't cry, didn't speak, didn't do anything.

"What did you eat today?"

I didn't answer. *If I'm just "sick," but don't actually have an eating disorder, then why do you care how much I eat?*

"Can we leave?" I asked her. "I don't feel good. I think it's my Crohn's. We don't have to stay for the awards."

My mom seemed happy to comply. I thought she was embarrassed by me. And now we didn't have any prize money to pay for this expensive trip, which was my fault. I had failed there too. I didn't know it at the time, but my mom had skipped out on paying the fees and dues associated with the Birmingham competition, so leaving quickly was an advantage.

I was too distraught to go to the after party. Instead I lay on the bed in our hotel room, curled around my painful belly. We wouldn't have gone anyway. After all, parties were sinful.

After returning home, I struggled to make sense of what had happened. I thought constantly of dying, imagining all the different ways of doing it. My climbing shoes lay beside the door, but I couldn't stand the thought of trying to climb in the cold garage alone, again, while whatever unknown illness that plagued me consumed my muscles.

Instead, I bought myself a car, a cherry-red Mitsubishi Eclipse. My family wondered why I would buy a car before getting my driver's license, but I knew the truth. I wrote it down, for my own proof, if nothing else. *I bought it because it makes me feel as though I can escape at any moment, should I need to.*

I decided to take January off and not climb. About a week into my hiatus, however, my agent told us that there were rumors that an eating disorder had affected my performance at Birmingham, and that we needed to address it.

"Somehow I knew," I wrote in my journal, *"when I fell off that wall that people wouldn't let me make a mistake. I knew it would be bad."*

In hindsight, I should have used the opportunity to open up. After all, I wanted so desperately for someone to notice. But I couldn't bring myself to say that I had an eating disorder.

My mom exploded at the news.

"You have a seed of discontent," she yelled at me. "You are so negative, your bad attitude ruins everything for everyone around you. All you do is think about bad things instead of looking at the positive, being thankful for the ways that god has blessed you. We have given up everything for you. No one will like you if you keep this up."

I was already aware of all my sins, but she wasn't finished.

"You are so selfish."

Then she shifted gears.

"You shouldn't care what people say. That shouldn't matter. The only thing that matters is what god says, his will. Living unto him and being a testimony for him."

"God is a god of grace," she told me. "He will forgive you as many times as you repent. He only punishes when you turn your back on him. Right now he is testing you, saying, will you trust me when it gets tough? Can you trust me even when everything seems wrong? You have to give thanks through everything, even if something happens that you don't want to happen. You have to have enough faith to believe that god will bring about greater things so you should be joyful. These trials will make you stronger. You should be looking to help others rather than being selfish. With each hold say, yes Lord, your will, not mine, be done."

I didn't even know how to make sense of her lectures anymore.

"Instead you only think about yourself. Everything has to be according to you. And for what. So I can sit in this shitty house with a husband who is never helpful, never around. He's allowed your father to depart as head of the household. He's allowed your brother to go down the path of sin. And he's allowed you to be sick. I should just leave, walk out on all of this like you've departed god's ways."

I had heard it all before. At least I could dream of driving off.

"Right now I'm living in sin," I wrote. *"Why can't Mom understand? Why does she hate me so much? Where is god? Is it god, or satan, making me feel like I'm sinning no matter what I do? Who is who?"*

My head was pounding, and my stomach was killing me. There was no way I could eat now.

CHAPTER 13

FED TO THE WOLVES

My brother came home periodically during my late teen years. Sometimes when he looked at me, I could see a deep sadness flash in his eyes. He cared, but he couldn't say or do anything—that wasn't how our family worked. But I knew that Scott saw the pain I was in, which was the solace I needed to get through that phase of my life. I can't thank him enough for that.

Once, many years later, I said to him, "I feel like I need to apologize. I feel like when I started climbing, all the focus got put on me and you were left in the dust."

"That's funny," he responded. "I feel like I need to apologize to you. I feel like I escaped and you got fed to the wolves."

At the end of 1997, my parents bought a house a few miles away from the one we'd been renting. I didn't yet have a climbing wall in the garage of the new house, so I didn't have a place to train. My dad said, "Well, you're going to have to find a plan B." It felt like plan X at that point.

Luckily, I now had my driver's license in addition to my car. I basked in the solitude and independence as I drove the thirty minutes to the local community college where I took classes. When I had enrolled the year before, my mom decided to do the same. My need to be away from her and to be alone had become so strong by then that I'd feel as though I was going to explode. She still got angry if I went running without her, but she couldn't get angry if I had to get to an early class. Other times, I would at first decide to spend the day alone, but then sit in the car crying because I felt like I was somehow doing something wrong.

My agent urged us to dispel the eating disorder rumors so that I could maintain my sponsorships. One way to do that, he said, was to win my third X Games. As the two-time defending champion, it would redeem my reputation after the disaster of Birmingham. With no place to train, I was to do this climbing almost exclusively outside.

The pressure of proving myself to the world made me want to run away. At one point I wrote a press release addressing the rumors.

"What bothers me most," I wrote, "is that nobody has ever confronted me directly about the issue, given me the chance to give explanation. It's pathetic of you climbers who, for the most part, pride yourselves on your strong character." I didn't stop there. "As for Birmingham, I am human. I am fallible. Am I not allowed to have bad days like the rest of the world? Apparently not."

In truth, I wished someone would ask me if I needed help.

That spring, a TV crew came to our house to film a commercial for the X Games. The commercial starts out with slow, sad music and water dripping from a cliff. You can hear me say with a slight catch in my voice, "I don't have much in common with other people." The video pans to a close-up of my eyes, slightly red around the rim. Then the narrator says, "It is hard to be seventeen years old. It is hard to be the best sport climber on Earth. It is hard to be Katie Brown." More sad music follows as the video pans to me climbing on the holds we had bolted to the underside of our deck, where I would do lap after lap.

I had to fight back tears during the interview. "Sometimes I feel really old," I said, my voice wavering, "even though I look really young." Depression had made me feel leaden and I could hardly speak, let alone talk about something as far-fetched as being a competitive athlete. I felt like a joke.

At one point they asked me about friends, and I mentioned that I had recently gone to visit an old friend from elementary school. What I didn't say in the interview was that the visit, and the reminder of all that I had left behind in childhood, had shattered me. I had become so distanced from the experience of a typical teenager that when confronted with the joking and camaraderie, their lightness and freedom, I couldn't relate. Instead, I felt exhausted. What I said on national television, though, was that hanging out with her just "hadn't been that much fun."

One night, after taking a shower, I looked in the bathroom mirror. There was a long, pronounced bulge on the side of my abdomen. I gingerly pushed on it, which caused excruciating pain. I swooned, retching as I agonized over what it might be. Then I searched online for possibilities: a hernia or tumor—something bad, I was sure.

Sobbing, I ran to my mom and we ended up in the emergency room. An X-ray revealed that I had an "excess of stool" blocking my intestines. It was a complication from gastroparesis, or delayed gastric emptying. Starvation is one of the things that can cause gastroparesis, but either no one knew this back then, or no one considered it. I was given a laxative and sent home.

The next day I was back at school. I took a test and went for a run, despite the pain I was in. Ignoring the sensations and needs of my body had become so commonplace that I didn't even think twice about it. I hadn't planned to eat anything until I went to the bathroom, but inerita took over and I frantically ate a candy bar and cheese crackers in the privacy of my car. I stuck my fingers down my throat, trying to bring the food up, terrified that it would get stuck in my intestines and explode. Nothing worked.

That night, in my daily Bible reading, I came to Psalm 119:71, which said, "It is good for me that I have been afflicted, that I may learn your statues." I threw the Bible across the room. I didn't want to be afflicted anymore. The devotional book I was reading said, "God will spare you from suffering, or he'll give you the grace to bear it." I threw that too. I didn't want to bear it. I didn't want to just accept all the shit and be ok with it.

In the book of Lamentations in the Bible, Jeremiah says god is angry at him because he rebelled. Had I rebelled without even realizing it? My mom said that god was leading me through a wilderness to prepare me for what he had planned in my future. I thought, if that was the case, then maybe I could bear it. But if I'd sinned and this was god's punishment, if he wasn't giving me another chance, I didn't think I could bear that.

I wished fervently that I could have energy again, feel hungry again. I thought back to my days at the Red, and then looked at what I had become, what I had deteriorated to, and decided that my sin was that I hadn't been grateful back then. Now the collapse of my body and spirit was all my fault, due to my ungratefulness. I asked and begged god for forgiveness. I begged him for another chance. I had no one else to turn to, no one else to talk to. The thing about religion as I knew it, was that this thing—climbing—was a gift from god. I had no personal agency in the sport at which I excelled. God had given me the gift of climbing, and he could just as easily take it away, almost on a whim, it seemed to me. And yet paradoxically, it was up to me to use that gift to glorify him.

Training more or less, having a bad day, needing more experience, or any of the innumerable reasons something might happen—reasons would have given me control over my success and destiny—those were not things that I ever even considered. To the world, I was still technically a champion climber, but inwardly, I wanted to die.

———————————

I trained for my third X Games that winter and spring exclusively outdoors while my dad and brother built a new bouldering wall in our garage. I can never thank them enough for the effort. One benefit of climbing outdoors was that I got to climb some with people other than my mom. I tried to be friendly and outgoing, but by the end of each day, I was thoroughly drained from the effort.

In the spring, I went to the Phoenix Bouldering Contest again. I told the organizer that I had Crohn's disease, so I wasn't planning to compete, but would be there as a spectator, and climbing for fun. I went with my brother—my mom wasn't there, although I can't recall why. The whole experience of being at a competition, surrounded by incredible athletes but without the pressure of competing myself, was liberating. Scott and I had fun picking boulder problems that looked appealing, rather than being worried about the point value.

After the competition, Scott stayed behind and I flew home. I felt great, until I got to the airport. As I thought about trying to find my mom, my fear of angering her came flooding back. She wasn't at baggage claim, where she usually picked people up at the airport. So I waited. And waited.

Since my mom was almost always late, it took me a while to realize something was amiss. She wouldn't be that late. I decided to check outside at pickup, and there she was, seething.

"I'm really, really sorry, Mom," I said. "It was an accident."

"You just never think about how your actions are affecting others." Later that night, she followed up with a letter.

Dear Katie,

Are you camping out in Phoenix? Especially Saturday night when Sunday you travel in a plane all night and then go to school. You will have no rest. What will your stomach do with no rest for two days and two nights? To say nothing about how you will behave with no sleep.

What is going on here? You're unable to do hardly anything in the evenings and you are going on this two-day epic. For what?

I talked to Scott and he said that is what is happening. Scott will take you down the path of the sinners if you let him. One little insignificant slip at a time and without you thinking he is. Not that he wants to do that, but he will. It will all make sense in human reasoning but not with First Corinthians it won't.

It is like Scott is deceiving me about taking care of you at all. But only if it doesn't inconvenience himself or his buddies? Bob is deceiving me in other areas. He took rolls of film of you and only brought 15 slides over.

Deception.

Never the whole truth, always leaving out the details so to elude me into thinking something different. Always the same things but different circumstances.

Nobody really cares about others. Only to use for personal gain. Or discard when they can't gain anymore from you.

It is like this house, what will really get done. Nothing. I gave up more, a kitchen, a bathtub, for a garage to boulder in that will never happen. Everything is for nothing. A dark cold house with a few antiques. Carpet that is ugly. All for what?

Why should I bother to clean, to put things away, to do anything? The only redeeming thing I have is my Lord, nothing else. He has allowed my son to depart from his way. He has allowed my husband to depart from being a father and spiritual head. He has allowed you to be very sick. He has allowed you to go your own way too.

Should I join you all? Forget who I was without Christ and just not care anymore. The pain is great that I feel for those I love. Yet my pain is nothing compared to what my Lord in heaven felt. Oh! But it hurts so.

She was mad that I'd gone to Phoenix without her. The joy I'd felt during the weekend away crumbled down around me. No matter how much I tried to please her, I would never be enough. At the same time, I thought, no one else was trustworthy—not even my brother. The letter, so light in my hand, carried a crushing weight. I slipped it into my journal.

Throughout the spring, bumps appeared on my abdomen that hurt when touched. They'd occasionally move around, leaving me quaking with chills. I searched for my symptoms online all the time, trying to figure out what was wrong with me and reading all kinds of worst-case scenarios. I went back to the hospital twice, once getting an ultrasound where they accidentally looked at my ovaries instead of my guts, and shortly before the X Games, getting an X-ray. I drank barium beforehand so that the doctor could get a better look at my intestines, which later resulted in excruciating pain as my body, in its gastroparesis state, tried desperately to process the liquid.

Despite all the pain, once I did start eating, it was as though some internal switch flipped. No matter how hard I tried, I couldn't stop until I was incredibly full. My desire to no longer be in pain started to win out over the control that anorexia had on me. The tide had begun to turn.

I experimented with different foods, trying to figure out what made me feel better, and what made me feel worse. I found that if I ate high-fat foods, I felt better, stronger, and my stomach hurt less. At seventeen, I finally started to gain weight.

I started running more too. When I was running, I felt free, like I could express myself. My thoughts felt less jumbled. But my transformation didn't come without challenges. At one point, my mom commented that all my muscle was transferring from my upper body to my lower.

"Climbing might be harder right now because you've gained weight but haven't gotten stronger to compensate for it," she said.

I looked in the mirror, terrified, and saw a flabby butt that wasn't even there.

Nonetheless, I somewhat impulsively decided to enter a national competition in Denver. The comp was held at a gym in Thornton called ROCK'n and JAM'n, whose 40-foot walls were unusually tall for the time. I knew a lot of people there, and many of them noticed and commented on the change in my body, telling me that I looked great. At the same time, I felt strangely separate, as though I had spent years on another planet, only to come back to Earth to find that I no longer fit where I had once belonged.

I was out of shape, and for the first time, I felt nervous about how I would perform at a national. Would I still be able to win? As I climbed the finals route I heard every rustle from the crowd, and I felt my arms grow increasingly pumped as they tried to support my heavier body. As I neared the anchor, my elbows rose in the desperate chicken-wing position that climbers recognize as a classic sign of imminent failure. Sure enough, I fell just shy of the finish. And yet, I had still managed to eke out a victory. I felt intensely grateful.

As the year progressed, I grew increasingly disillusioned with doctors, and eventually stopped talking about my symptoms altogether. To this day, I have debilitating anxiety around anything health-related, and I become defensive in the doctor's office, assuming that whatever issue I'm in there for will be categorically dismissed.

I spent my teen years waiting for someone to notice what was really wrong. But eventually it became clear that if I wanted to feel better, I had to figure out my eating issues on my own. I couldn't handle any more examinations, or another test or procedure that showed nothing.

During one internet search, I discovered that laxatives could be helpful for people with Crohn's. I decided, since I couldn't seem to control how much I ate anymore, that I was allowed to take laxatives. Then I could eat as much as I wanted, and the laxatives would keep my weight down. The problem with gastroparesis, though, is that laxatives don't always work the way they're supposed to. I took more and more until I found a dosage that worked, but then food passed through me undigested, leaving my whole body clammy and sweaty, shaking with chills as the pills worked to combat my body's innate need to hold onto the food. I was terrified that I had done something really bad, that something was seriously wrong with me. But all the same, I resolved to not tell anyone, knowing that nothing would come of it.

One night I had a dream. A man was holding my arms, swinging them back and forth. "I'm going to pop your back out," he said. "And then ask you questions while you're in pain."

"What are you going to do after that?" I asked him.

"Love you and marry you," he responded.

"Why don't you just do that first? Why do you have to hurt me first?"

At that moment, he popped my back out. At first I felt nothing, but then I moved and a blinding pain ripped through me. I woke up gasping for air, sweating into my sheets.

The next day, feeling off-kilter from my dream, I asked my dad about the contracts I had with my sponsors. They were all coming due and would need to be renegotiated or re-signed. Some were for one year, while others were up to three years in duration. They also varied in how much they paid, and in what I was expected to do. Sometimes, for example, it was to feature a logo a certain number of times in print media; other times, it was to attend the Outdoor Retailer trade show and sign posters, or attend a certain number of events. My agent handled most of the negotiations, and he was pushing for a more mainstream sponsor that could pay me more and alleviate some of the financial stress on my family. But that idea terrified me, especially with how I was feeling and how little I was climbing.

We weren't close, and I felt somewhat uncomfortable opening up to him, but I knew my dad to be rational, and I knew if I shared my concerns he wouldn't just tell me what *he* wanted.

"Well," he said. "You have enough money in the bank that you could go to college for two years. Maybe you should just write a press release and say you are stepping back for a bit and going to school."

His idea stuck with me, and I mulled it over. It sounded nice to be relieved of all the pressure, maybe move away from home, be normal.

"We could build an apartment over the garage and you could live there," my mom added. Inwardly, I vehemently disagreed.

"I had a dream," my dad mentioned slowly. I was surprised, given my own recent dream.

"About what?" I asked.

"In my dream a voice came to me and said that your body was starving you." He stopped, looking sad.

I nodded slowly.

"I'll think about it," I said. "The press release thing."

I gathered up the contracts and my homework and left the room, wishing that someone would come and make the decisions that were in my best interest for me. I couldn't seem to figure out how to do it for myself. I desperately wanted someone to say, "I see you are hurting. Let me help you."

I have no memory of the 1998 X Games. When I reread my journal and watch my old VHS tapes, none of it feels familiar.

I know that on the way there we either missed our flight or it was delayed, and we ended up having to stay in Salt Lake City overnight. When we made it to San Diego, my mom and I got into a huge fight the day before the competition, then we made up and went for a run on the beach, chatting about how we were so sick of the fake climbing scene, and how maybe we should leave it behind, try something new. For my part, it was easier to hate the climbing community than want to join it—something that would never be allowed. Hate them, and they can't hurt you. Hate them, and you aren't missing out on anything.

I fell in the preliminary round going for the final hold—my first fall at any X Games. I tried to grab the hold by slowly reaching farther than my arm could go. It probably would have been easier to lunge for it instead. "This fall shows that Katie is, in fact, human," said one commentator.

I somehow returned to form in the finals, which was held on a 45-foot-tall, 45-degree overhanging wall. I climbed last. Move by slow-motion move, I gained height, reaching smoothly between holds where others had lunged, lurched, and fallen. None of the moves seemed too challenging and, before too long, I had reached the top of the wall—the only competitor to finish. Somehow, I had won my third X Games. Maybe there was a god, after all.

CHAPTER 14
THE ROAD TRIP

After the X Games, buoyed by my dad's suggestion, my mom and I decided to skip all the fall competitions and head out on a road trip, ostensibly to look at colleges. At least, that's what I said the trip was for. I wasn't planning to go to college any time soon; that kind of thing was reserved for other, lucky people.

On our first stop in Boulder, we met up with Christian Griffith from Verve. He offered to take me up *The Naked Edge*, a classic 5.11 in Eldorado Canyon and one of the most revered multipitch climbs in North America. I eagerly accepted.

I had done one low-angle multipitch in Vegas the year prior, at Red Rock, but otherwise, this was all very new to me. Christian is a night owl, so we left the ground at five o'clock. Slowed by my lack of experience, it was well and dark by the time we reached the final pitch. As I sat at the anchor belaying, waiting for him to top out, I heard a voice in the dark. A light summer wind had picked up, and I strained to hear what Christian was saying. I thought he was yelling "off!"—meaning that he was clipped in to an anchor and it was safe for me to take him off belay—but I wasn't sure.

I looked down at my belay device. Should I take him off? What if I was just hearing things? Something tugged hard on the rope, pulling my belay device up sharply, locking the brake mechanism. The rope went a bit slack after meeting resistance, so I hastily pulled it out of the belay device. Sure enough, the coiled rope at my feet began to move upward as Christian pulled it toward him, until it became taut again, this time at my knot. I heard another muffled yell. It was my turn to climb.

I winced as I pulled on my teeny-tiny sport climbing shoes. I was used to wearing these shoes in twenty-minute bursts up a sport route, then taking them off in between attempts. Wearing them for six pitches and several hours was painful. Unclipping from the anchor, I yelled as loud as I could, "Climbing!" *I really hope he has me*, I thought as I climbed in the dark.

Toward the end of the pitch, just as the rock grew more overhanging, I started to feel fatigued. Climbing in Eldo is technical and precise, with slippery sandstone, small, hidden holds, and airy exposure. In the dark I couldn't tell where to go. I couldn't see Christian either, and had no idea if he had me on belay.

When I fell off the steepest section, I screamed in pure, unadulterated terror at the hundreds of feet of air below my feet, convinced that he would not catch me. But instead of falling six pitches down to the bottom of the canyon, I swung lazily in the dark. Pulling back onto the rock, I tried to control my shaking and told myself that it was ok, that I was ok, that I could trust Christian.

Not long after the adventure in Eldo, I was sitting in my tent in Rifle Mountain Park, a beautiful, narrow limestone canyon on Colorado's Western Slope. Rifle was among the first sport climbing areas in the US, and it's where climbers like Christian, and later, Chris Sharma and Tommy Caldwell, would establish difficult and severely overhanging routes. I reached back to scratch an itch, and something moved under my fingers. I knew what it was. Without thinking, still holding my breath, I yanked the tick from my back and threw it as hard and far as I could. My only other experience with ticks had been after climbing in Castlewood, all those years ago, when I had sworn I would never go climbing again.

Several days later, in a hotel room outside of Lander, Wyoming, my mom noticed that I had purple splotches all over my back and torso when I came out of the shower. We headed straight to a walk-in clinic, where they told me that I had Lyme disease. I was prescribed a ten-day course of the antibiotic tetracycline. After my last experience with antibiotics, which I felt had effectively ruined my life, I could barely bring myself to take them. I stared at the bottle, hesitating before swallowing the first pill.

"It's ok," my mom assured me. "They use this antibiotic to cure Crohn's disease." I'm not sure if I believed her or not, but either way, I took the pills.

The antibiotic left me feeling nauseous and unwell. It was harder to eat because I felt like throwing up most of the time. Still, though, we kept climbing. I moved slowly, afraid that any sudden movement would make me vomit. I halfheartedly wondered, *Isn't Lyme disease supposed to be, like, kinda serious?* But I couldn't handle one more thing going wrong in my body, so I shoved that thought to the back of my mind. I tried to take myself out of my body each day rather than think about how awful I felt. En route to our climbing destination each day, I would follow several steps behind my mom and whomever we were climbing with. In videos from the time, my face is slack and expressionless, almost zombie-like. Like flipping a switch on a breaker box, I disconnected my mind so I could ignore the pain.

The next time I weighed myself in front of my mom, I was down a pound.

"You're cutting back again," she yelled at me.

"I'm not, Mom, I really don't feel good."

I should get fat, I thought. *Just so you'd leave me alone.*

On our way to visit a small college in Redding, California, we stopped at Donner Summit to climb with Beth Rodden, who had become a friend of mine. Beth and I had met at our very first Junior Nationals, back in San Diego in 1995, and had subsequently traveled to many of the same competitions. We were in the same age group and had hit it off right away, despite my awkward shyness.

I got to climb one day with just Beth and her friends, sans parents. Most of our time together had been at either competitions or trade shows, so in a way, this was my first glimpse into her real life. When Beth and I were younger, I saw that she struggled with the same food demons that plagued me. One time, when Beth had come to climb at the Red, whether from a misguided sense of competition, or maybe solidarity, we had both starved ourselves to within an inch of sanity. We were climbing at the Motherlode that day, which held the highest concentration of 5.13s at the Red, with the steepest routes right up the middle. The image of her, sitting in the car next to me as we drove back to my house, eyes glassy with hunger in the same way mine were, will haunt me forever. Why didn't we talk to each other? Confide in one another? Support one another? Instead, we waited in painful, hungry, mutual silence until we arrived home, where we immediately set to carefully doling out whatever meager dinner we had planned for ourselves.

That day at Donner though, I realized how different our lives were. I marveled at her teenage freedom. She had high school. And friends she chose and whom she was allowed to climb with. And parents who loved her. And boobs. At the end of the day, she ate loads of pizza. She seemed so free, so normal. I would give up all the competitions I had won, just for a minute in her life.

I longed to go to her and say, "Please, please take me along with you. Let me join in your adventures so that I can feel a part of something. I'll do anything. I'll belay you for eight hours on your project. Just let me into your life. I need someone, and you are my only friend."

But instead, we kept our friendship carefully on the surface, neither of us really saying what we wanted to. The next time I saw her, en route to Maple Canyon after a trade show, we still tore our pieces of Extra gum (2.5 calories each) in half, piece after piece after piece, until we had gone through an entire pack, all the while rapping along with Eminem as loudly as we could, drowning out the negative internal voices.

Eventually, my mom and I made it to Yosemite, where I had been wanting to climb for a while. I couldn't wait to learn how to trad climb—the moniker used for "traditional" climbing, in which a climber places protection and then removes it after climbing, rather than clipping permanent bolts. The antibiotic I was still taking for Lyme disease, however, made me extremely sensitive to sunlight, so I climbed in long sleeves and a wide-brimmed hat. Only my hands were exposed, and at night I lay in my tent, sleepless, feeling as though the skin on the back of each hand was on fire.

Under each fingernail I developed what looked like a blister. If I pushed on my nail, I could squish the fluid around. As the blister pushed up, the skin under my fingernail grew tight. At first it felt like my nails were going to pop off when I grabbed a climbing hold. After a while, my fingernails deadened, but the fluid remained.

Months later, at a competition in New York, I asked a fellow competitor who was also a dermatologist what I should do. "You'll have to drain the fluid," he told me.

After the competition, I used a needle to poke a hole under each nail bed, draining the clear fluid. They had been that way for a while, so the top of each nail was detached from the nail bed. When I trimmed those back, I saw that there were new nails, super short and thin, growing in underneath. They grew in quickly, but my fingernails have never been quite the same.

In Yosemite, my mom and I decided to do a multipitch 5.9 on the south side of the Valley, near Leaning Tower and Bridalveil Fall. The approach was heavily forested, the climber's trail tough to follow. We got lost, but we eventually found our way to the rock. I had little idea how to place gear, and the route was all but devoid of fixed protection, such as bolts. I felt like I was free soloing—that if I fell, all the gear I had placed in cracks would rip out and I would crash onto a ledge or the ground. At one point, I fumbled with a medium-sized cam, and it dropped hundreds of feet to the forest floor, glancing off rocks and bushes. We had topped out by nightfall, but got lost again trying to find the way down. Fortunately, some climbers we had met previously were kind enough to hike all the way up to look for us.

While my mom and I were away, my dad interviewed for a new job in Colorado. The family consensus was that Georgia was not working for us. When I asked my dad years later why he had moved us there in the first place, he said that he took the job at PMI/Petzl because he thought that working for a climbing company would make him feel more included in our lives.

More than anything, my dad wanted to make my mom happy. She had never liked the South, and was very vocal about it. There were a million things wrong with the house we bought, and she hated it. If he could find a job that would move my mom back to Colorado, maybe he could make her happy.

"Are you happy to be moving back?" he asked her after he was offered the job.

"Kind of, I suppose."

My dad, as I've said, rarely showed emotion or talked back. But this time, he snapped.

"You have been complaining about the South for so long, I thought you would finally be happy, but you're not! Nothing I do, nothing, is good enough for you!" he yelled.

As I listened to my parents argue, it all sounded familiar. Truths were twisted into strange almost-lies, until you couldn't tell if you were crazy for remembering it differently. Until you were convinced that whatever was wrong was all your fault, that she had an unbearable load and you were dragging her down. What started as a little tickle in my mind began to worm its way through my consciousness. My understanding of how I had been raised began to shift underneath my feet.

CHAPTER 15

ADULTHOOD

At the end of 1998, I turned eighteen, alone, in my bedroom. Birthdays usually passed without much fanfare in my family, and although I had thought I wouldn't care, for some reason, knowing I was now eighteen brought only a deep sadness. This was adulthood.

I looked down at my arms. On the inside of my right forearm, the same arm that I stroked at night to self-soothe, were thin, red lines, up high close to the elbow. Little droplets of blood would bubble up out of those lines, until I used climbing tape to strap toilet paper over them to stop the bleeding. The same lines existed on the inner side of my right thigh.

Sometimes I ridiculed myself because I wasn't even cutting deep enough to leave a scar. I wasn't even brave enough to get it right. But at the same time, I liked those red lines, so tidy and uniform, marching up my forearm as if a large cat had taken a swipe at my pale, sinewy flesh. The cuts comforted and soothed me. Sometimes in class I would flip my arm under my desk, tracing a finger along the lines and feeling the soreness as they healed. The cuts made my pain physical and tangible. So much pain lived inside me, invisible to others, but those thin red lines were visceral proof—even if no one else saw them.

Around that time, *Rolling Stone* called to tell me I'd been inducted into their Sports Hall of Fame, and asked me to do a photo shoot near Boulder, Colorado. My dad had already moved to a small apartment in the Denver suburb of Golden to start his new job, while my mom and I stayed in Georgia to wait for our house to sell, so I flew out and stayed with him through the holidays. Christmas with my dad was a far cry from the fudge and summer sausage Christmases of my childhood, and I couldn't help but feel that climbing was what had made it all fall apart.

My dad accompanied me to the hotel room where the prep for the photo shoot would take place. He stood off to one side, as though trying to melt into the wall, while the stylist presented me with some clothing options, including the tiniest string bikini I had ever seen.

"You just have this Lolita vibe that we want to play up," she said. "This, like, super innocent but also sexy thing."

I may have been eighteen, but I was so sheltered she might as well have been talking to a twelve-year-old. I had never worn a bikini. I had never been on a date. Anorexia meant that I didn't have breasts yet. My fellow climbers were the closest I had come to having male friends. I didn't even know what she meant by "Lolita." After the shoot, I looked it up online and sat there, aghast.

"Sexy" meant evil in my mind. I burst into tears in the hotel room as a war raged inside me. On the one hand, I wanted to grow up. There was a part of me that wanted to try on that bikini, to see what it felt like to be sexy instead of a little girl. But on the other hand, I had been taught my entire life that this sort of thing was evil, and if I wasn't careful, people full of satan would pull me in.

"You have to be on guard," my mom would tell me. "Satan is everywhere at these things, and you will be tempted. If you are not on guard, you will be pulled into their sin."

I didn't know how to advocate for myself or express what I was feeling. My dad stayed quiet in the corner, not offering advice or support, as I stood there, confused and uncomfortable.

"Oh gosh," said the stylist, looking uneasy. "Don't cry." Realizing what she had gotten herself into, she continued, "Don't worry, we have other things."

She put away the bikini and laid out another option, a crop top and pants that ballooned out. The entire thing was pink and completely sheer. It looked like something Jasmine would have worn in *Aladdin*.

I was flummoxed. *What would I wear* under *it*? More tears.

The stylist and the other crew members were getting annoyed.

Finally, we agreed that I would wear the black North Face sports bra I had worn to the shoot, and blue swim shorts.

When the magazine came out, one woman athlete is pictured lying naked on a locker room bench. Another poses topless in a studio shot, her arms crossed over her breasts. And in still another, a skier wearing a bikini top rides a dolphin ice sculpture, bucking bronco style. In my photograph, I'm crouched on a small boulder. Since it was the dead of winter, a giant heater was set up to blow warm air on me. The hot/cold sensation left me feeling like I was going to vomit, and I grimaced into the camera, hating every second of the experience, for many reasons. Years later, a friend looked at the image and said that I had, "cunt-y face."

After the shoot I journaled that I was angry at my dad. *"For all the ways that my mom is messed up, at LEAST she would have stood up for me. She would have done SOMETHING. He did nothing. Nothing."*

That time in Golden, like every other memory I have of my dad, felt stilted and awkward. It was like trying to relate to a total stranger. I found myself trying to avoid unnecessary interactions with him. It seemed like he was making an effort to "hang out" with me, but that just left me feeling angry and rebellious. I couldn't help thinking, *It's a little late, buddy.*

Back in Georgia a few months later, my mom and I went to the Red for the weekend. I was going to college full time by then, but still climbing every weekend at the Obed, Tennessee Wall, or the Red. During the week I would climb on the wall in our garage or on the rotating climbing wall, which was like a vertical treadmill. I did lap after lap, then hung from random holds for up to five minutes. I just made stuff up that felt challenging, with absolutely no structure. I was scheduled to compete in my fourth X Games and third Arco competition later that year, as well as a couple of world cups. I had taken a step back from national competitions, though, so I was traveling less.

On that Friday I redpointed *Ultraperm*, a 5.13d, on my second try. The next day I did another 5.13+. Then on Sunday, at the very end of the day, I decided to try a route that Bill Ramsey had just put up called *Omaha Beach*. A philosophy professor at Notre Dame, fourteen hours round trip from the Red, Bill was there almost every weekend. As obsessed with sport climbing as he was with academics, he was—and still is—a respected climbing pioneer and mentor. While Chris Martin had discovered and bolted the line of *Omaha Beach* the previous autumn, Bill was the first to climb it bottom to top without falling. I was sore and tired from three days of climbing, but someone mentioned that I might do well on it, so I decided to give it a try, see how far I could get before I fell—my usual approach to onsighting.

The route follows a line of sculpted sandstone for more than 100 feet out a very long, steep wall called The Madness Cave. The hardest moves are near the ground, but the true difficulty lies in hanging on through the relentless overhang. Bill and others who had tried it had rated it 5.13d, but I didn't know that. I hadn't bothered to ask about the grade—I just tied in and gave it my best effort.

I'm told that when I began climbing, others at the cliff stopped what they were doing to watch. At the upper crux I climbed up and down several times, trying different sequences, returning to an inadequate resting position in between. On several clips, I struggled to get enough slack to clip the quickdraw, and expended extra energy yanking on the rope. Despite this, I fought my way to the top, at the very end of three days in a row of hard climbing. The Motherlode erupted with applause, then Bill approached and told me the grade. He added that I had just made history as the first woman—and one of only a few climbers—in the world to onsight 5.13d.

Physically, I was clearly capable of redpointing 5.14. But mentally, well, I didn't believe I could do it. Even though it was only the tiniest bit harder than 13d, I could not envision it. Mindset, you see, is everything.

My first big competition of 1999 was the X Games. Organizers had changed the format to bouldering, hoping to invigorate viewer interest in the sport. I felt like I was probably partly to blame for viewers losing interest. All the other X Games sports involved speed, daring tricks, big personalities, and bigger crashes. Then there was climbing, where a tiny, silent girl climbed so agonizingly slowly that the audience couldn't even tell where the hard part was. Bouldering would be more dynamic, and when competitors fell, we'd hit the ground—a better fit for ESPN.

Organizers built the walls tall, with thick pole-vaulting pads below. There were four walls, so that more than one competitor could climb at a time. If a climber made it to the top, they could either top out, climbing over the top of the wall and exiting around the back, or drop down, landing on the pads below. At the athlete meeting prior to the competition, organizers urged us to be dynamic, enthusiastic, and most of all, to jump down rather than topping out, as it made for better television. They made it clear that they were trying to save climbing from being cut out of the X Games altogether.

In the semifinal round I surprised myself, performing well enough to be in first place going into the finals. On the final problem, however, I decided to take the organizers' advice, and instead of topping out the way I'd done every other time, I dropped from the top of the wall. I should have landed on my back, pole-vaulting style, but instead I dropped straight down, stiff and unyielding. I landed on the hard foam on my feet and my knees popped up, connecting with my chin. My head snapped backward, teeth clacking together hard. Pain shot through the back of my neck, straight into my head, and a pounding headache developed instantly.

The next morning, the day of the finals, I woke early and realized I was unable to turn my head. My mom and I went to the medical tent, where they took a cursory glance at my neck and decided I had definitely strained, and possibly torn, some ligaments. They gave me a couple pills to take that I thought were anti-inflammatories, like ibuprofen.

The pills were actually muscle relaxants, designed to release the muscles holding tight to the damaged ligaments in my neck. As I headed out for finals, I felt strangely lethargic and unable to concentrate, but I could swivel my head from side to side and up and down with only minimal pain.

I sat at the bottom of the first boulder problem and looked up. *Blah.* Two moves in, I dropped off. That wasn't all that unusual in bouldering competitions, where the difficulty of each individual move means that climbers rarely get to the top on the first try. Competitors are given time limits to solve a bouldering problem and lose points for taking multiple tries, rather than being eliminated as soon as they fall.

On the floor, my body seemed unwilling to exert effort. I sat down and said out loud, "Come on, Katie. Try. You have to try hard." Up I went again, willing my brain to connect with my body, but it was no use. I dropped off again.

I was in first place going into finals, and pretty close to last place coming out. And that was it. My X Games run was over.

Next came a World Cup in Leipzig, Germany. My mom and I arrived at the airport late, only to discover that her passport was expired. After much ado, we decided that I would go on ahead, and my mom would try to expedite her passport renewal application.

I was deliriously jet-lagged when I arrived at the World Cup. In recent competitions, my mind had been so disconnected that it was as though I wasn't there at all. Rather than tuning out anything extraneous and focusing solely on the task at hand, I now seemed to just tune everything out. Everything.

The men's and women's routes ran parallel to each other, so close that they almost met, and before I realized it, I had veered off the women's route and onto the men's. I could tell something was amiss from the whispering of the spectators below, and I paused to glance around. Stunned, I realized my error and jumped off the route.

My mom, who had arrived just in time, recorded the competition. Watching the tape later, I found footage of Liv climbing, but once I started up the wall, the video cut out. I suspect that she erased my mistake from the record, perhaps in an attempt to rewrite reality.

Later, I wrote in my journal, *"I did not sin by jumping off the route, I did not sin by jumping off the route, I did not sin by jumping off the route,"* over and over on the page, like a kid stuck in detention and forced to write his or her transgressions on the chalkboard.

In June of 1999, my mom and I headed to Besançon, France, for another World Cup. After the X Games and Leipzig, I was feeling downtrodden but also strangely liberated. Now that my winning streak was well and solidly broken, there seemed to be less pressure. It was no longer a foregone conclusion that I would win. I was also just so tired of it all that I had stopped caring what happened.

Sitting in isolation at Besançon, I looked around. There was one small bouldering wall for warming up. Competitors swarmed over it, climbing on top of each other. It held little appeal. Instead, my mom and I headed to a nearby crag. Eschewing the indoor warm-up wall to go find real rock was unheard of, but I didn't care. For whatever reason, we were getting along well, and I felt good.

The beautiful part about climbing in Europe is that there are small, bolted, limestone walls nearly everywhere. This particular wall was softly overhanging, light-gray limestone that swooped up from the ground like an ocean swell. It was situated in a low, quiet, wooded area and felt like the secret garden games of my childhood. I warmed up, then hopped on a beautiful 5.13 that called to me, falling at the crux. Coming down, I looked at my watch to see when I needed to check in for isolation. If I tried again right then, I'd have enough time to redpoint the route and make it to isolation. The competition, for once, felt far away and inconsequential, and I decided to go for it. I managed the redpoint, but my forearms felt swollen and pumped—a little too pumped. Almost like a flash pump that sets in when a climber tries too hard too soon, and doesn't dissipate like a normal pump. It can sometimes ruin an entire day's climbing.

Back in isolation, I tried not to worry about how my forearms felt and instead lay down on my pack to rest until it was my turn. I felt different, climbing in the finals at that world cup. I wasn't dissociated, as I had been in my early competitions, but I also wasn't terrified—distracted and hearing every little noise—either, as I'd been in Leipzig. My arms felt tired, but not overly so, more like I felt at the end of a long day at the Red, where I discovered that endurance was my strength and I could keep going and going. I felt more at peace than I had in a long time. I wasn't trying to find some divine reason or sign or wondering what it meant if I did or didn't win. I just felt *there*.

After a superfinal, Besançon became my first—and only—official world cup win. It's probably fair to say I'm the only world cup climber in history who cared enough about a random sport route—and so little about the competition—to try to redpoint it right before isolation. That little crag will always hold a special place in my heart, a rare moment during those days when, however briefly, I was able to let go and just be in my body and enjoy the experience of climbing.

Midway through 1999, our house in Georgia finally sold, and my mom, my dad, and I moved into a small house in a canyon in Colorado. That fall, I headed out on my first solo international trip, traveling with my friends Mark and Sierra, a climbing couple that my mom and I had initially met at the Red, and then again in Yosemite while on our road trip.

The first time we met, Sierra gave me a ride home. She recalled her thoughts of me on that ride: "I had never met a person who so, it seemed on first impression, wanted to melt into the car seat and never be noticed, like a broken seat belt, tucked deep in the fold of the car seat. For the girl who was such a sensation, who produced both joy and jealousy, compliments and vile contempt (depending on the ego of the person giving their opinion), you seemed hopelessly unhappy—when I expected excitement and joy."

Despite my recent losses, *Climbing* magazine named me "Best Female Climber of the Millennium." Not of the year, or decade, but of the millennium. My self-worth, however, was so low that it didn't even register.

Our road trip that fall started with the Rock Masters competition in Arco. The pressure to succeed was back, and while I was eager for the independence of a solo road trip, I felt lost without my mom. My guess is that most people learn how to be independent and their own person in small bursts, gradually increasing their time away from home and family as they grow up. When they finally arrive at adulthood, they are prepared to function within it. I, on the other hand, had experienced very few bursts of independence, so I had almost no framework for understanding how I fit in the world, how to relate to others, or who I was as a person. But now I was eighteen, and suddenly independent. I wasn't at all sure how things worked, or where I fit, or how to do it alone. To further complicate things, I was also in the throes of a binge-eating whirlwind as my body struggled to restore itself.

In Arco, other competitors would say hello, wave or smile—but I was so lost in my own sadness and confusion that I couldn't imagine anyone would want to be friends with me.

We stayed at an Italian hotel run by an older woman who everyone called Mama Marisa, the same place my mom and I had stayed in previous years. She was exactly what you would imagine an Italian grandmother to be like, kind and soft and always cooking. My first year in Arco she had showed my mom and me around the hotel. She didn't speak English, but she gestured and managed to communicate anyway, showing us where Lynn and Robyn had stayed when they'd come to compete, emphatically pointing at their photos on the wall like a proud mother.

When I returned in 1999, she smiled at me but seemed concerned, pinching my cheeks and gesturing out to the pool. She seemed to be saying that I was too pale and needed to sit in the sun. She also fed me a lot of soup and other delicious meals. *"Mangia, mangia,"* she would say, indicating that I was too thin, even then, after I felt like I had gained so much weight.

One evening one of the organizers walked in right in the middle of dinner to get me for an athlete meeting. Mama Marisa walked

straight up to him as he stood next to the table where I was eating, smacking him lightly on the arm. She spoke rapidly and dis-
approvingly in Italian, gesturing at me and my bowl of soup. The
organizer turned back to me. "I'll just come back after you've eaten
dinner," he said sheepishly, deferring quickly to Mama Marisa and
hurrying away.

One warm, sunny day prior to the competition, I tagged along with
Sierra on one of her runs. She was training for a marathon at the
time, and we ran tempo repeats through the vineyard-lined streets
of Arco. I managed to keep up, but just barely. As we ran, I started to
feel looser and my mind and body relaxed. I found myself chatting,
smiling, and laughing in a way that I rarely did, speaking freely and
with abandon. Sierra, running alongside me, let me talk.

"You actually laughed!" She would tell me years later. "Like a real
laugh!"

———————

All my levity had disappeared by the time the competition started,
but still, as finals wrapped up, it looked like I was somehow, mirac-
ulously, in the lead. Then suddenly I was disqualified. Apparently, I
had stepped on a bolt during my climb. My score would only count
up to the point where I had touched the out-of-bounds feature.

The routes at Arco were hard, with very few extra holds—the
footholds, especially, were tiny and sparse. I had carefully calcu-
lated each move, including where I would place my feet. I couldn't
imagine how I could have stepped on a bolt and not noticed, and
several people encouraged me to refute the claim, which would have
forced the officials to look at the tape to confirm what had happened.
I didn't refute it, and it wouldn't have mattered if I did. A couple
from a German climbing magazine had it on tape. Apparently, low
on the route, with my body fully extended, my toe pressed on a bolt
while bumping its way up the wall. In truth, there's little chance that
it affected my performance, but nonetheless, there it was. My toe
had touched a bolt.

I pretended that I didn't care. In a photo from that day, I'm crack-
ing a joke, my smile almost a grimace, stretched so wide that my eyes

are squinted shut. I can see it for what it was—an attempt to not cry. But I didn't want anyone to know the pain that I was in. More than anything, I needed everyone to think that I didn't care at all.

After the competition, Mark, Sierra, and I went to a small gelato shop run by an older Italian man, a place all the climbers went. A couple years earlier, at my second Arco, there were posters of me, advertising the competition, plastered all over town. It had been strange to walk down the cobbled street and see my own face on doorway after doorway. One of those posters was still hanging inside the gelato shop.

As we entered, the cool breeze blowing through my hair, the shop owner spoke loudly and animatedly in Italian, welcoming us, smiling as if I was still, in fact, the champion. At first the attention embarrassed me, but he swung his arms jovially, saying, "Come, come," in Italian and then, "for you, no money," in broken English. His face was so welcoming that I couldn't help but smile. Then I began to laugh. A real, true laugh. I felt lighter in his grandfatherly presence.

The feeling didn't last. Paranoid over the amount of competition money I had squandered by messing up so many times that year, and struggling to figure out who I was outside of my mom's influence, I was mostly silent and closed off for the rest of the trip. But while I pretended that everything was ok, inside I was struggling. I would sit in my tent and write letters to my mom, eating and eating, then writhing in agony, so lonely that I wanted to claw my skin off. I hated climbing.

It was so easy back then to blame all my pain, both physical and emotional, on climbing. I had to cast blame somewhere. It would take years, and nearly a decade of not climbing at all, to rewrite the narrative I had constructed about my relationship with climbing and understand why I felt so broken inside.

PREVIOUS PAGE: *Climbing at Lake Louise, Alberta, Canada* (Photo by Ben Moon)
TOP: *Trying to keep a straight face for the camera with my brother, Scott, at our home in Paris, Kentucky* (Katie Brown personal collection) BOTTOM: *Gathered outside Robyn Erbesfield-Raboutou's house with some of the climbers who competed in the Junior Worlds in Laval, France* (Katie Brown personal collection)

TOP, LEFT: *Looking out at the crowd from the top of a comp route at Arco. This photo reminds me that a part of me loved climbing and competing, despite being largely unanimated throughout my teen years.* (Photo by Marco Scolaris) TOP, RIGHT: *The girl in this photo feels like someone I've never met, but her relaxed, determined expression in such a precarious stance is the look of someone doing what she was born to do.* (Photo by Marco Scolaris) BOTTOM: *A moment of levity while tying in, wearing Mickey Mouse earrings and my mom's sweatshirt, at the Red River Gorge* (Photo by Jim Thornburg)

TOP: *Grimacing with pure determination, when there was no f-ing way I was letting go, at Arco, Italy* (Katie Brown personal collection) BOTTOM: *I will forever love the red dirt and vistas of Canyonlands. Cody and me, enjoying the day.* (Photo by Ben Moon)

TOP: *A sunset photo session the day after climbing* Hydrophobia, *a steep 5.14a near Montsant, Spain* (Photo by Jorge Visser) BOTTOM, RIGHT: *Constantly reading or writing in India, while trying to make sense of life* (Photo by Corey Rich) BOTTOM, LEFT: *One of the many perfect boulders sprinkled throughout the landscape of Hampi, India* (Photo by Corey Rich)

Trying to avoid running out of appropriately sized gear on Tricks Are For Kids *in Indian Creek* (Photo by Cory Richards)

TOP: *Climbing the classic* Blue Jeans *on a beautiful day on Yamnuska in Canmore, Alberta* (Photo by Ben Moon) BOTTOM: *Cleaning a route in stunning El Potrero Chico, Mexico* (Photo by Ben Moon) NEXT PAGE: *On one of the upper pitches of the Leaning Tower in Yosemite Valley with Lynn Hill* (Photo by Jim Hurst)

CHAPTER 16

HYDROPHOBIA

After Arco, Mark, Sierra, and I headed to Céüse, France, home to some of the world's most famous sport climbs. It took an hour to hike from our camp to the crown of a crag set atop a steep hill. The cliff is an enormous half-circle of tall, smooth, overhanging walls of limestone with gray, blue, and tan stripes sweeping upward. The spans between bolts are sometimes far and intimidating, but the climbing is impeccable.

In between bouts of unpredictable weather, I sat in my tent, alone, eating an entire jar of Nutella and then hating myself for it. I longed for clarity. Why was it that I was finally getting to climb with other people, and yet I missed my mom? It made no sense. I had wanted nothing more than to get away from her. I wanted friends, but I couldn't figure out how to connect with other people. No matter where I was or who I was with, I felt like I was on the outside looking in.

Despite everything, my mom was still my best friend. The lines between parent and child had become so blurred that in many ways I felt I needed to take care of her. And because she knew everything about me, she was who I went to when I needed to talk. I didn't know how to confide in anyone else. It was only years later that I learned the phrase "trauma bonding," and how the cycle of fighting and then talking had created a strong—albeit extremely unhealthy—connection.

In Céüse we met up with some people from the Red, and it was nice to have a bit of familiarity—although I didn't share my feelings with anyone. It was enough to sit on the periphery and watch their camaraderie and obvious joy from climbing.

During the day I would try to eat as little as possible, even though that left me feeling weak and tired at the crag. But then at night, once I was alone, I would eat and eat and eat. My stomach hurt constantly.

From Céüse we headed to Spain. Some of the people I'd been climbing with went home, and others arrived. I was in Europe for almost three months, which wasn't unusual in the climbing community. Most of the climbers I knew would go to a destination and camp there for two or even four weeks. In fact, I can recall when, as an adult, I learned that most Americans go on vacation for only one week at a time. The concept of such a short trip was foreign, and I wondered how on earth they had time to do or see anything.

I didn't write consistently in my journal while I was in Spain, and my memory of that time is fuzzy. I know we eventually ended up at a climbing area set atop a plateau, where a winding road led to a small, almost abandoned village called Siurana, the ancient buildings and narrow roads still evident. We rented a *refugio*, which is like a hostel, that was an easy drive from several world-class crags. In Siurana, I could walk along the road and pick fresh figs off roadside trees.

One day most of the climbers I was with decided to head to Barcelona for a rave, while they let the skin on their fingertips, worn thin from days of climbing on abrasive rock, recover. I somehow convinced a friend to go climbing first, at a nearby area called Montsant where there was a 5.14a, *Hydrophobia*, I wanted to try. Once we got to the crag, however, I chickened out. We did three pitches, but by the time we got back to the refugio, everyone else had already left for Barcelona. My friend was stuck with me.

The next morning everyone had made it back from Barcelona, but they were in no shape to climb. I convinced my friend to go back to Montsant with me to try again. *Hydrophobia* is a 150-foot journey up a steep wall of white and orange conglomerate. Since it was so long, my friend agreed to hang the draws for my attempt, so that I wouldn't have to carry the weight of over twenty quickdraws. Partway up, however, he found himself unable to pull over a crux lip and came down. I transferred the remaining draws to my harness.

Up I went, nearly falling at the low crux and totally missing the arm bar rest that would have allowed me to recover before the top portion of the route. Past the lip, I ran into the top crux, and just as I felt my fingers slipping, my body going slack in preparation for a fall, I saw it. It was as if the path I needed to take just appeared in front of me. I knew exactly how to get through, and before I knew it, I had clipped the chains. It was my first, official 5.14. At that time, no woman had done a route of that grade on her first try. Because my friend had hung half of the draws, technically I had seen him climb some of it, so my climb fell in the murky area between flash and onsight—half of it a sort of flash, and the remainder a full-blown onsight, while hanging my own draws. I was worried that the route would be downgraded because I had done it, so I wanted to be as factual as humanly possible. I called it a flash, even though in my heart I felt it was basically an onsight. For once, I felt I had done a good job.

The following day we went up to the route again to take sunset photos. Afterward, my friend took me "rallying," which was basically driving very fast on extremely windy European roads. I had always loved roller coasters, and I loved every minute of our car ride, whooping and hollering as we careened around bends.

It turned out that my concern about a potential downgrade was accurate. When the story of my climb of *Hydrophobia* broke, industry publications said that the route was possibly overrated. They went to a male climber, Daniel Andrada, who had redpointed the route. He had spent months memorizing each and every move, learning how to climb it the most efficiently, how to best utilize each and every rest. They asked him, "Do you really think it's as hard as they say? I mean, really? Is it maybe soft for the grade?" The implication was that if a young female climber had accomplished it, could the climb really be that hard?

It was 2005 before *Hydrophobia,* or any other route of that grade, received another onsight. The climber was another woman, a strong Spanish climber named Josune Bereziartu. What added to my heartbreak regarding this particular route was that Josune's ascent was reported in 2005 as 5.14a—no questions asked. That same year, another article referred to my ascent of Hydrophobia as a 5.13d. The only difference between the analysis of my climb and Josune's, it seemed, was not even based on gender, but more about me. It was less hard because I had done it. I felt singled out, disliked, just like my mom had always said I would be, and once again, a failure, no matter what I did.

At the end of my trip, I competed in one last world cup in Osp, Slovenia. Everyone I was traveling with had decided to leave rather than stay and watch the comp, so for the first time I was truly alone *and* the only American.

Isolation was in a long, narrow hall that twisted and turned. It was packed with competitors on either side, and smelled of various body odors. There was very little space, so again, climbers warmed up nearly on top of one another. Not wishing to come into contact with another human, I avoided the warm-up area. I no longer cared about anything. Even the competition felt flat.

In all of my previous world cups, I had been a bundle of nerves, clenching my jaw, not sleeping, praying feverishly. This time, though, I felt nothing. In semifinals I climbed so slowly that I ran out of time before I reached the top of the wall. I didn't really care, leaving the competition and going shopping in Osp, where I found a cool pair of Doc Martens and a pair of orange fleece pants festooned with brightly colored flowers. That evening I sat around in my lovely hotel room, alone. The shower had a six-inch lip around the square pan, so I stuffed a plastic bag in the drain and filled it up, sitting in the hot water as though it were a bath. I laid my head down on my knees and stared at the tiles on the wall, feeling nothing.

In finals, I didn't even look at the route during our allotted time to preview. I walked back to isolation while all the other competitors scanned the route, pantomiming moves and making a plan. Despite my apathy, I climbed well enough to end up in fourth place. *"I'm not even sure what happened,"* I wrote. *"But that's just it. Nothing happened. I had no desire to try. Nothing. I tried to give thanks for being there, but I felt nothing."*

At the end of the competition, Yuji Hirayama, a kind and thoughtful competitor and one of the most accomplished all-around rock climbers in the world, told me, "I have always gone up and down, but I find that even when I don't have a good placement, I have learned something." The thing was, I wasn't sure I was learning anything anymore from competing. I felt like I had to place first, and if I didn't it was because something was inherently wrong with me. And since I was no longer placing first, it must mean that I was intrinsically worthless.

After the competition, my mom wrote me another letter, which said in part:

> I am praying for you specifically to have the attitude of a great competitor. Which is attitude not to focus on not doing well but on doing your best as unto the Lord. To keep looking up with the joy of the Lord no matter what and not to look down in whatever negative feeling. But up as you would look upon the Lord if he was present and will be.
>
> For it is not the competition that matters in the long term or the big scheme of things but attitude that is pleasing to the Lord. If you waver let it be only a short time and then refocus on Jesus once again because that is forever.

Not long after this, I took first place at the Wasatch Open Climbing Competition in Salt Lake City, alongside Chris Sharma. I have no memory of this competition, but it tells me that in spite of what I may have felt, I did not suck. At the time, though, all I could focus on were the things that had gone wrong. All I could think about was the pain in my heart, and in my brain, and my crushing obsession with binge eating.

For so long I had wanted nothing more than to get away, but now that I had, it felt like I had nothing left. Even though, despite everything, I was *still* one of the best climbers in the world, it felt like I had already lost it all.

CHAPTER 17

DANCING UNDER
THE STARS

As another new year began, I started cleaning houses in the canyon where my parents lived, to earn money. In spite of my status in the climbing world, I thought very little of myself. I didn't—couldn't—see the position I was in. All I could see were mistakes. Cleaning houses was a better fit for me. One afternoon, after a morning spent scrubbing playdough-encrusted floors and wiping toilets, I found myself standing in the Boulder Rock Club. Climbing was as natural as breathing, so even when I tried to walk away from it, I somehow always found my way back.

I was tying my knot underneath the steep, sweeping lead wall of the gym when a tall, dark-haired boy approached me with a smile. His eyes were a deep brown, so dark you almost couldn't tell where the pupil ended and the iris began. He started to talk to me, and seemed keenly interested in what I had to say. It was all I could do not to glance over my shoulder to make sure he wasn't talking to someone taller, prettier, and more grown-up standing behind me.

At nineteen, I still hadn't gotten my period, which concerned a doctor I went to see after moving back to Colorado. I was put on birth control and, I swear, within thirty days I had both boobs and hormones. My body still felt childlike though, soft and squishy from disordered eating, my face round and puffy. I felt ridiculous talking to that boy.

Even though I was technically an adult, there were so many things that I had not experienced. I had not gone to high school. I had never been on a date. I had never been to a school dance. I had never been to a movie theater, arcade, or bowling alley with friends. When most teenagers were at their prom, I was alone in my garage trying to retain my status as world champion while my body disintegrated before my eyes. But I never felt these missing parts of my adolescence more deeply than in the presence of the man now standing in front of me.

Why is he talking to me? I wondered. *He actually seems like he's . . . flirting with me.* I could not fathom why a guy like that would be interested in someone like me. *It must be because I'm "Katie Brown."* In a way, the idea that he might "like" me made me hate him—and myself.

Still, I welcomed his attention, which opened a whole new world to me. Now I had potential friends, people to climb with. People that *I* chose, and it felt good, even though things that felt good also seemed somehow wrong. Nonetheless, I was completely wrapped up in the whirlwind of emotions. It was heady, exhilarating, addicting.

We started hanging out more, going running and climbing—I suppose we were dating, although I didn't realize it at the time. At one point the boy-with-brown-eyes sat me down and asked me "what we were," but I didn't know how to answer.

That summer felt magical—bouldering in Chaos Canyon outside of Estes Park, climbing in the gym, starting friendships, making plans with people I was excited to be around. I also began to find my voice as I grew increasingly strong and competent in my new body. I had enough money that I could have rented my own place and learned how to be a functioning adult, but it never occurred to me that this type of independence, the kind my peers had, might be available to me.

All the while, I had a secret that left me awash in shame and embarrassment. In private, I would eat and eat and eat, unable to control or stop myself, overwhelmed with hatred for my body and personality. The day after a binge, I would starve myself, going for long, grueling runs alone in the mountains, needing to atone for the loss of control the day prior. Combined with my confusion over my rapidly changing body and the feeling that I was sinning just by wanting to be around the boy-with-brown-eyes, I was too distracted to see the potential life opening up before me.

At one point I felt so out of control and frustrated that I went to a nutritionist. I was disconnected enough from my body that I didn't understand what it was telling me or even what hunger cues felt like. She helped me create a chart. I had five goals for each day: avoid the scale, don't compensate for what I ate the day prior, wear my own clothes, stop comparing myself to others, and eat two snacks without it leading to a binge. Every day that I accomplished a goal, I put a sticker next to it on the chart, like a child getting a gold star.

Because I struggled to ask for, or even identify, what I needed or wanted, the nutritionist also introduced me to meditation and the DESC model of communicating assertively. DESC stands for describe, express, specify, and consequences. It's a framework that was developed to promote effective and assertive communication, while also decreasing the potential for defensiveness in the other person. I had drawn so far inside myself over the years that I wasn't sure how to communicate at all, let alone assertively. I felt stuck.

———————

Because my body oscillated between binging and starving, my blood sugar yo-yoed constantly. I had been hypoglycemic for years, but now the fluctuations in my blood sugar were wreaking havoc. One day I'd feel fine and be able to climb well, and the next day I'd be unbearably shaky, falling off the warm-ups and unable to focus. Sometimes when my blood sugar plummeted, it was all I could do to stay awake. I struggled to make sense of what I was feeling but didn't connect it to my eating habits. I often wondered if god had taken away my talent because I was living in sin. Or if there was even a god at all. Desperate for a way to increase my energy levels, I began to look into diet pills.

I found myself in a grocery store. I knew what I was there for, but I didn't want it to be obvious, so I picked up a few random items and put them in my basket. Soon, I headed up the aisle I had been

aiming for all along. On the shelf sat the diet pills, the main ingre-
dient of which was pseudoephedrine. Today products containing
this drug are kept behind the counter at the pharmacy, but back then
they were more readily available. I stood in front of the rows of pills,
protein bars, and other diet products and imagined going through the
checkout lane. What would the cashier think, ringing up diet pills for
an already thin teenager? *They'll know what I am,* I thought. *They'll
know what's wrong with me.* I couldn't do it. But I had to have the pills.

I glanced up and down the aisle, then slipped the pills into my
pocket. Finishing up my shopping in an attempt to not appear obvious, I headed for the checkout lane, sweating slightly as the cashier
rang up each item and announced my total. I picked up my brown
plastic bag, breathing a sigh of relief, thinking I had made it. But
as I exited the store, two men came up on either side of me and
instructed me to enter a surveillance room near the entrance.

The room was small and dark, with a row of black-and-white
TV screens monitoring every corner of the store. I hiccupped. I
had been caught. *Was I going to jail?* A man seated in front of the
cameras played the security footage of me slipping the pills into my
pocket while the guards stood by the door. I was mortified.

He never asked me why I was stealing diet pills, but he did fill out
a report and instructed me to call a parent.

"How old are you?" he asked me.

"Nineteen," I said, looking at the floor. "What's going to happen
to me?"

"You don't look nineteen," he said. Then he sighed deeply. "Call a
parent, ok?"

I choked on a sob.

"Just pay the fine, and you'll be ok. It's $300. If you don't pay it
though, they'll put out a warrant for your arrest."

I knew my dad was the better parent to call in this situation.
He didn't know me well, but he also wouldn't say or do anything
to me. My dad arrived and signed the papers, and we left. When
a letter detailing the fine arrived, I paid it. Nothing else was ever
said about it.

It felt as though a pendulum had swung when we moved back to Colorado, from so many rules and so much control to, suddenly, nothing. I was free to do whatever I wanted, with whomever I wanted. Once again, the rules had changed, and I didn't understand them. To me it felt as though I wasn't as shiny anymore. Living my life, having everything I had, no longer held as much appeal, or any appeal, really.

My mom was working at the post office now and, although initially upset that our family's financial situation had made such a job necessary, she soon started making her own friends, cycling a lot, and pursuing her own athletic activities. Her eyes still scanned my body when she saw me, up and down, assessing, comparing. But the power I had felt over her when I was younger and starving myself was gone. I felt I had lost all control, and given it to her. I was just a girl who no longer won competitions and was no longer on TV. She no longer wanted, or needed, what I had.

During that summer, Beth came to stay at our house for a month. One day while she was there, a fan called. He had been exchanging emails with my mom, and because he was a Christian, she had given him our phone number. I still froze up in certain situations, especially on the phone, so I stood silently, the phone to my ear, while the boy talked.

"You sure don't say much," he said.

No comment.

"Here, give me the phone," said Beth.

I handed it over.

"What's shakin', toots?" she said to the fan, a mischievous grin on her face.

"We're not allowed to shake here," he pointed out. Before long, he had launched into the full Christian diatribe, telling Beth that she was going to hell when she died, that dancing was evil, that every time she had an unclean thought about a boy she was committing adultery in her mind. By the time he was done, she was in tears.

I took the phone from her and hung it up without saying a word to the boy on the other end. I'll never forget her asking me if that's what I believed, too. In that moment, I was ashamed of the religion I had tried so hard to measure up to.

"Of course not," I said. "You are a good person." Beyond that, I didn't know. My whole life I had been taught that if a person was not "born again," they were going to hell. But somehow that didn't seem right anymore.

While Beth was in town, a group of my climbing friends decided to go to Indian Creek, a beautiful, red-dirt area with an endless supply of perfect crack climbing, outside of Moab, Utah. To get there, we drove a twisting, narrow road that follows the curves and bends of the river. It was late at night by the time we hit that section of highway, and our headlights illuminated the desert that opened up on either side of the road. Heavy, dark shapes—towers and other rock formations—littered the horizon. It felt so expansive, this alien landscape. Impulsively, we pulled off to the side of the road, flooded the area with headlights, and turned up the Paul Oakenfold mix CD that Beth had brought. This was my first road trip with friends, my first time listening to this kind of music, my first time having a *dance* party. At first I was afraid that I wouldn't be able to join in, that I'd be the silent, catatonic person that I had been for years. But around those people, a piece of the real me finally slipped out past the bars I had put up so many years ago. I danced in the floodlights of the cars, my feet kicking up dust that looked like smoke. On that trip, I fell in love with Moab, vowing to someday live there.

In Indian Creek the boy-with-brown-eyes and I kissed and cuddled on our first night of camping. The next morning, though, I saw that he looked happy. Too happy. Was *I* making him happy? The thought made me hate him. It was the same feeling that cut through my gut when I saw my mom on old VHS tapes, her face glowing with pride—no, ownership—as she raises her arms, pumping the air while she screams, "Yes!" as I reach the final hold in a competition.

I was suddenly repulsed by this boy that I had been so infatuated with only twenty-four hours ago, who I had planned to travel to Europe with, train for world cups with. Now I could barely look at him, let alone be around him. How *dare* he use me for his happiness. If I was making him happy, then he could end up needing me, and when someone needs you for their own happiness, it leads to immeasurable pain. I didn't want to be needed, not ever again.

The boy-with-brown-eyes looked at me, hurt and confusion written all over his face, but I could not explain how I felt. My reaction was automatic, as much a nervous tic as the movement I made around my leg loops each time I put my harness on, judging how wide my thighs were. I spent the rest of the trip trying to avoid him. I can only imagine his confusion at my sudden switch from hot to cold.

———————————

The next night we drove into Canyonlands to use the pay phones at the visitor center. When we got there, a dark, wooden ladder was leaning up against a wall. Someone had the idea to climb on top of the building, which had a flat, mesa-style roof.

As the last of us scrambled up, someone said, "Hey guys, look at the sky."

We all lay on our backs on that roof in the middle of the Utah desert, staring at a sky that spilled out as far as east is from west, nearly purple in its blackness, every star brought to piercing clarity by the contrast. Night had bewitched us, the quiet, thick magic blowing over us, settling and pressing its weight on our prone bodies.

It felt dangerous and exciting to break the rules, and I thought, *So this is what it feels like to be happy. To have friends.*

Despite all the good happening that summer, the freedom and friendship I had spent years longing for, I was already plotting an escape—from myself more than anything. My whole life I had been told that this kind of happiness was wrong and immoral. That the people I was climbing with were evil, not to be trusted. I still felt that no matter what I did, it was wrong. I needed to go somewhere far away, reinvent myself, become someone else. Be around Christians, even if I wasn't sure anymore what to believe. Then things would make sense, and I would feel ok.

I started researching colleges on the coasts, as far away as I could get from Colorado. At the Outdoor Retailer trade show at the end of the summer, I delivered letters to my sponsors that said I was quitting the sport of climbing to go to college full time.

If that sounds abrupt, well, it was. I still don't understand my motivation for leaving everything from that summer behind. I didn't think I was worthy of all of that wonderfulness. Selfish people like me didn't deserve that kind of happiness, didn't deserve to do what they wanted to do, just because. If I wanted it, hoped for it, and believed in it, it would be taken from me. So I had to self-implode. There really was no other option.

CHAPTER 18
COLLEGE GIRL

I packed up my belongings and headed to the West Coast, to Seattle Pacific University. It was a Christian college not far from where my grandfather lived, and about as far from Colorado as I could get.

On the way there, I drove through Tuolumne Meadows, with its alluring beauty and openness, and then on to Yosemite. I was still fascinated by the place, even if I no longer considered myself a climber. If I wasn't ever going to climb El Cap, I told myself, then I'd settle for hiking to the top.

I found a trail that started somewhere between Tuolumne and the Valley, about eight miles to the summit. I had decided to hike out late in the day, camp on top, and then hike back the next morning. Carrying an overnight pack, I started out around three or four o'clock in the afternoon. With dusk approaching as I neared the end of the trail, I rounded a corner and nearly ran into three men. One of them, outfitted in flannel and sporting a beard, grinned.

"You out here all by yourself?"

I remember he had a Southern accent, and something about the way he looked at me gave me the creeps. *Perfect.* I thought. *Straight out of a movie.*

Thinking fast, I stuttered, "N-no, my friends are right behind me!"

I quickly walked past them and headed to where I had planned to pitch my tent. It was a beautiful vista, but I couldn't appreciate it because my mind was racing. There was no way I could camp now. I would never be able to relax.

I looked at my watch. It would be dark soon. If I turned around, I'd be hiking back in the dark. My mind conjured up the Yosemite brochure I had read on my way in. It had said that "mountain lions are more likely to attack women and small children." *Or women who look like small children,* I thought. The brochure continued, "If a mountain lion attacks, fight back aggressively."

I definitely did not want to run into a mountain lion, but it felt like the better option. Spinning on my heel, I headed back down the trail. Not five minutes later I again ran into the men. They had turned around and were headed back my way.

"Where are you goin', little?" asked the same man as before.

My heart thudded in my chest and adrenaline coursed through me as I nearly ran past them.

"Just going to see what's taking my friends so long!"

I hurried around a bend and as soon as they were out of sight, broke into a full run. I cut into the trees, veering off the trail but keeping it in sight. I figured I was strong, and worst-case scenario, there was a good chance I could outrun them. If I was off-trail, I could hide, too, if they came back into view.

I kept running and running, eventually looping back onto the trail so I wouldn't get lost as darkness fell. It seemed the men weren't coming for me. Now, however, I had mountain lions to contend with. I grabbed two sticks and started clapping them together as I ran, singing at the top of my lungs.

Long after darkness had fallen, I reached the trailhead. There I saw headlights shining bright over the creek bed near the end of the trail—a couple had decided to drive their car down the trail and were now stuck. I had never been so excited to see normal people.

"Hi!" I yelled enthusiastically to them as I splashed past their stuck car, oblivious to their plight, giddy with happiness that I had made it. I threw my pack in my car, hopped in, and locked the doors. Safe at last.

My grandfather lived on the Washington coast, near the border of Oregon, and I stayed with him for a month or so before school started in Seattle. He was quite eccentric, but we had always gotten along well, and his odd ways made me laugh. He was always researching, always learning. There were stacks of papers all over his house, newspapers and printouts everywhere. It was information overload.

For example, while I was at college later that year, my brother got very sick. After three days back and forth to the hospital, with no diagnosis and nothing but heaps of medication for migraines, Scott couldn't bear to leave a darkened room and wasn't able to keep food or water down. Finally, my grandfather, who had been searching for information about his symptoms online, demanded that someone take Scott back to the hospital and get him tested for spinal meningitis. The test came back positive, and I have no doubt that it saved his life.

My grandfather also kept mannequins in his house, dressed and carefully posed in front of windows to keep intruders away, which I always thought was funny, given that he lived in the middle of nowhere. Getting up to pee in the night, however, could cause quite the fright.

From the house, it was a short walk downhill to an inlet where my grandfather kept two small, solar-powered boats. We'd take his boats around the many tiny inlets, stopping here and there. He taught me how to forage for and identify edible mushrooms— chanterelles and oysters and others. He'd collect them and sell them to local restaurants. It was 2001 by then, and I watched the twin towers fall while sitting in his newspaper-strewn living room, staring at the TV, feeling very far away from anything real. Later that fall, when I turned twenty-one at his house, he gifted me a box of wine, six pack of Coors Light, and bottle of Kahlua.

When the semester started, I moved into the dorms at Seattle Pacific. I was truly on my own for the first time. My mom was no longer just a few minutes away. Now she was half a country away, with her own life and interests.

During orientation, the university dean announced that there was a "world-champion rock climber" in our midst. I sank down in my seat as people around me whispered and looked around, trying to spot the climber. Still, I was thankful for her comment. Because of her, sometimes a fellow student would knock on my dorm room door and invite me to go do things. Those friendships kept me going, even though I still felt I was on the outside looking in.

Unchecked, I quickly lost control of my eating, and the shame and self-loathing I felt over my inability to stop bingeing left me deeply broken. I also couldn't figure out how to connect with people, how to "let them in." If I let them in, I believed they would see a dark, dark place. A place where the pain from my latest binge made me want to die. They would see me bang on my chest and claw at my stomach to make it go away. I felt so low that I couldn't imagine how anyone could like me.

To "burn off" the calories from my binges, I continued to run. The difference in altitude from Colorado meant I could run for hours without being out of breath, and near Seattle there are trails that go on for what feels like forever. Despite everything, those runs felt peaceful and I remember them fondly. The canopy of trees overhead felt secure, a silent protection, and my feet landed softly below me on trails covered with wet leaves. I'd dodge slugs crossing the trail and listen to my heartbeat creating a syncopated rhythm with my footsteps, like a drum beating out a prayer somewhere far away, soothing my soul.

Hours into the run I'd feel like I was flying, sunlight hitting me in shafts through the dense canopy overhead. That feeling, a runner's high, is caused by endorphins flooding the body, but at the time all I knew was those runs helped me put myself back together again.

———————————

What must my friends and dorm mates have thought of me during those months in Seattle? Was I short and brusque? Was I funny? Was I quiet? Rude? I formed relationships, but I was so lost in my head that it felt as though I wasn't really there. I only remember glimpses, snapshots of moments in time, but I don't know what, if any, impression I made.

At one point I got a job at the flagship REI store in Seattle, which had an enormous climbing wall set in a large, heavily glassed, circular room. There, I'd belay school groups of kids. One day, my head began to itch, and then it itched desperately. I went to class and tried not to make a spectacle of myself, sitting on my hands to avoid scratching my scalp.

I'm not sure how I found out I had head lice. I think I asked my roommate to check my head—she had had it as a child. When she confirmed the bugs, I panicked, throwing away all my bedding. Mortified, I drove far out of Seattle in the middle of the night, to a grocery store I was sure I would never frequent again, to buy lice medication. After putting it on, I combed through my hair, starting at the root. When the bottom was a giant tangle, I flipped my head over and cut off all my hair. When I flipped my head back again, the front of my hair was up to my chin, while the back hung somewhere below my shoulders, mullet-style. I looked in the mirror and burst into tears.

The medication worked though. Nobody around me on campus contracted lice, and I quit my job by never going back—avoiding any possibility of confrontation.

CHAPTER 19

HOW TO HAVE A LIFE

Seattle Pacific University was a Christian school, but it was a lot more liberal, socially and theologically, than what I had been raised with. During my time there my professors encouraged me to study other religions. At one point, I went to watch Tibetan monks complete a sand mandala at a local Buddhist temple. They worked for hours to create something beautiful and elaborate, each grain of sand lovingly blown into place as an act of meditation. Then, in just a moment, they let the mandala blow away in the wind. The whole process signified the impermanence of everything, which spoke to me on a deep level. I wished I could figure out how to be ok with life's impermanence, rather than agonizing over every decision as though the world would implode if I made one misstep.

What I didn't know was that for all my agonizing, I was making not one misstep, but a multitude of them. Much of my life had been spent making decisions based on what someone else wanted, but now, as an adult, I was suddenly adrift in a sea of decisions that I had no idea how to make. I had no internal compass. Decision-making felt more impossible than ever.

I sat on the outside of life, watching other people live and trying to figure out how they did it. How did they know what they wanted? How did they know what was right? How did they fit themselves into the world, and connect to others? I felt like a bird on a windowsill, peering into the windows of other people's lives.

After my first year of university ended, I went back to Colorado. At first I tried to recreate the magic of the past summer, but it was gone. I hadn't been climbing, I had abandoned the relationships I had begun to forge, and I no longer had sponsors. Sometimes I would go to Beth's house in Estes Park, but regardless of whatever plans we had made, she almost always had a reason not to climb that day. Each time, I felt a bit more hurt by it.

I decided she was being secretive, hiding something from me. The only reason that I could think of was that she saw me as competition. The way I saw it, if we were in a competition, then she had won a long time ago, maybe at birth. I wished that we could just be real, true friends who could climb together and push each other to be better and stronger. I was lonely, and I needed a friend, and she had known me the longest. What I didn't know, and wouldn't know for many years, was that she was in the midst of her own trauma during that time. We had never talked about our internal pain. I wasn't even really aware of how my life experience had affected me at the time and, as far as I know, neither was she.

I spent the summer tortured, trying and failing to make decisions. Ultimately, I decided not to return to Seattle. The gray, cold winter in Washington had been challenging, and the school was so expensive that even with scholarships, I was in debt after just one year. Four years like that felt insurmountable. My brother had recently moved to the Colorado mountain town of Gunnison with his new wife, on his own mission to figure out some kind of education. Without a better plan, I followed them.

I found a small two-hundred-square-foot cabin in a tiny community called Almont, not much more than an intersection halfway between Gunnison and Crested Butte. My new home was rented out nightly to tourists during the summer, but in the winter I could get a month-to-month lease for not much money. There was a small front porch, and inside, a bed on the left and a small table on the right. There was a hot plate, a microwave, and a mini fridge. At the back there was a decently sized bathroom, with terra-cotta tile that I liked.

When I had moved to Seattle, school had, in effect, created a life for me. There was the structure of class and the community of dorm living. But now that I was attempting to create one for myself, I was at a complete loss. Consequently, I didn't have much of a life.

That winter, alone in my tiny cabin in Almont with few friends and very little social interaction, I wrote maniacally in my journal, creating elaborate love stories about broken girls who were saved by kind men who "saw" them and helped them heal.

As a child I had lived within an imaginary world. As a teenager I had filled pages of my journals with stories about how my life would be so much better once I was free and independent. That was my escape, and it gave me enough resilience to keep pushing. But then I carried that into adulthood, where it no longer served me. Throughout that long winter, my thoughts continued to veer toward the fantastical, as though I could live in a novel that had a happy ending if I just focused hard enough. It was unhealthy, but at the same time, it gave me hope, something to look forward to when I couldn't stand to be in the present anymore.

I often cried myself to sleep, rocking and clutching my sides to try and quell the aching loneliness. Upon waking in the morning, I would feel a moment of peace, but then a crushing weight would drag me down as I thought about facing another day. Some days I just wanted to stay asleep so that I could live in my imaginary world rather than trying to navigate the real one.

Mentally, I thrashed about, searching for someone who could save me from my pain and confusion. I eventually landed on the time I had sat in isolation with Chris, chatting about all the things we hoped to do in the future. Perhaps that boy, who had seen something in me way back then, could help me now. I wrote him a letter and mailed it off.

After Chris received my letter, we talked on the phone for a long time. He even called me again to wish me a happy birthday. In that first conversation, as he told me about his life, I began to miss climbing. I asked if I could go with him on a climbing trip he was planning, and he said yes.

I had tried to walk away from climbing, but sitting alone in that cabin, I decided that climbing was really the only thing I had. It was the one thing that I understood, that gave me value and identity. The only "life" I knew. Without it, I couldn't figure out who or what I was, how to exist and function in the world, or how to relate to people around me.

A couple of months later, Chris and I set out to drive to California together, en route to our ultimate climbing destination in India. We spent the night in his truck outside of St. George, Utah, and shared a kiss. I was unsure and inexperienced, and I had built up the moment in my mind, which was terrifying. It felt dangerous to want something.

In the morning, Chris said that he was just "a hard guy to pin down."

"You're a nice girl," he told me. So, he didn't want to hurt me. He wasn't sure what he wanted to do after our India trip. The fantasy I had imagined, where this boy would save me and teach me how to live, dissolved. I felt alone again. Unable to face what I perceived as rejection, I turned cold, angry, and juvenile, finding fault with everything about his personality. As we were already committed to this five-week journey, we continued to travel together with an added layer of tension.

In Santa Cruz, we packed our bags. We each had a carry-on, and checked only our crash pads. It seemed like Chris was telling me what I should or should not bring in my single backpack, and I felt a rising resistance to anyone trying to control me.

Chris had been to Hampi, India, the year before and had wanted to make a film about the place and all that it represented physically, emotionally, and spiritually. The main purpose of our trip was to make that film. Chris also wanted to return to climb a particular boulder—a one-move problem he hadn't been able to complete on his first trip.

We arrived in Chennai (Madras) late at night, but in India, life continues full tilt at all hours, as though there is one population for daytime and one for nighttime. The airport felt claustrophobic and tight, full of unfamiliar sounds and smells, from body odor to cumin.

Cars honked and voices yelled over one another in fast, lilting and bobbing languages. As we drove, we passed everything from slick, black cars to bicycles piled high with people. Cinder-block buildings lined the streets, some of which looked bombed out while others showcased tattered awnings over produce-filled bins. Groups of people squatted around open fires here and there, just off the sidewalk, cooking food over large pots. This, next door to an expansive, tree-lined estate with perfectly manicured lawns, glistening white gates, and golden figurines guarding the entrance.

Culture shock set in quickly for me. Overstimulated, my fight-or-flight response kicked in and I unintentionally shut down. It was the first time I had been this outside my tightly controlled and judgmental worldview. In addition, I was overcome with health-related anxiety. One morning, shortly after our arrival, I held a glass of water but was unable to drink, my mind racing with irrational thoughts about what could be in it.

"Have faith," Chris said, ever patient. "There's only so much you can do and at some point you just have to have faith."

In that moment, I realized that for all my "religion," I had no faith. I had begun to deeply question the idea of god, but I was still afraid of what he would do if I stepped out of line. One slip, one wrong move, one moment of letting my guard down, and I would be vulnerable. I was trying to mentally hold onto all the bad things that might happen to me, ever wary. So armed, I thought I could then control any situation I was in. The first thing I learned in India, though, was that I had no control.

Unable to function, I let Chris take the lead and handle everything, including the arduous task of arranging travel and accommodations. He hired a car to take us to Hampi, but after many setbacks we ended up stranded in Bangalore. The trip was taking much longer than anticipated, and the driver did not want to go any farther. He charged us more than we had expected, too, and this at least partially snapped me out of my frozen state. *We got ripped off. I should be helping more. Chris is too trusting and takes everyone at face value.* I, on the other hand, was suspicious of everyone. After that, I tried to be more involved in bargaining and haggling.

In Hampi we met the film crew, another climber, and later, the photographer. Once we were all together, the tension eased between Chris and me. We settled into a beautiful spot across the river from the town, which was a destination for Hindu pilgrimages. Often, lines of people could be seen, slowly walking through and around boulders and rice fields. Cows roamed the streets freely, festooned with necklaces gifted by traveling pilgrims or painted with saffron and other bright colors, a red dot marking their third eye.

Toward the horizon was the reason we had come—fields of golden boulders as far as the eye could see, piled on one another like a game of Tetris. There were also skeletons, both animal and human, buried in those fields of rock. In Hampi, I felt as though remains from my own past were bubbling up, threatening to crawl out of the closet I had tucked them in. Here, I was forced to face the parts of myself that I most disliked, that I was most ashamed of.

I could scarcely do an interview for the film without crying. In the final video, my voice wavers and nostrils flare as I struggle to rein in emotions that I don't understand.

The days were hot in southern India, so we frequently got up before dawn to boulder, rested in the shade during the heat of the day, and then climbed through sunset and into the dark, our bodies mirrored by lengthening shadows on the rocks. Sunsets and sunrises were spectacles to behold, the colors rich and cosmic, from deep burnt-orange to the palest pink.

The owner of the cottages where we stayed would rise before dawn to make us rice porridge with milk delivered straight from the cow. I fell in love with the chai that I purchased from the many street vendors. The flavor was like nothing I could find in the States, a decadent sweet treat complemented by raw, unpasteurized milk.

The guys on the trip, for their part, accepted me and included me, despite my obvious angst and inner turmoil. Nate, also known as Biggie, was so warm, open, and jovial that being around him eased my worry and overthinking.

One evening at sunset, we were sitting at the base of some boulders when two Indian men walked up a long slab of rock toward us. Dressed in loafers, dress pants, and button-up shirts, they were much larger than most of the local people we'd met. They approached two smaller Indian men who stood nearby, and began rummaging through their pockets, shoving and jostling, even hitting them once or twice. Alarm bells went off everywhere in my mind.

The men turned their attention to us, and although they didn't speak English, they communicated that they were police. Gesturing, they noticed my backpack, which sat half open, and indicated that they wanted to search it. I froze, unable to breathe, imagining drugs being planted in my bag, imagining myself in Indian prison, imagining that Claire Danes movie where she and her traveling companion are stopped in a Thai airport while unwittingly carrying drugs onto a flight to Hong Kong.

Nate stood up, shirtless and undeterred, as the two men approached my bag. Despite their stature, Nate was bigger and imposing. He punched one fist into the palm of his other hand while telling them that we were Americans, and that they weren't going to look in my bag. The two men quickly backed down, hands in the air, saying "No problem, no problem." When they had retreated a fair distance, Nate turned around, a goofy grin on his face—he could never hurt anyone—then turned back and yelled something ridiculous about coming after them.

———————————

"Hello friend, one photo?" a small boy asked, jogging alongside us as we walked down the dusty path. The crash pads on our backs made it obvious that we were outsiders. Word had gotten out that we had a Polaroid camera, and now children surrounded us everywhere, asking the question with relentless repetition. Most had never been photographed before.

A tiny girl clung to my leg and I looked down at her. She was beautiful, the darkest of eyes surrounded by long lashes and an impish grin on her face. One of her hands was already digging in my pocket, searching for treasures. I let her. Maybe there was a rock or a stray rupee in there that she'd like. She pulled out a couple of small things and I smiled at her.

Another boy, closer to my height, pointed at me and then himself. "Hello friend, my photo?" He pronounced it "fota," his lyrical accent making the request sound like a song or poem. Realizing that I was not the keeper of the camera, he and the other kids changed tactics.

"Hello friend, school pen?"

"One chocolate?"

"Water bottle?"

"Friend, one rupee?"

I emptied the remainder of my pockets, finding sticks of gum and a few rupees, and handed my water bottle to the small girl at my side.

As the guys produced the camera, the kids clambered off in their direction. Their eyes grew wide, mouths forming a large O when they saw their face magically appear in the photos. With huge smiles, they ran off, pictures in hand, their bare feet kicking up dust as they took the treasure back to their family. I marveled at the incredible luxury I lived with back in the States. My privilege seemed vast—earlier, when we had crossed a river, I'd made Nate carry me on his back to avoid what I saw as dirty water. I was ashamed that I couldn't just get over my fears, that I had the audacity to feel sorry for myself in a place where a single photo was a life-changing experience.

During our time in India, I read books such as *Atlas Shrugged, Autobiography of a Yogi, Les Misérables,* and *The Brothers Karamazov.* I struggled to reconcile my close-minded worldview with the new ideas I was learning. That, coupled with all that I saw around me, the beauty and the pain of India, made me realize that not everything I had been taught was true, right, or even good.

I wrote at length in my journal about the different reasons I had essentially invited myself on this trip. The answers changed frequently over the course of those five weeks, until I realized that I didn't understand why I made certain decisions or clung to certain beliefs.

When the film, *Pilgrimage*, eventually premiered, it inspired an entire generation of young boulderers. For them, it was more than just another climbing film. It was an intimate look at what drove Chris Sharma and his friends to travel, climb, meditate, and explore beyond the niche world of bouldering. The film started out with Chris's one-move dyno project and then zoomed all the way out to culture, humanity, and beyond.

In truth, I don't like the person I was then. We are ultimately responsible for the decisions that we make, for the choices and reactions we have to the things that happen to us. For years I turned all my bitterness and anger on the people I was around, on climbing—anything other than myself.

I had effectively turned into the person my mom had always told me I was—selfish and discontent, regardless of my situation.

CHAPTER 20

FIRSTS

The candles were lit, David Gray played in the background, and the thing I had been told my entire life was both sacred and taboo was officially gone. The last petal had fallen. I had returned from India feeling changed, and headed straight back to the boy-with-brown-eyes in Colorado. My knowledge of "such things" was rudimentary at best, and I hardly knew or understood what was happening. I had studiously avoided that part of my body my entire life. In the end I felt nothing.

I left his condo the next morning. As I stepped out onto the blacktop of the parking lot, the sun hitting my skin, I wondered if I looked different. I definitely felt different, but not in a bad way, like religion had taught me. I didn't feel like I had lost something or given something away. What I felt was more grown-up. I had felt like an outsider my entire life, but now I was part of some kind of club. At last, I told myself, I had arrived at adulthood.

Not long after that, the group that had traveled to India together headed out on a road trip to promote *Pilgrimage*. With my recent foray into adulthood, something tightly controlled inside me had loosened. I had broken the most sanctimonious rule of religion, so why was I holding onto so many others? For me, the movie tour would also be a tour of firsts. First night club, first time getting drunk, first time feeling like I was a part of something. I felt liberated, finally free. Maybe *this* was who I was.

Partway through the movie tour, we passed through Tuolumne, California, and Chris took us up a route he had previously done called the *Matthes Crest Traverse*. We woke before dawn and stumbled into the darkness. Even midsummer, there was a hint of frost and the air was crystalline in its purity, scented with pine, glacier runoff, and granite.

We packed small day packs with water, snacks, and climbing shoes and drove to the trailhead. Before we left, Chris and Nate smoked a joint. This habit of theirs used to make me jealous—angry even. It seemed so much easier to go through life stoned rather than battling your mind every day. But I wasn't jealous anymore. It was just who they were, part of what made them, *them.*

The sun came up as we walked, its warm hand pressing against my cool skin. All around me there was dirt and rocks and trees, and my mind settled into the peaceful reverie that I sometimes found on long runs. My brain and body were finally releasing, letting go of their vain attempt to ward off an unknown danger.

I listened to the sound of my feet crunching underneath me, birds lighting from trees as we approached, and the guys chatting and laughing amicably. They had become almost like family on that trip, and their presence and acceptance meant so much to me, even if I didn't know how to tell them.

Eventually we reached the base of the climb. After a snack, we followed Chris along the route to a ledge about 60 feet up. From here, the route began to traverse the actual crest for nearly a mile, across a razor-thin peak. At times, I could look down from where the rock cut away sharply, as though I was leaning off the edge of a diving board, peering down into a swimming pool so vast and expansive that I could barely comprehend the bottom.

The only "real" climbing on Matthes Crest is one 12-foot section, but it's more than a thousand feet off the ground. I saw that we needed to use a hand jam—cupping the hand to slide it in a crack in a rock, effectively creating a wedge to pull on—to pull through the move. Nate had never crack climbed before, so we coached him through, cheering as he climbed through his fear. Later, we traversed on our butts across the steepest part of the knife-edge crest. As we scooted, our legs dangled over the edge, swinging in empty space.

There's a time-stamped photo of me from that day. It was taken at the end of the long traverse, and you can see the jagged granite ridge stretching out behind me. In the photo, I'm high in the air, arms outstretched for balance, heels clicking together Charlie Chaplin–style. A moment of pure happiness, caught on film.

After descending, we all sat in the dirt, eating the remainder of our snacks and marveling at what we had just done, before beginning the long walk back to the cars. I felt at peace and content. My body was tired, satisfied to be still after a big day, and my mind, for once, felt still too. I did not feel an urge to fill the gaping hole inside me with food, or external validation, or some other kind of self-harm. It was the best day ever.

One of the last stops on our movie tour was in New York. As I walked into the auditorium for the screening, I met someone named Liam. He was impeccably dressed in a navy puffy vest and khaki climbing pants, with wavy hair that held a hint of product and eyes that glinted with merriment. A waft of cologne hit my nose. I was thrown—this was not the kind of climber guy that I was accustomed to. He was too charming and clean, and he smelled good.

After the screening, several of us headed back to the hotel where we were staying to hang out. Liam and I chatted about our plans for the future. He sat on the floor, flipping through a book, and I lay on the bed on my stomach, my hair slipping over the edge to brush his arm. He mentioned trying to decide between going back to school and hitting the road to climb. He stood on a potentially life-altering precipice. All in, or all out.

In a burst of energy I said, "Climb! Come through Colorado and pick me up!" I had totaled my car on our movie tour, and I was unsure of what direction to take my life next. A road trip with this guy seemed like the perfect answer. Van life beckoned.

He mentioned Yosemite, but that the season was ending. Temperatures were dropping and days were getting shorter.

"It'll be fine," I said, without really having any idea. "Let's just go for it."

For climbers, asking someone to go on a road trip is often tantamount to asking someone on a first date. The problem with this is that it effectively skips a number of steps in the dating process. Climbing with another person, being roped together, trusting each other with your lives, inevitably speeds up the process of intimacy. Add in van life and the dirtbag culture that was prevalent back then, and we were all essentially going from zero to living-together-full-time-in-a-very-small-space. In my case, I was also quite a few years behind in maturity and experience, which made the whole situation with Liam confusing at best. Outside of the guys I'd traveled to India with, I'd hardly ever had a male friend, and almost no relationship with my dad. I wasn't ready for a boyfriend.

Liam and I embarked on our road trip together in his small white van, eventually landing in Yosemite Valley in November 2003. Each side of this gigantic, U-shaped corridor is lined with sheer, magnificent granite walls, culminating with the iconic Half Dome. Its northwest face, visible from the valley floor, rises an uninterrupted 2,000 vertical feet to the summit. When Royal Robbins, Mike Sherrick, and Jerry Gallwas first climbed this face in 1957, it was the most difficult big-wall climb in North America, if not the world. It took them five days and plenty of aid climbing to reach the top, which is guarded by The Visor—a final tiered overhang jutting out from the lip. If a stone falls from The Visor, it goes straight down, without stopping, to the valley floor.

In 1975 Jim Erickson and Art Higbee free climbed all but a short section of the wall below The Visor. Four years later, Leonard Coyne freed this section to make the first complete free ascent of the northwest face, which clocked in at 5.12b—an extremely difficult grade for a wall this size, especially back then.

The Valley seemed almost deserted that late in the season, as though we had it all to ourselves. We were traveling vagabond-style, living out of Liam's van and off as little money as possible, pursuing climbing for its own sake—a lifestyle that is still considered the holiest form of the sport. Liam taught me the art of picking up food in the supermarket to eat while we were still shopping, so that we wouldn't have to pay for it on the way out. This was especially important, as my bank account was basically empty. At one point, when I was climbing competitively, I'd saved a decent amount of money, but I had spent some of it on school, used some to pay back taxes that hadn't been paid when I was a minor, had given my dad my car and subsequently bought another, and had invested the rest with a broker at a local bank. The investments didn't do well, and I watched the account dwindle. Eventually, a few years later, I would pull out the little that was left.

I told Liam a bit about my past, and he quizzed me on singers on the radio while we drove, so that I could learn more about the decades of music I had missed.

"Led Zeppelin!" I'd guess. "Or, The Eagles!" I was always wrong. I never could differentiate one band from another. There's a picture of us from this time, where I'm standing several inches away, but leaning in at the shoulder so that I can put my arm around him. Trying to hug or be affectionate was a deeply uncomfortable experience. It felt wholly foreign and awkward, but it seemed to be what other people did, so I tried to learn and imitate the behavior.

Liam liked to sleep late and climb late. With winter daylight in short supply, our schedule felt reminiscent of my teen years, when I would wait for my mom to get up and get ready, and, not understanding my internal triggers, I struggled to remain calm and go with the flow. But, even as we slept side-by-side in his van, climbed, ate, and rested together, a gigantic mess was being stirred up inside me.

Back then, I thought that if anyone saw the real me, they would reject me. So instead, whenever I was in a new relationship, I tried to be the person I thought I was supposed to be—outgoing, brave, happy. Keeping up that façade was exhausting, as I could only relax when I was alone—something that wasn't possible in the close quarters of van life.

Although now round and soft in body, I still felt the whispers of damage from my years of starvation. My muscles burned and shook when I climbed. I was out of shape and unaccustomed to the additional weight on my frame. Sometimes I would hide food in strange places so that I could eat in secret, when Liam wasn't looking. Once, I asked him to get something out of my purse, and when he opened it a large chunk of cheese fell out. He didn't make a big deal about it, but it felt as though a bit of my bleeding insides had been exposed.

One day we found ourselves climbing at The Cookie Cliff, a sheer cragging wall in Yosemite with some single-pitch routes. Up until that point, I had kept my inner turmoil mostly tucked away, but on that day Liam finally got a glimpse of my self-hatred and darkness.

At times I could be brave, even reckless, on lead. At others, overwhelmed with fear of the unknown and my imagination running wild, I could be completely terrified. And yet, despite the fear, my self-loathing and desire to be "good enough" would make it impossible to turn back. What resulted was a screaming, crying, total panic meltdown, all while I continued to climb, my belayer helpless below me, unsure what to do. On that day, I thrashed about on the climb, too scared to keep going but unwilling to back down. I hated myself and my fear so much, and it all came out in torrents of tears and nasty words directed at myself.

Eventually, I used my self-loathing to overcome my fear, completing the climb amid sobs and yelps of terror. As Liam lowered me, I felt a familiar shame settle in. He had seen the real me, and there was no way now that he could ever love, or even like, me.

I untied the climbing rope and sat down to take off my climbing shoes, watching as my tears dripped onto the leather, sinking in and expanding on the material. It was over. He was going to reject me now. Instead, to my surprise, Liam came over and sat next to me, putting his arm around my shoulder.

"You're the coolest girl I've ever met," he said.

I looked up. "What? . . . Why?" I sniffled.

"Because you were scared but you kept going," he responded. As though he hadn't even witnessed my maniacal outburst.

"Ha," I scoffed, but I smiled at him and leaned into his embrace. I wasn't accustomed to feeling much of anything besides discomfort from the touch of another human, but in that moment I felt a little something else.

Some weeks later we were in Bishop, in a gigantic field of granite boulders called the Buttermilks, when Liam abruptly told me, "We have to leave. Somebody is coming who wants to kill me."

Shocked, I pressed him for the story. Liam told me his ex-girlfriend had broken off her engagement, and now the guy she had been engaged to was coming to Bishop to settle the score, believing Liam to be the reason behind the broken engagement. Liam was still in regular contact with his ex, and had even mistakenly called me by her name a couple of times. Hearing him talk about her had often made me feel that at any moment he might go back and choose her over me. I felt insecure and inexperienced, and this new development crushed my already low self-esteem, especially as we were about to part ways for Christmas.

As we said goodbye for the holiday, he told me, "Since I met you in New York, you've put a breath of fresh air in my life. I've never been so happy or content and I want to thank you for being you. I wish you could come with me and have a real Christmas."

Those words meant so much to me that I wrote them down in my journal verbatim. But so deep was my self-hatred and so innate my desire to self-destruct that I responded with little to nothing at the time.

CHAPTER 21

HOW TO SAY NO

On December 25, 2003, at the age of twenty-three, I got my period for the first time without the aid of medication. I relished in the feeling of being a woman, and yet I still struggled with hatred of my body. My face felt round and swollen when I looked in the mirror, and I hated every inch of it. How could someone possibly love me when I was this disgusting?

I was back in Colorado for Christmas at the time, and on that same trip I learned that my mom was moving out of the house in the canyon to get her own place in the mountains. My parents were considering divorce. *Finally*, I thought. How long had she been out of love with him? As long as I had been her confidante, nearly my whole life. But if she was going to get a divorce, what was the point of all the religion that had been imposed on me growing up?

After the holidays, Liam and I reconnected and headed to El Potrero Chico, Mexico, for a month. It's a playground of supremely tall, slabby-to-vertical limestone walls peppered with sport routes of all grades. Some of the walls are as tall as 2,000 feet. We were with another friend of Liam's, who also happened to be a fan my mom had exchanged emails with during my teen years. He had even been to our house in the canyon once.

I felt unsure about traveling with or being around him. I still thought anyone who had been a fan of mine during those years, especially those who went through the effort to send messages and then become friends with my mom—regardless of my lack of participation—was straight up weird. But what I discovered was that Liam's friend was a goofy, kind, insecure human, just like the rest of us.

I continued to struggle with my weight, bingeing in private, feeling shaky and exhausted while climbing, and, all too often, terrified of falling. My stomach issues continued to plague me, sometimes leaving me horribly bloated and uncomfortable and other times sending me running for the toilet at the most inopportune times. At the same time, I was still struggling with anger while climbing, crying or sometimes yelling when I got scared on a route, then feeling guilty that I was ruining the day for everyone around me, not to mention pushing Liam away, despite his constant patience and reassurance. I thought constantly about dying. About how I'd rather not exist. Despite this, I made a friend, Ben, in the Potrero, who supported me and is still in my life today. He was also experiencing some unusual stomach troubles, and I urged him to go see a doctor when we returned to the States, despite knowing that I would not do the same.

Eventually, Liam and I traveled from Mexico all the way to Squamish, British Columbia. Along the way, we stopped in Boulder and stayed with some friends, Eric and Julia, who lived in a basement apartment while they cared for Julia's elderly grandfather. They kindly let us stay free while we climbed locally. Alone in the apartment one day, I perused a large bookshelf that lined the wall filled with books belonging to Julia's grandfather, some of which dated back nearly a century. One book on "women's etiquette" instructing women on how to sit, and dress, and talk was fascinating. Eventually, I landed on a thick, dense book about sex education that presented information in a textbook-like manner. It was there, alone in that cool, dark basement apartment, that I learned all about my body parts, bodily systems, and more.

When we finally made it to Squamish, we rented a house with a couple of other climbers and I attempted to settle in. Days were spent climbing or writing articles for climbing publications to supplement our meager sponsorship earnings. Liam had several sponsors, and I'd added a few back after the publicity that came with the

India trip and film. Some even paid us small monthly stipends. Squamish, at the time, was an inexpensive place to live, not the outdoor mecca it is now. We were good at living very frugally, and had very few expenses outside of rent.

As life settled into a more normal routine, though, the issues in our relationship became pronounced. Liam thrived in our new life, pursuing his goals, while I, so wildly uncomfortable in my own skin, floundered. The monotony of each day felt like fingernails on a chalkboard. I was still unsure of how to make friends or connect with people, and I looked to Liam for guidance. He pushed back, wanting me to be independent and find my own passions and goals within our relationship.

I wrote, *"Liam wants me to be bold, energetic and optimistic, but all I feel is scared, tired and pessimistic. He says I don't have enough self-confidence because I don't believe him when he tells me that I'm beautiful. I'm going to prove to him that I can be energetic and optimistic."*

The effort, though, was exhausting, and I retreated into myself rather than trying to forge relationships with the people around us.

Liam dropped me at the airport in Vancouver at one point so that I could fly home to Colorado for a visit. "You're such a heavy packer," he said sweetly, poking fun at me as I hauled my stuffed bags through the airport. He meant it affectionately and he was right—I was a heavy packer, always indecisive about what I would need. But still, my mom was a heavy packer, and his comment made me feel like I was like her. He had no way of knowing this, but I fixated on that detail, making up all kinds of reasons I thought he may have said it, and what it meant about me. I barely said goodbye to him, adrift in my thoughts.

I'd been feeling like I needed to get away from the relationship for months anyway. I told myself that things weren't working between us. Honestly, had Liam been a different person, less smooth and more obviously enamored, I probably would have already left. Much of my energy was spent trying to figure out whether or not he actually liked me, whether or not I could believe his protestations of affection. It was stressful, and it left me feeling exhausted and lethargic at the end of each day.

Liam, unwittingly, kept me guessing just enough that I stayed for almost a year, an eternity in my limited experience. Climbing, I knew, was his first love, his essence, and I was jealous of that. My own relationship with climbing was confusing, and I was tormented by my oscillating feelings about the sport, its frequent highs and lows. I knew it bothered him that I had so little confidence. I was afraid I couldn't be the kind of person he wanted me to be. But this was my first real relationship, and it was the single most powerful bond I had formed with anyone besides my mom.

After we parted ways in the airport, I felt lost. Upon arriving at my family's home in Colorado, I had the eerie sense that I had gone back in time, back to a version of myself I never wanted to revisit. At the same time, the house was not the same. My mom was gone. What had been their house was now just my dad's, complete with the torn-down wall between the living room and the kitchen and all the things that my mom had left behind, either because she didn't want them, or she needed him to store them for her. I was also storing items that wouldn't fit in a road-tripping van at my dad's house, tucked away in the attic.

By that point, I'd mostly gained control of my eating disorder. I was still dealing with a host of what would become lifelong intestinal issues, and occasionally fell back into my old patterns of bingeing and restricting, but I had learned through trial and error how to eat intuitively. The problem was that my healthy body was some thirty pounds heavier than my former self. It felt to me like I was inhabiting a stranger's body, and climbing in this new body felt foreign and awkward.

Ironically, neither of my parents talked at all about their new living situation. No one mentioned my new, much larger body. It was as if the past, for both of them, had been erased, and this new reality had always been there. Apparently there was nothing odd about new men in my mom's life. And despite all the years I had been taught about purity culture, nothing was said about me living in a van with a guy.

For my part, I didn't bring it up while I was there. I could barely wrap my head around how little communication there had been about all of the changes in our lives, not to mention the fundamentalist rules that were seemingly gone. I headed back to Canada feeling even more alone and emotionally lost.

Back in Squamish, I headed to the Petrifying Wall, a small cragging area just uphill from a lake where climbers cooled off on hot and muggy summer days. It was there that I met Charlie. His attention was immediate, intense, and palpable. He seemed completely unfazed by the fact that I had a boyfriend.

When he talked, full of plans and big ideas, he gestured wildly. I would watch his knobby-knuckled hands flail about and wonder if I could ever be attracted to him. He had brown shaggy hair, pale skin, and sad, puppy-dog eyes that belied his outward energetic nature and buzzing energy. There was something about the sadness in his eyes that I recognized. *Maybe it doesn't matter if I'm attracted to him. Maybe his sad eyes mean that he'll accept my sadness. Maybe his obvious brokenness means that he'll accept me as I am.* It sure would be easier than constantly striving to feel worthy of Liam.

Charlie had a big, old truck. I did not have a car. The math added up. I repressed the niggling doubt in the back of my mind that something wasn't quite right.

Over the past year I'd grown comfortable with Liam. We lived together in Squamish, we'd grown close and intertwined our lives; being with him felt like home. But how I felt was usually not a reliable source of information, by my estimation, anyway. How I felt didn't really matter. It never had. I broke up with him, coldly and abruptly.

Suddenly I was in another car, with another boy. I missed Liam's smell, his warmth and comfort, almost immediately. I didn't feel that with Charlie. I sat on the bench seat of his truck, the dash dusty and littered with random objects, and missed the feeling of being in a van that had felt as if it was mine too, almost like it was ours.

As we drove eastward into the night, toward the distant Rocky Mountains, Charlie put on a song for me. "This is how I feel about you," he said, as Tracy Chapman's smooth, deep voice drifted through the cabin, singing about someone giving her a chance. It gave me shivers. I felt overwhelmed, bombarded by this near-stranger's deep feelings for me. At the same time I thought, *How could I not be with someone who feels this strongly about me? Isn't this what every girl wants?*

We drove through the night, him behind the wheel and me in the passenger seat. I got a little sleep, but mostly I wondered what the hell I was doing in this car, with this guy. By morning the truck had turned off the highway toward the mountains. We followed dirt roads leading up through forests, passing occasional logging trucks parked in muddy pullouts. After an hour of slowly driving deep into the wilderness, we arrived at the Canadian Mountain Holidays Bugaboo Lodge—a luxurious, if not seemingly out of place, hotel for heli-skiers and adventure tourists. Charlie and several of his friends were there to guide a boisterous and friendly man up some moderate alpine climbs in the Bugaboos.

Not long after our arrival, we boarded a massive helicopter with room for the five of us and our gear. I fastened the seatbelt, slid headphones over my ears, and felt the quickening *thrump, thrump, thrump* of the powerful rotors. Moments later we hovered, rotated toward the mountains, and were off—cruising above the forest. My first helicopter flight was magical. At one point we flew through a canyon, so close to the rock it seemed I could reach out and touch it. With windows all around, I saw the ground, then the sky, alternating as the helicopter swooped and dipped in a way that felt more carefree than flying in a plane.

After a fifteen-minute flight, we landed on a grassy knoll beneath massive gray spires jutting up from the snow. To hike here from the trailhead with climbing and camping gear would have been exhausting, a full day with steep scrambling and glacier travel.

Broad slabs of rock were interspersed with patches of grass, snow, and ice. Rugged peaks surrounded us as we set up our tents near a

large boulder. This would be our basecamp for the next week, where
we would sleep, cook, and hang out.

———————————

The next day, I invited Charlie into my tent. Things escalated
quickly. "Wait, stop," I said, suddenly tormented and feeling like
this was all wrong. "I don't think I want to do this. I don't think I'm
ready. I don't know ..."

"Ok," he said, "ok. There's no rush." But then, a few minutes later,
we were having sex anyway. While it was happening, I thought, *This
doesn't feel right. I should have insisted, should have said "no" harder.*
But I didn't know what I wanted, or what I was supposed to want. I
didn't even know *how* to say no.

Besides, I thought, maybe this was how love was supposed to feel.
I wondered if maybe god was punishing me because I'd turned my
back on him. I'd spent a lifetime trying to figure out what the other
people in my life wanted, and then working to make it so. I'd silenced
myself over and over in order to avoid anger. I'd listened when I'd
been told that my needs and desires were selfish, wrong—even evil—
and that another person's needs and desires were what mattered.
Now, having stopped listening to or trusting my own feelings a long
time ago, I was applying that same thinking to my new relationships. As an adult, if something felt wrong or "off," I assumed it was
right, or fine. If something felt good, I assumed the opposite.

When it was over, I cried and cried. Charlie seemed to feel awful
as he comforted me. I'm sure he didn't know why I was bawling—I
didn't even know why. He was damaged in his own way and in
those days probably fantasized that being with "Katie Brown,"
whomever that was, would fulfill him somehow, or save him from
himself. We were like broken mirrors, reflecting each other's
anguish.

Charlie seemed over the moon about me, so obsessed that he
couldn't sense my profound ambivalence, so the next morning I
attempted to brush off the incident. After all, I had invited him into
my tent, so technically it was "my fault" that things had moved too

fast. I didn't communicate how I was feeling, carefully smashing down and attempting to hide my confusion.

For our first alpine route in the Bugaboos, we soloed the west ridge of Pigeon Spire late in the day. It was warm and beautiful, with snow and rock everywhere. I crossed my first glacier and jumped my first crevasse, which felt wild and foreign. The route itself was easy, a modest 5.4 at the hardest, yet the position, high above the glacier on a sharp arête leading to a pointy summit, proved sublime. After the climb, Charlie helped me search for a climbing partner for the next day, out of the group who had just backpacked in, since he'd be out guiding. I never had the courage to ask total strangers to climb, so I felt incredibly supported. It was another "pro" on my imaginary list of pros and cons as to why I *should* like him.

It felt strange to climb the next day with someone I had just met: a twentysomething guy with longish brown hair, who seemed experienced. The landscape also felt foreign. One pitch up a five-pitch granite tower, I found myself staring out over vast fields of rock and snow. I may as well have been on another planet. My mind swirled with fear. I pictured us stranded on the route in a snowstorm—an irrational fear on that particular route.

For once, instead of burying my anxiety and saying nothing so that I didn't inconvenience someone else, then having a panic attack or meltdown later, I told my climbing partner that I wanted to go down. It was one of the first times I listened to my needs and stood my ground as a climber, and I was relieved when he seemed fine with it. We rappelled and went to climb single-pitch routes instead—a better warm-up for an alpine newbie like me.

———————————

The following day I again climbed with people I didn't know in an alien setting. The climbing community is small, but since climbers tend to focus on a "genre" (alpine climbing, sport climbing, competition climbing), they often run into the same people in their micro-community time and again. Where I had once seen the same faces over and over at crags, here everyone was new, although they all still knew who I was. I was new to alpine climbing, but I was still a sponsored sport climber who had won competitions and been featured in magazines. This was my first introduction to those on the outskirts of the competition and sport climbing world.

With these strangers, I did a route on Snowpatch Spire so easy I could barely even call it climbing. Still, I grew fatigued over the course of the day. I struggled with how to be, who to be, around strangers, especially in this intense, high-altitude environment. Partway up, the temperature dropped and it started hailing, then the clouds broke and the sun came out. Then it rained again, and back and forth. I didn't have proper mountain boots, so I'd strapped crampons onto my approach shoes. My toes turned into tiny blocks of ice.

Our group finally reached the summit, where we saw an oncoming wall of dark clouds. We descended immediately. Thunder boomed and lightning flashed as we rappelled. It all felt exciting and dangerous, and took my mind off being cold.

Once down, we huddled under a rock to stay dry while waiting for Charlie and his client to return from their route on Bugaboo Spire. On the hike back to camp, the sky cleared and the sun came out. It felt like heaven after being cold and wet all day.

After that climb, it rained or snowed every day. That was normal alpine weather, but I found it intolerable. At one point I wrote in my journal, *"To be honest, it seemed like a lot of work just to go choss-aneering,"* as in, climbing poor rock on moderate mountain terrain—to me, the worst of both the rock and alpine worlds. I preferred being challenged by the climbing itself, rather than all the random variables, like weather and loose rock, that the mountains throw at you.

I had no way to escape, though. I either sat in the rain or in a tent, trying to stay dry, eating too much and thinking too much. Charlie wrote me elaborate love notes, while I wrote to Liam. I missed him.

Finally, the weather cleared enough to go bouldering. I was immediately drawn to one edge of the most prominent basecamp boulder, where a conspicuous arête overhangs about 15 degrees. I could see just enough fingertip edges and tiny footholds to imagine how it could go. It was tall, though—about 15 feet high at its top—and jagged talus guarded the landing beneath the arête. A fall could easily result in a broken ankle.

Still, a few of us tossed backpacks over the sharpest rocks and stuffed ankle-eating holes with sleeping bags, clothing, and whatever else was handy. Tentatively, we took turns on the first few moves over a bulge, spotting each other while the climber found solid edges and footholds. After a few challenging moves, we each dropped off.

Finally, my fingers latched onto the holds, and I felt strong and secure. The first time I made it past the bulge, I knew I could do it. "Watch me," I said, noticing the outstretched arms below, ready to catch me if I fell. I balanced upward, leaning off the razor-edged arête, smearing my shoe rubber on nothing but texture. With each move I risked a harder, more unpredictable fall that my spotters might not be able to check. But I felt no fear. Once again, the only time I felt safe was when I was actually in danger.

I grabbed the lip and pressed onto the top of the boulder. A feeling of satisfaction, almost happiness, filled me. Years later I learned the boulder problem was named "Katie Brown Arête" and rated V8.

After leaving the Bugaboos, I went back to Squamish to wait for Charlie to finish guiding before we headed to Yosemite together. I felt terribly restless, with nervous energy and an ugly feeling that something wasn't right. A nameless anxiety had taken root deep inside me, although I wasn't completely aware of it at the time. I wrote a letter to Charlie, the tone angry, saying that we had moved way too fast. I had been hearing rumors that he was a "player." I stuffed it away, too scared of the confrontation giving it to him might cause.

I also felt weird and confused about Liam. I missed him, and felt better about myself and the world in general when I was around him. But, at the same time, Charlie seemed like the better fit. It would be years before I understood that if a person carries childhood trauma into adulthood, they subconsciously seek relationships that reinforce the ways in which their boundaries were violated as kids. The relationship Liam had wanted with me was healthy, but I chose trauma bonding with someone else. I would repeat this pattern over and over.

Charlie and I set off for Yosemite's Camp Four—a broad, flat campground so packed with tents when we arrived that they were almost touching. The scent of campfires permeated the pine forest, dotted with boulders large and small. Neither Charlie nor I had much money to speak of, so we hiked up above the campground to sleep under a giant boulder.

It was illegal to sleep outside designated campgrounds, but Camp Four was both expensive and always full, requiring a reservation, which we did not have. Sleeping in your car was illegal as well, and if the rangers caught you, they'd boot you out of the Valley. So the boulder was our best option. I lay in the dirt, a rock digging into my back, and listened to small rodents scrabbling around in the dark at our feet.

The next morning, Charlie taught me how to get free food from the cafeteria by scooping up other people's leftovers. On our way into the Valley, we had stopped at Trader Joe's near Fresno, where we climbed into the dumpster with headlamps and fished out food still wrapped in plastic. We also frequented the "dented can store," where we bought expired canned food for cents on the dollar. I was officially getting a taste of the ultimate dirtbag Yosemite experience.

We decided to climb a few of the classic routes in the Valley. We started with The Rostrum, a 900-foot-tall pillar of vertical granite splintered by long, parallel-sided cracks. It was my first time up, and I managed to onsight it. I even led some of the pitches without getting scared, which felt reassuring considering how all over the place my emotions were. I wrote in my journal, *"Charlie is such a good person, has a really big heart, takes good care of me and has similar goals, but I just don't feel right being with him. I'm not sure what to do about it. Plus, I keep thinking about you know who, which I always do, and which really confuses me. I've been in such turmoil it's been crazy. Up and down."*

One morning we walked through Camp Four to discover that a bear had broken into the truck while we were asleep. I had left energy-bar wrappers in my pack, a rookie move. Bears can smell anything that has even touched food, and they'll try to get to it. Our climbing packs were strewn across the parking lot. Off to the side sat several well-known climbers, and my heart stopped when I noticed that one of them was holding my journal, leafing through it. "I keep thinking about 'you know who,'" he taunted, his hair blowing lightly in his face as he and his friends softly cackled. He handed me my journal, smirking. I couldn't say anything. I would have probably toppled over if someone had pushed me with one finger, so I just glared at them. Better to pretend that I didn't care, that I felt nothing. I knew how to do that. I hastily stuffed my journal and all my displaced gear back into my bag and walked away.

After another night of bandit camping beneath the boulder, we climbed one of the Valley's most famous long free routes: *Astroman*.

Rising 1,300 feet in a gentle, right-leaning arc, *Astroman* is steep, sustained, and unforgiving. Its modest 5.11c rating belies the overall difficulty of ten strenuous pitches of crack climbing. Of all its pitches, the Harding Slot is the most feared. A slick, overhanging tight hands crack leads into the belly of the slot—a steep, blank chasm just wide enough for a human body to slither up. Near its top, the squeeze chimney pinches down so tight that many climbers pass through only with a choreography of properly timed exhales and panicked pushing upward.

In the slot, claustrophobia hit and something cracked inside me. I began to cry and scream. I hit the rock and tore at my clothes in anguish. I hated myself and everything around me. I was such a mess that Charlie had to lead every subsequent pitch, which made me feel even worse.

Later, I found myself crying hysterically again, with heaving sobs. I thrashed about, trying to pull, claw, and rip my heart out of my chest. All the confused feelings in my head were torture—I felt heavy and awful, as though I'd done something terribly wrong but didn't know what. I felt this way so often during those weeks that I was completely drained—empty—to the point of giving up.

It was Charlie who gently, persistently, urged me to see a doctor and get on antidepressants. He was familiar with those medications, and listening to him, I started to feel hopeful about the idea. Maybe I would feel less shattered and confused. Maybe medicine would fix me.

We left Yosemite and drove to a clinic in Fresno, an hour away. Thankfully, my dad had drilled into me the importance of health insurance, so even though I didn't have a permanent address and lived on seven thousand dollars a year, I still had at least basic coverage.

After a very brief conversation with a doctor whose name I never learned, I was prescribed forty milligrams of Prozac, and it kicked in fairly quickly. I felt revved up, impatient, and ready to move on from all the turmoil I had been feeling with Charlie. I broke up with him unceremoniously in Camp Four.

As he sat on a log in Camp Four crying, I stared at him coldly. Being with me had been annoying anyway, so why was it such a big deal? I was frustrated that he couldn't just get over it and move on, that the whole thing was taking so long. Plus, people were staring.

CHAPTER 22
WHAT GUYS WANT

After Charlie, Liam and I began an on-again, off-again relationship that would last for over a year. I would break up with him, usually in some kind of letter, then sleep with someone else, only to go back to Liam later, begging him to take me back. It was a toxic cycle, and after each iteration, the bond between Liam and I was further eroded. Crying jaggedly, I would beg for forgiveness, wishing he would look at me the way he used to. He would turn away, his once merry eyes filled with pain, and go somewhere to process his feelings alone.

When he walked away, I felt abandoned and confused. I could not understand why a physical act like sex meant so much to him, could make him look at me with such disgust, hurt, and betrayal. To me, sex had become just that, an act, something I did because someone wanted it, because it seemed like it made others like me, and because, ultimately, I didn't know how to say no. With Liam, I had had an emotional connection, but with the rest I was just playing a part, trying to be what I thought others wanted me to be.

In the midst of one of our breakups, I went to Bend, Oregon, to see Ben, who had become one of my closest and most trusted friends since I met him in the Potrero. He had gone to see a doctor about the stomach problems he'd had on that trip, and the diagnosis was a shock to everyone—cancer. He met the diagnosis with unfathomable bravery and optimism, but when I found out that he was going through painful surgeries and treatments all alone, with no one by his side but his dog, I headed to his house.

Ben was the one guy who never let our relationship get romantic. He never wanted more from me than who I was, and I felt like he accepted me, ugly bits and all, as an equal. As I slept in his basement, I struggled with how to express my love for him, my appreciation for his presence in my life. I didn't know how to tell him in words. The only thing that I could think to do was to show him. So I brought him tea in bed (accidentally scalding him in the process) and brought his favorite food to the hospital. I decided that I needed to get my own car, thinking that going car shopping with me would distract Ben. What I failed to realize, however, was that after his most recent surgery, each bump caused him excruciating pain.

Ben graciously accepted my attempts to show him I cared, despite my obvious bumbles and inexperience, and I loved him for it.

When Ben's situation stabilized, I tried to go back to Squamish, only to flee again. I had seen a dog on the Humane Society website in Boulder, Colorado, that I liked, so I drove straight there from Squamish, stopping only to pee and get gas. More than twenty hours and many caffeinated beverages later, I arrived at the shelter window. A black-and-white border collie puppy lay there quietly, watching me watch him, while dogs all around him barked and wiggled and jumped. I loved him for his aloof indifference.

The Humane Society almost didn't let me adopt him, since I was essentially homeless and living out of my car, but I eventually convinced them that being out at a crag with me was better for a dog than a house and a fenced yard. As we drove out of the parking lot, the puppy quaked with fear and attempted to squeeze in between my back and the seat. He had come with the name Ratchet, but I had always wanted to name something Dakota. That seemed like too much of a name for my tiny, timid puppy, so I settled on Cody.

I didn't have a home or a place to go, so Cody and I ended up at my mom's condo in the mountains for a few days while I trained him. She and I weren't close anymore, but we still corresponded regularly, and whenever I was in Colorado, I would stop in and visit. My dad had helped her buy a tiny condo at the base of a ski mountain, and she had finally returned to her first love—skiing.

I longed for someone to talk to about my relationship with Liam. I had thought I'd marry the first guy I ever kissed, and that certainly hadn't panned out, so where did that leave me?

We sat in my car in the dark, and I attempted to explain how I felt about Liam. I don't remember exactly how she responded, but our brief, stilted conversation wasn't what I needed, and I walked away feeling worse about myself and the situation rather than soothed and comforted.

At twenty-four, I finally came to terms with the fact that going to my mom for solace and advice was never going to work. That was one of the last times I attempted to confide in her. We still communicated, but the unspoken divide between us deepened as I pulled further away.

––––––––––––

Eventually, I made my way to Moab, where I had wanted to move since I was nineteen. I headed to the home of the one person I knew who lived in Moab, Lisa Hathaway.

There are a handful of women I consider some of my first true adult friends. Of course, I had childhood friends, but once I started climbing, they fell away. It was just me and my mom for so long that I forgot how to get to know people, how to bond with them and forge friendships. Then a handful of women I met in my early twenties welcomed me and taught me how to form and keep friendships. They stuck with me through all my ups and downs, not to mention all the times I showed up and then disappeared without a word—a habit that earned me the nickname "the Vaporizer."

I met Lisa at a trade show, and from the beginning, she welcomed me into her life with open arms. Lisa is one of those people who is unapologetically herself, and she showed me how to start to live my own life that way.

Lisa's house, where some of my best, freest memories have taken place, is tucked into a discreet corner of Moab. To get there, you enter a narrow, barely noticeable drive, which takes a 90-degree turn past a cinder-block wall. The small, squat, stucco house sits on the left as the driveway opens into a large, dirt parking lot, usually filled with trucks and campers—some that Lisa's friends are storing at her house, plus a couple of others filled with climbers who are passing through. Lisa's house was essentially a climber KOA, where all were welcome. It was a safe place for more than just me.

There was a storage shed next to Lisa's house, filled with carefully organized, neatly labeled climbing gear and other sporting equipment, and behind that another A-frame shed, dubbed "the woody," home to some of the only indoor climbing in Moab. Mattresses lined the floor, and steeply overhung plywood walls were scattered with a multitude of holds and labeled routes.

According to lore, Lisa's house had once housed chickens before she had completely overhauled it. It had a low doorway, ironic given her height, and the inside was colorful and quirky, with lizards for drawer pulls, a wood-burning stove in the kitchen, and owl paraphernalia scattered here and there. She had tucked the expired passports of friends, baby faces grinning out from the pages, into the doorway that led from the living room into the kitchen. At the start of any chilly winter climbing day, climbers would cluster into the kitchen, brewing coffee and tea in her ceramic pourover and soaking up the heat from the wood stove.

One evening I was lamenting that I didn't know how to find people to climb with. "I don't know how to make friends. How do people do it, just magically find people to climb with?" I asked Lisa, who never seemed to have a problem and could make friends with anyone.

"You just ask them," she said, nonchalantly.

"But . . . how?" For some reason this baffled me.

"Just say, 'Hey do you want to go climbing?'"

"To a stranger?" I balked.

"Yes, Katie," she responded. "There's some people outside right now who are going to Indian Creek tomorrow. Ask them if you can join them."

I was terrified, but I wanted to climb, and at least it was dark so they wouldn't be able to see my face if it turned bright red. I went outside, stumbling in the dark parking lot, and walked up to a small cluster of guys standing near the woody. I had met them before, but I felt awkward and unsure.

"So, Lisa said you guys are going to the Creek tomorrow?" I asked. They responded yes.

"Do you mind if I tag along?" I stammered.

"Well," one of the guys said. "I'd have to ask my girlfriend how she feels about it."

I shuffled back, confused. What did his girlfriend have to do with it? Did he think I was going to slow him down? Seduce him? I just wanted to go climbing. If I were a man, he wouldn't have to ask his girlfriend.

"Uh . . . ok. Yeah, actually never mind. It's fine." I turned to go. Not only had my worst fear come true, but now I didn't want to climb with them anyway if that's how they saw me.

"Dude," one of Lisa's friends cut in, a large figure who resembled a Norse god and towered over the smaller, lighter climbers. "She just wants to go climbing. So lame."

The guy started mumbling, backtracking on their previous comment, but I was already long gone, back to Lisa's house to hide from my embarrassment.

Despite the awkward experience, I stayed in Moab, and Lisa helped me find a room to rent. Still too unsure to meet my own climbing partners, I mostly went with her to climb at Mill Creek or boulder at Big Bend. But over time, the crew of women I knew in Moab grew, thanks to Lisa's introductions, and often there would be three or four of us up at Mill Creek, dressed in our thrift-store delights, goofing off and laughing as we climbed.

Give a desire a name, and you've given it power over you—including the power to hurt you. But a desire with no name is an amorphous thing that you can guard and protect. No one can steal it from you. I preferred not to want anything too much—not belongings, which I left everywhere with abandon, not my past accomplishments, the remnants of which I told my dad he could throw out (he did not), not relationships, and certainly not myself.

This became my motto of sorts during the years I spent in Moab, a time when, in a way, I grew up. It was, however, in direct conflict with another of my beliefs: that I had to keep pushing in order to prove that, unlike what I had been told, I was not like my dad. He just let life happen to him. I refused to give up. The problem though, was that this was paradoxical thinking. I was trying to force my way through life, to become an unrealistic ideal, while at the same time refusing to need anyone, care about anything, or have any goals.

I had thought about dying for years. Every emotion felt too large to hold, every decision too hard to make. I didn't know to call it depression and anxiety until Charlie had helped me get the treatment I needed. As I approached twenty-five, my Prozac-laden brain cared less about everything. It felt nice to feel good, when I had spent so much of my life struggling to keep going. But sometimes people would notice.

There's a photo of me at a trade show from this time. In it, I'm holding a plate out for food. I'm biting a Red River Gorge Climbing Coalition patch between my teeth and grinning maniacally. My eyes look crazed. I remember a friend commenting that I seemed "strung really tight" that weekend.

I was no longer bingeing, and had begun to settle into my body, but I had traded in one addiction for another—the new one being male attention. For whatever reason, it seemed that I was the kind of girl that guys liked. I told myself that men liked the *idea* of me more than they liked the actual me. Many of them didn't even know me when they decided they were smitten. Even after I stopped competing, I received love letters, emails, photos of T-shirts with my picture printed on them. Once I was told by a guy that dating me would be like "winning the world cup of girlfriends." So I dated him, because, why not? Another time, when asked what he was projecting—lingo for a climb that requires many attempts before potential success—that season, a man that I was climbing with said that he was "projecting Katie Brown."

Knowing that men liked me became my new power. It gave me some sense of control, just like starving myself had, and it was just as misguided and damaging. In fact, it was an addiction. A less definable addiction than something like alcohol and pills, but an addiction nonetheless.

In my mind, guys liked girls who were outgoing, funny, brave, and sexy, so I set out to be that kind of girl, at least for a while. My relationships were based on farce, with me acting out a part. When I was exhausted from trying to pretend that I was the bold, happy, energetic girl I thought every guy wanted, I left, unceremoniously, brutally, and without explanation.

Throughout my midtwenties, I also started and stopped my antidepressants cold turkey, without telling anyone and without realizing how dangerous that can be. A thought would creep into my mind, the way anxiety does, that I was suffering some imaginary side effect from the Prozac. I would decide to stop taking the medication. This, in turn, would plunge me into a low low, which was usually followed by some kind of ugly meltdown on the rock. Then I would decide I was braver when I was taking Prozac. So I'd start taking antidepressants again. Sometimes I'd think, *I should stop taking Prozac. I should be strong enough to be able to climb without drugs.* I'd wonder if Prozac was bringing me up to everyone else's "normal" or taking me past normal to a place where I didn't care anymore. I didn't know. And so the cycle continued.

Sometimes, when it became too much, I would check myself into a hotel in Moab, where I'd stay for upwards of two weeks, not talking to a single soul. I'd spend long days hiking in the red desert with my dog, until I felt ready to re-enter the world. Only alone could I be the real me—broken, jagged, scared, confused, and sad. And only my dog, as far as I could tell, would accept that part of me.

It was at this time that I met Robert. Our first interaction was via email, where he introduced himself as a newish photographer who wanted to document people in the climbing community. He exuded charm and a self-deprecating humor that made me laugh. Plus, to keep my flagging climbing career going, I needed to be photographed. I quickly saw that he had a crush on me and assumed it was based on who he imagined me to be. He had never even met me in person. Like many of my other flings or relationships, it seemed like we would be a good fit on paper.

Robert drove from Canada to Moab to pick me up. My friend Sascha and I were with another friend in a bar when he entered, bobbing with excitement, a wide grin on his lightly freckled face. A wide, pink headband pushed back his blond hair.

"A pink headband? Really?" Sascha giggled into my ear.

"Oh my god, who is this guy?" said our friend.

I blushed. Suddenly I was unsure. What had I gotten myself into? I still didn't understand myself well enough to know what I was feeling, so although they were just joking, I used their first impressions as a barometer. This did not bode well.

Robert sensed my apprehension and pulled back a little, wounded, when I greeted him coldly. I wasn't accustomed to sensitive men, which made me feel even more off-balance. His insecurity was palpable, and I recognized myself in it. I didn't like that mirror.

Nonetheless, we headed out on the road together. I'd recently developed my first celebrity crush, on a Scottish musician named Paolo Nutini. I know this typically happens a little earlier than twenty-four. I had also never been to a concert. When I found out that Paolo was playing in Seattle the very next day, I convinced Robert to drive me there, straight through the night. On the way, we listened to Paolo's music. His words, about madness, fighting with his brain, and a sadness that creeps up his spine—sung in his signature raspy tone—spoke to me.

Robert and I arrived in Seattle shortly before the concert started, delirious from the drive. I found myself in a cement-filled space, jostled about by a crush of bodies as we waited for what seemed like forever. Someone spilled a beer on me and it dripped down my leg, onto my shoe. Finally, Paolo appeared onstage, so drunk he could hardly sing, his accented voice slurring the words together as he waved about, leaning on the mic to keep himself upright.

I wasn't sure what to do with myself while we listened to him sing, and I looked around, watching all the people crammed together, bobbing in time to the music. *So you just stand here, listening?* I thought.

It was so different from the nighttime dance party in the desert I had experienced years before, with the stars twinkling overhead and plenty of space to spread out and kick up dust. I suddenly wanted to just sit down. Or better yet, go to sleep.

Robert later told me that when he was around me it felt like he never knew who he was going to get. He remembered "a profound amount of sadness, but also a profound amount of light. That's what made you so intoxicating. The light—the positivity—you would have when you would allow yourself to just be you was so stunning. And then the sadness came from this place of almost a sense of entrapment . . . almost like you didn't deserve to be happy."

He continued, "As soon as you were that free, amazing, beautiful person, you'd shut it down, as though you didn't deserve that happiness. You didn't deserve to feel that good. Having seen that brightness, people would be like, 'Why can't you just be that person?' It was, understandably, an unfair ask, without knowing the depth of everything that had brought you to that point."

Robert's assessment hit home. Hearing someone else's view on my behavior, rather than just my own judgmental recriminations, felt strangely liberating. As though, maybe, there was good in me—maybe there was light in me. I had been told so many times that people didn't really like me, that they only wanted things from me. That view had become so fundamental for me that I couldn't believe that anyone truly liked or loved me, myself included. But in the end, don't we all deserve happiness? And aren't we all not *just* bad or good, but some of both?

CHAPTER 23

THE LEANING TOWER

In the Valley, across from El Cap, is the Leaning Tower, the steepest big wall in Yosemite and one of the most sustained overhangs in the world. To me, overhanging climbing is the best kind of climbing (I blame this preference on the Red River Gorge), so the feature drew my attention right away.

I was traveling a lot in the lead-up to the summer of 2005—a couple of months here, a few weeks there, back to Squamish, then Moab, then Yosemite. At some point, I had decided that it would be fun to try and redpoint a 1,000-foot route called *Westie Face*, rated 5.13a. Given my chronic stomach issues, I wasn't sure about sleeping on a wall, but I enjoyed being high off the ground, and the Leaning Tower was small enough that it felt like a big wall that was still doable in a day.

I was a bit strung out from navigating male relationships, and desperate to climb with a woman. I decided to call on the Yosemite master herself, Lynn Hill, a climbing prodigy whose time in the Valley harkened back to the seventies. Since she was a mom with a toddler at the time, I didn't really expect Lynn to say yes, but surprisingly, she did. I had been on the route the season prior, so I knew a little about it, and Lynn had a short window—less than a week—when she could come to the Valley. There wasn't much wiggle room, just a couple days to rehearse the pitches, a rest day, and then a day or two try for the redpoint. I felt a bit of self-imposed pressure to keep up with Lynn's skill and experience, but I was excited to try.

Westie Face starts out with a bolt ladder, so technically it's not a free climb. I had never really thought much about the bolt ladder though. It just seemed like part of the route. Lynn and I worked the bottom crux pitches one day, then rested for a day before giving the whole thing a go. We decided not to rehearse the upper pitches to save on time, since they weren't as hard and were well protected, unlike the lower pitches. On our rest day we went down to the river with my dog Cody and Lynn's son. Cody had been terrified of the water when I got him. He would panic paddle with his paws above the water, splashing himself in the face and looking like he was going to drown. I decided that the solution was to throw him in, over and over, until he learned how to swim. That day at the river I tossed him in, time and time again, until suddenly something clicked, and he could paddle with his paws underwater. Although my teaching tactic is not advisable, from then on, Cody was a water-loving dog.

The morning of our attempt we got up early: our plan was to get as high as possible before the sun hit the route in the afternoon. *Westie Face* is accessed by an hour-long hike through a pine-scented forest sprinkled with boulders. We traversed a fourth-class ledge system with a few low-fifth-class moves (protected by fixed hand lines) to the base of the route: a beautiful, overhanging wall of yellow, gray, and orange. Some two hundred feet up a line of closely spaced bolts, the actual free climbing began. Cody came with us and hung with the packs until the heat chased him back down the trail to a shady spot near the car.

Yosemite seemed particularly mosquito infested that summer, and we were each peppered with red welts. We decided to alternate leads, and I led the first free pitch: a 5.12c dihedral, complete with wide stems and the occasional finger jam in the corner. Lynn took the next pitch, a steep corner to vertical face with some fixed gear and bolts. At 5.13a, it was the hardest pitch on the route, but because it came early on, when the temps were cool and our energy fresh, it didn't really feel like the crux. As I watched Lynn climb the pitch, I marveled at her skill. I felt overwhelmed by how short I fell of her ability and how much experience I lacked by comparison.

I was still very much in awe of and intimidated by Lynn. She is a very pragmatic climber, almost scientific in her process, whereas I am all feeling, both on and off the rock. I tried, for a long time, to hide that part of my personality, not realizing that was what made me an intuitive climber. I couldn't explain the how or why of what my body was doing on the rock, but I almost always could feel how a climb would work. I couldn't appreciate that part of myself at the time, so I spent a lot of my time with Lynn worried that I was going to let her down. The responsibility bore down on me as the sun crept closer to the wall. I wanted to be an equal partner to Lynn—even more so than with the men I climbed with—to carry my weight, find my own verve.

After Lynn climbed, it was my lead again. The next pitch involved a dynamic heel hook, followed by slapping movement across a slick, sloping rail. Even though it was rated "only" 5.12b, it took me three tries to get the pitch clean. Lynn took the next pitch, rated 5.12a R, which meant that the lack of solid gear placements in the middle of the pitch required care and precision to prevent a long and potentially harmful leader fall. We had broken a key hold off during our practice day, but Lynn breezed through the tricky reimagining of the sequence. It took me a few tries to follow her.

My repeated tries had slowed our progress and the sun was now baking the remainder of the route. It was my lead on a steep, 140-foot crack with several poorly protected moves at the base on thin and polished rock. This was just my style, and I was finally able to turn off my mind and let my body take over, almost reveling in the self-inflicted pain bearing down on my muscles and skin as I ascended the crack.

The last pitches were steep and sometimes coated with bat guano, the aroma radiating in the now-hot sun. Lynn fell a couple of times on the steeper sections before successfully pulling through the roof, ripping off duct tape left by aid climbers (left in place over sharp edges to prevent rope abrasion while ascending fixed lines) to find extra holds. We topped out the climb in the dark after more than twelve hours, exhausted but successful.

Well, Lynn was successful. She freed the whole climb in a single day. But ultimately, I fell on one of the final pitches, and there wasn't time for me to lower to the start of the pitch to try a second time. I just started climbing again from the point where the rope caught me. Technically, that means there was a break in my ascent, rather than a clean line from bottom to top with no falls.

It felt like choking at the finish line had become a habit. We returned the next day so I could redpoint the pitch and "finish" my climb, and Lynn assured me that my climb still "counted," but I walked away feeling like I had fallen short yet again.

CHAPTER 24
THE ORBITER

During those years, Lisa had begun to affectionately refer to me as "the Orbiter." I would leave Moab in search of inner peace, only to come back after circling through the western states and Canada. Around and around I went, trying to escape myself. But wherever you go, there you are.

After one such orbit, I rented a tiny studio apartment in Moab for four hundred dollars a month. Of all the places I have lived, this was my favorite. It was my own space, not shared with a roommate or a boyfriend, and it felt divine. But at the same time, being alone meant that I had to sit with myself rather than run, and the solitude and lack of movement meant that my anxiety crept in with a vengeance. My mind spun with illogical, horrible things that could go wrong, until I'd curl up into ball, my hands grasping inward as I hyperventilated, riding the tide of terror and waiting for the panic attack to end.

It was during this time, though, that I found a couple of people to climb with in Indian Creek on a regular basis. One of them, Jack, and I started to climb together a lot, which allowed me to hone my crack climbing skills and learn a variety of sizes, even projecting some routes that were hard for me and onsighting a few 5.13s, including *Winner Takes All* and *Tricks Are for Kids*. Some of the onsights went smoothly and I never felt like I would fall. Others were full-on screaming battles where, unable to stop to place gear, I ran it out as far as I dared.

Crack climbing worked for me, and I enjoyed the punishing pain
it left in and on the body. There was something about the hurt I
inflicted upon myself as I wedged fingers and toes into the crack
and then twisted them, bearing down and pulling upward, that rang
familiar and comforted me. Mentally, this style of climbing was not
taxing—the cracks required little thought, and there were always
gear placements if you had enough energy to stop and place them.
This kind of climbing suited me just fine.

There was a lot of laughter during those months, and I needed
the camaraderie. Cody would sometimes explore for hours at a time
while I climbed, always returning as dusk approached. I'd catch
glimpses of his black tail during the day, far below us as he wandered
the red earth in search of something gross to roll in.

Perched on a piece of red stone at the base of a climb, I'd look
out over the expanse of open nothingness and see crowns of rock
sweeping up from the earth, as though a giant god had dropped them
so that the pieces split into perfect, seamless cracks. They looked as
if they were ready for someone to fill them in the style of *kintsugi*,
the Japanese art of filling cracks in broken pottery with gold to highlight the imperfection.

While in Moab I became intrigued by a route called *Epitaph* (5.13),
which scales a sheer 375-foot wall split by a single crack, right up
the center of the middle Tombstone. Just outside of town, and situated barely off the road, it felt like the local coffee shop version of
crack climbing—convenient, homey, comfortable. I'd heard about
Dean Potter and Steph Davis doing something called rope soloing
on it, where they would independently self-belay with the security of a toprope without the need for a partner, and the concept
appealed to me. Maybe if I could project a route in that manner,
where I didn't have to navigate the complexities of climbing partners and relationships, I could finally find some success.

First though, I tried for the onsight. Partway up the wall I could
feel the pump in my forearms; my breath and heart rate quickened.
I wanted to place another cam, but I had run out of the only size that

would fit. My best option, a split-second decision, was to punch it upward until I could place another piece. With every move I risked a longer fall—my last gear hidden in a corner well below my feet. Desperate now, I pawed at the orange sandstone, smearing my sticky-rubber slippers on ripples and texture. I lurched my right hand into the thin crack above, thumb up to get as deep as possible. I stuck it for a moment, but then my body sagged slightly—just enough to tear my hand right out of the crack and into the air. In a flash I looked down and saw the slack rope slithering below, attached to gear a long ways away. I screamed bloody murder as I fell. The rope weighted the piece below me and ripped it out of the crack. After a long arc of flight, the rope finally went taut on the cam below. I softly hit the wall with my right side—a harmless whipper, but as I swung back and forth in midair, adrenaline buzzed through my veins.

It was a solid effort, but afterward I decided to work the route by myself, on a toprope. I could easily rig it with a quick hike to the summit, a popular BASE jumping location, rappelling down the route to fix a rope all the way to the ground. The wall stayed shady long into the season and there were rarely other climbers there, so I spent many mornings or afternoons by myself, climbing as much or as little as I wanted—sometimes just hanging from my rope, listening to the soft pop of a BASE jumper's canopy opening above me. I rehearsed *Epitaph* here and there over several months, until I finally felt ready to lead it again.

When I finally succeeded, I climbed easily through the section where I had fallen on my onsight attempt. I knew the moves, the holds, the body positions, and crucially, I had memorized exactly where to place gear. I redpointed it in four pitches instead of linking the two crux pitches together as Dean had done on his first free ascent. Since there was a no-hands rest at the anchor point between the two pitches, it felt pretty similar to the linked version, but in the end it didn't matter. I had done the route for myself. Spending the season out there, swaying in the breeze, climbing one move or ten moves, just me and my self-belay setup, had meant more to me than what anyone thought of my ascent.

———————

Once, while climbing in Squamish with Robert, a long time after we had become friends rather than romantic partners, I became despondent and started sobbing mid-pitch, the physical effort of a long, strenuous pitch on the Stawamus Chief bringing up emotions that I otherwise kept carefully hidden. My shoulders and core sagged beneath my hand jams, and I cried as I climbed.

At the anchor, I said to Robert, "Do you know how many guys I've slept with this year?"

He laughed, "Do you know how many girls I've slept with this week?"

I couldn't help but laugh, too. I sniffled, choking on snot and wiping my nose unceremoniously on my sleeve. I was definitely no longer trying to impress Robert.

"Yeah, but it's ok for you. You're a dude."

Back in Moab, I was still climbing a lot with Jack in Indian Creek, but had managed to keep our partnership on a friendship level. Unlike the way things had gone with Robert, I hoped to keep that climbing relationship strictly platonic. I enjoyed the way things were with Jack and wanted more than anything to learn from past mistakes. I knew that he wanted things between us to be "more," but he also seemed ok with climbing and being friends. He seemed to be ok ignoring the elephant tucked quietly in the corner, for which I was immensely grateful.

I had a long history of disregarding my physical self, starving it, cutting it, reveling in the pain inflicted upon it by sport. I really wanted Jack to simply be a friend and climbing companion. Such an arrangement usually felt impossible in the climbing world.

It can be easy to confuse a good climbing partnership with a romantic relationship. Climbing is a sport that bonds you to your partner. You are literally tied to one another, holding each other's lives, witnessing the other person at their most scared, most jubilant, most vulnerable. It can be easy to think, *Well, it works so well here, it should work romantically, too.* But the relatively few number of women in climbing compared to men can lead to problems, and my trouble with setting boundaries compounded the issue.

I always thought my confusion stemmed entirely from my own mixed-up ideas about relationships and religion. And while that part was true, I now understand that it was also due to the lifestyle of the sport I was in, and I wasn't the only who sometimes mistook a climbing partnership for a romantic one.

By spring, however, the pressure of the elephant felt unbearable, so I wrote an email to Jack saying that I couldn't choose between him and someone else in our small, Moab community. "For some reason the whole thing is tearing me up inside," I wrote, "so I think I need to get away from both of you and clear my head. . . . I'm so, so sorry for behaving this way, but I'm really trying to do the right thing and not do anything I'm going to regret later. I hope you can understand."

What I really wanted was to just be friends with all of these guys that I found myself climbing with, but I couldn't understand why I couldn't figure out how to keep my climbing relationships from turning romantic. It felt hopeless.

Jack wrote back, angry, his message long and rambling and filled with hate. In part, it said:

The other day in the height of my anger and hurt I thought, "SCREW THIS, she's not even that good of a friend . . . I mean what has Katie ever done for me, when has she ever gone out of her way to do something nice, you know be a good friend?? And all I could come up with was a couple rides to Indian Creek, and an espresso maker . . . !" And honestly I don't see you doing much nice for anyone . . . that doesn't have selfish motives. . . . So really it comes down to the fact that you are doing me a favor by pushing me away . . . in fact it's one of the nicest things you've ever done . . . you just aren't that nice or considerate . . . to anyone. . . . I'm not trying to be mean I'm trying to be honest . . . sure you are selfish, self absorbed, and capable of being an uber bitch . . . but I've always seen that forty percent sweetheart doing battle with that sixty percent psycho, callous, user of souls . . . and I've always cheered for the sweet katie that shows up at my house all teary eyed and remorseful for the bad things she's

done. . . . We can climb . . . You need friends like me . . . because
most people just want a piece of you . . . or a piece. I'd just like
to see you pull your head out of your ass.

The letter went on and on. It hurt me deeply, but in some ways, it was like coming home. I had grown up with my mom calling me some of the same names, and everything he said to me was something I said to myself. All the time.

Ultimately, what I took away from it was that trying to be just friends with this guy had failed. I also wondered if he was right. Had I been selfish as a friend? Maybe. I knew I could be cold and callous, not considering how my actions affected others. But what was a normal amount of selfishness, of give and take in a friendship between a man and a woman? I had no barometer for what normal was supposed to look like. Jack and I had swapped belays, laughed, enjoyed each other's company. The only thing I had withheld, as far as I could tell, was my body. Had I been a man, would our climbing relationship have felt so unfair to him?

Not long after that, I started corresponding with a man fifteen years older than me. In spite of the fact that he was no longer a climber, I eventually convinced him to come to Moab and go to Indian Creek with me. The lure was mountain biking, his now-preferred sport.

Mac was one of the few who, I think, saw past my surface persona to the teetering brink my mental health was on. I joked in an email that I couldn't seem to sit still long enough to focus on the book I was under contract to write, saying, "I have to keep moving otherwise the wall of depression that is my craziness overwhelms me. Needless to say, sitting down and writing anything longer than a brief email is out of the question. I must be in motion at all times. I'm thinking about heading down the road of drug abuse."

I joked like that all the time back then, calling myself crazy and psychotic, trying to explain away my inevitable actions before they happened. I knew I wasn't well, I just didn't know how to stop it, and I didn't want people to be surprised when I did things that didn't make sense. This man, however, after joking back, offered a bit of serious advice before signing off. He had had his own experience with potential addiction, self-hatred, and a desire to run from himself, and he was able to see through my joking to how serious the situation was.

I wish I could have heard and absorbed his words, but they mostly fell on deaf ears. Instead, I turned back to what I knew how to do.

One night after Mac arrived in Moab, we were sitting in Lisa's kitchen, waiting for her to get home. I sat curled up on his lap. I felt small and cherished. His age and wisdom, and the fact that his pain "saw" my pain, made me want to stay curled in his arms forever. I felt safe. But there was also a small, tiny voice in the back of my head screaming *This guy is way too old for you.*

Lisa walked into the house, her eyes opening wide at the sight of us. She quickly tucked the surprise away, welcoming Mac and I with her characteristic open arms, but in that brief moment, I saw how skewed my decision-making was. I still, it seemed, struggled to make choices for myself and instead relied on validation from others. Lisa would never have judged me or told me one way or another how to proceed, but in her eyes I saw what I was doing, and I quickly pushed Mac away, literally and figuratively.

It was at about that time that I finally stopped communicating with my mom. It had been years since our fight in the kitchen, but ever since then we'd grown further and further apart. At the time we had settled somewhere in the realm of polite, but distant. I knew very little about her life, and she, in turn, knew little about mine.

On one of my many orbits, I passed by my dad's house for a visit. While I was there, I wanted to pick up a bike that I had stored in his garage. I have a thing for vintage bikes, even though I'm not a cyclist. As soon as I'd seen this particular vintage blue road bike in a dusty thrift-store window while driving through the desert of California, I made a U-turn. I bought the bike on sight for ten dollars. It was tiny, almost too small even for my five-foot-one frame, but in perfect condition. I loved it. It lived on the tailgate of my hatchback for a while, but since I was always moving here, there, and everywhere, my dad agreed to store it for me until I finally settled.

On that trip to my dad's, however, I couldn't find the bike anywhere. He didn't know what had happened to it. I drove up to my mom's condo in Summit County, to have dinner with her, my current boyfriend, and someone who I assumed to be her latest boyfriend.

As we sat casually at the table, I asked if she had my bike. Since she also often stored things with my dad, I thought maybe she'd picked it up by accident, not realizing it wasn't hers.

"Yes," she replied.

"Well, can I have it back?" I asked.

"No, I've already put fat snow tires on it. I'm going to use it to ride around the village."

I sat back, surprised. *No?* I thought. *Just like that? She hadn't asked to take it, and now I can't even have it back? Does she not see that I have the right to have ownership over something? That not everything that is mine is hers too?*

And that was it. That was the last teeny, tiny straw. I tried to tell myself that squabbling over a silly object was petty and materialistic, that it shouldn't matter. It was just a bike after all. But it felt symbolic somehow. In my mother's world, there was no division between what might belong to her and what might belong to someone else. There were no boundaries, and my dad, for his part, had let it happen.

After that dinner, I stopped reaching out to her. I stopped calling. I stopped emailing. And as was the custom in my family, nobody asked me about it. Just as no one had asked when I was dying of starvation, or when my brother battled his own demons—no one said anything. When my parents divorced, no one said anything. When my mom showed up with new breasts, a new car, or a new man, no one said anything. Just like those other times, we all started acting like my mom and I did not have a relationship, as if that was the way it had always been.

CHAPTER 25
JUST START DRIVING

Later that spring I was invited to film a climbing movie on the south face, or back side, of Half Dome in Yosemite, which, while not as sheer as the face visible from the Valley, would make for an impressive climb. For this gig, I would be paid, and they even rented a house for the climbers and crew in Yosemite West. I couldn't turn it down, despite not knowing anyone on the crew or my climbing partner. Already in the past year I had bailed on a trip to Australia while on the way to the airport, the tickets paid for by sponsors. I'd also moved to a new city and left after two weeks, gotten a job at a coffee shop then promptly left with no notice, and made a myriad of other impulsive decisions, both with my life and with men. What I didn't realize at the time was that those were warning signs of a mental health crisis.

Not long after my arrival in Yosemite, the darkness that I struggled against threatened to overwhelm me. Normally I would look to friends or a romantic connection for traction, but I was surrounded by strangers here. To those around me I probably just seemed aloof and disinterested in the project, but internally there was a riot of racing thoughts and a strong desire to escape the pain by any means available.

Finally, one night, I walked out of the house where we were staying and into the dark Yosemite forest. Pine needles crunched underfoot as I made my way to my car. I looked up at the stars peeking through the trees, so bright without light pollution. Not even the expansiveness of the sky provided solace. My brain felt like it was pulling apart at the seams and I wanted nothing more than for it to be over, for all the pain to stop. I felt exhausted from trying so hard, and failing so hard, every day.

I tripped and fell, my hands splaying out in front of me. Unable to see through my tears and too exhausted to get up, I crawled the rest of the way to my car. Pine needles and rocks dug into my knees and palms as I went.

I climbed in and sat in the driver's seat, the silence deepening as the door clicked closed. Leaning my head on the cool plastic of the steering wheel, I started crying in earnest. I felt done, but I didn't know how to end it. I couldn't even get suicide right.

Fishing my phone out of my pocket, I flipped it open and its dim light lit up the car. I scrolled through phone numbers, desperately searching for someone, anyone, who might be able to tell me what to do. I had long since stopped praying. I was nothing but an empty, bottomless pit of despair, self-loathing, loneliness, and need.

I wished I had a mom. Someone. Anyone.

Cody had traipsed out to the car with me and jumped into his seat on the passenger side, staring at me quietly. Sometimes he would look at me if I asked him a question and tilt his head to the side, as though listening and understanding. He watched my choking, guttural sobs and crept over the emergency brake, laying his head on my leg. I rubbed his soft ears as I clutched my phone. I wasn't a great dog mom, but I didn't want to leave him.

Eventually, I landed on my brother's phone number, and without thinking, I dialed. We weren't close and had never really talked about our struggles. But I didn't have anyone else.

My dad had been receiving my mail and depositing checks for me as I bounced maniacally around the country and beyond, so we were still in touch. Once, he had asked if I was ok. Bless his heart, he had an inkling, but I had responded that of course I was ok and that was the end of the discussion.

It was the middle of the night in Tennessee where Scott lived, but he answered the phone groggily. I sobbed into the mouthpiece.

"I just don't think I can do it anymore," I said. "I think I'm done ..."

"Done with what?" he asked, probably still half-asleep.

"Done … with life." I responded, almost in a whisper, afraid to say it out loud.

"Where are you?" he demanded.

"I'm in Yosemite."

"Get in your car," he told me. "And start driving."

"I am in my car," I sobbed. "Drive where?"

"Here," he said. "Memphis."

I paused. It was the middle of the night, and I was supposed to be doing this movie project. None of it made sense.

"Ok," I said finally. "Ok. What about all my stuff? I'll wake everyone up if I try and load up my bike."

"It doesn't matter. Just start driving."

I didn't think I was up to the challenge of packing. "Ok," I said again. Without bothering to gather much of anything, I drove out of Yosemite, in the dead of night and headed east.

In the morning, I sent the movie people a message stating that I'd had a family emergency and had to leave. They called, but I knew what I had done was cowardly and unbearably selfish. I didn't want to examine that part of myself. So I didn't answer the phone.

In Memphis, my brother set up a room for me in his house, helped me get a job at Starbucks, and found me a therapist. I had a semi-job already, working for a website posting climbing content, videos, and blogs, but I essentially dropped those responsibilities as well. When they emailed me, I sent back ambiguous answers. Someone from *Climbing* magazine also emailed, saying that an editor position was opening up and offering me the job. I never even responded.

The next couple of months in Memphis felt like a dream. When I put on my Starbucks uniform, my name pinned to the front, I knew I was wearing the façade of an ordinary girl, a pretend person who worked at Starbucks and lived in the South. The inner me was an ugly climber person who bailed on responsibilities and hurt people who cared about her.

The façade was "doing the work"—more pretending—but the inner me was already being drawn back to the comfort of the climbing world and its lifestyle. I could not relate to anyone that I met in my brother's world.

Eventually I packed up what little I had and left Memphis. I didn't tell anyone, didn't even let my brother know. He had worked so hard to get me help, and in the end, I decided it didn't matter. All that mattered was escaping, yet again. I wasn't ready for the help that he was offering me.

Once I was back in Moab, the therapist I had been working with sent me a message:

> How is your community going? Maybe your island like existence is not working for you, as Dr. Phil would say. It works some and then it doesn't. That is why you were surprised when your brother was angry when you left without face/face or voice/voice communication. In community, there is trust and accountability. There is also respect for others and their behaviors because everyone's behavior affects another. It is just like in school. If someone acted up in the cafeteria, the whole class was punished, not just the one who acted up. That functions as community so that the parts affect the whole. Your whole is alone!!!!!! There are great things about being alone and there are not so great things about being alone (not being comfortable in your skin in Yosemite when you were alone).

Her advice was profound, but I couldn't hear it at the time, and I never responded. Instead, I decided to register for fashion school.

———

I've always loved clothes. When I was young, I would draw outfit after outfit, coloring in the patterns and designs, putting them on little stick-figure characters, and then giving each outfit a name. Alongside these outfits I would write elaborate stories, frequently about a girl escaping an orphanage or a kidnapping, and in each story I went into detail about what my character wore. Once, I think in eighth or ninth grade, we were instructed to write a short story, and mine turned into a forty-five-page tome about an indentured servant whose father beat her and who escaped to start a new life. I described the rags she wore in detail.

I love how, with clothing, you can express who you are, what you value, what activities you choose to pursue. Or you can reinvent yourself, try on a different persona for a day, and see how people in the world respond differently to you based on your dress. I love how clothing can evoke a feeling—warmth and safety in a cozy pair of sweats, confidence in a blazer, playfulness in a romper.

I knew that what I had been doing over the past few years wasn't healthy. So, even though I wasn't ready or able to take the advice of that therapist back in Memphis, I began to look for a way to break the cycle I was in. The only thing I could think of was to get out of climbing. In my mind, all the pain in my life eventually came back to climbing. If I could break up with the sport, then maybe I could break up with all the other bad habits in my life.

I had been working with the company prAna as a sponsored athlete for a year or two, and part of my role was to provide product feedback, which I really enjoyed. Their headquarters were in San Diego, where there is very little climbing, but there is a fashion school.

By that point I had been to nearly as many schools as I had had boyfriends, amassing enough credits for a bachelor's degree, minus the degree part, but I decided to try one more time. In my fantasy-driven life I imagined going to fashion school, then working for prAna designing clothes. I didn't want to work for minimum wage forever, and I barely made any money climbing. I had lived on something like 10K a year far too long.

I found a place on Craigslist where I could live with a few other girls and enrolled in the fashion school with zero planning. I strapped my mattress to the roof of my car, loaded up my dog and belongings, and headed west.

I quickly discovered that although I was familiar with the outdoor industry, I actually knew nothing about fashion. I might know about Gore-Tex and what a shelf bra was, but I didn't know about designers, or even name brands. My idea of style was some quirky find at WabiSabi, the thrift store in Moab. I could count on one hand the number of times I had ever been in a department store. I had certainly never been in a store as glamorous as Nordstrom. Despite this, I did work with prAna a bit in San Diego, and Pam, one of the founders, was kind and welcoming, inviting my feedback on athletic apparel.

San Diego was vastly different from anywhere I had previously lived. I was once again a fish out of water, diving into something wholly unknown in an attempt to figure out who I was and where I belonged.

One day while my roommates and I were on the beach, a tanned, sun-bleached-blond, blue-eyed surfer came up to us and asked me out. I stumbled inwardly. After all, there was no way this guy knew I was "Katie Brown the climber," and without that I was sure I was wholly unremarkable as a human. I said yes, purely out of curiosity.

He took me on what felt like my first "real" date, the kind you saw on TV. He took me surfing, patiently pushing me into each and every wave. We got to know each other in the way I imagined people dating in the "real world" did. There was no small, insular community helping to shape our ideas of each other before we even met. No gossip. No pictures in magazines. It was all very nice, but did little to feed my love addiction, and we ended up fighting. He told me that he was "disillusioned" with me and felt like my sidekick, just someone to have around whenever I felt like it. The thing was, I was still on my island.

I left that relationship, probably with very poor communication and little explanation, thoroughly disgusted with the person I had become. Being with someone solely because they liked me, whether because I was a climber, or in spite of the fact that I was a climber, without any thought at all about how I felt about it, was no longer working, and I vowed to make a change.

As my first quarter of school ended, I tried to figure out what to do with myself over the academic break. I moved out of my room with

no notice and stashed my belongings at the house of someone I knew
through prAna. I had one foot out the door of San Diego already, even
if I didn't realize that's what I was doing.

I left and drove north toward the Needles, a world-class climbing
area in Sequoia National Forest, where granite pinnacles shoot up
from the ground amid a fragrant pine forest. Climbing was pulling
me back in once again. It was where I felt the most at home, where I
felt the most identity and belonging, the most valuable.

I loved to drive. I had everything neatly packed and in one place.
I felt liberated and free behind the wheel, in control of my destiny,
safe in my tiny, self-contained space. But as I left San Diego, driving
also allowed space for the loneliness to creep back in.

The sadness that had haunted me ever since I was a teenager
itched in my throat, threatening to bubble up as I careened down
the highway in my solitary safety bubble on wheels. Clutching the
steering wheel, tears streaming down my face, I screamed into the
windshield until my voice was hoarse, my foot pressing down on
the pedal.

"Whhhyyy?!" I screamed, fist pounding on the wheel. It was an
empty question thrown out at the universe in general, a longing to
know why I lived with so much pain and sadness, all the time.

As I rocketed toward the Needles and away from fashion school,
through the vast, barren deserts of California, I thought about all
my past mistakes and poor decisions and the weight of all of them
pressed down on me.

An empty house appeared on the horizon, where the air shim-
mered in the heat. The paint of the house was chipping, the windows were boarded up, and a decrepit horse paddock listed to the
side in the back, tumbleweeds sticking to it like Velcro. I imagined
the long-gone inhabitants of the house as it receded in my rearview
mirror, then admonished myself.

"How DARE you feel sorry for yourself!" I said out loud. Cody's
ears perked in the seat next to me, but he was accustomed to and
largely unfazed by my outbursts.

I pulled the rearview mirror down to see my reflection. Any one of my lives would have been amazing compared to the lives of the people who lived in that house.

"You should be grateful," I told myself. "Stop complaining. A lot of people have had it a LOT worse. The life you got was one people would dream of. What a selfish bitch you are."

CHAPTER 26

HALF DOME

I first met Sam while climbing in the desert outside of Las Vegas. Robert introduced us. Sam was somewhat new on the climbing scene, at least to me. He was goofy and awkward, with big ears, greasy dark hair, a wide, genuine smile, and chocolate-brown eyes that held no pretense. I liked him immediately.

When I climbed into his van, I saw a half-built plywood bed in the back and a lone unfurled sleeping bag. It smelled of dirty socks, and I couldn't help but tease him. "Oh. My. Gosh. Have you ever been laid?" I asked, fully aware of the shock value of my words.

Sam, startled, snapped to attention in the driver's seat.

Why did I just say that? It was like this whole other persona would sometimes pop out, unbidden.

"Psshhht," he hemmed and hawed in response. "Pffft." Finally he spit out, clearly ruffled, "Yes. Yes I have."

"Huh," I said, grinning flirtatiously and stretching my arms overhead as though a neon sign were plastered to the side of his van. "Cuz your van screams, 'I've never been laid.'" Robert chuckled as he loaded photo gear into the back. "This is going to be fun," he said.

After I left fashion school, I climbed in the Needles with Sam, and then headed north to meet him again in Yosemite. My school break was drawing to an end, and I needed to go back to sort out my next semester, find a place to live, but the draw of climbing was too strong. Climbing with Sam, especially, felt more natural than it had for a long time.

I was fascinated by Sam's well-thought-out atheistic view on life, so different from the ultrareligious way I had been raised. When he spoke of his decisions or why he did certain things, it made sense to me. His humor was somewhat cynical and self-deprecating, and yet he was still open-hearted and warm in a way that I adored. And I never had to wonder if he was telling the truth or had ulterior motives—he always said exactly what he was thinking. After a lifetime of being told that people couldn't be trusted, he was a breath of fresh air.

Still, I fretted constantly about what people would think if we were to get involved. What if my own feelings weren't to be trusted, and this ended up as just another mess for the climbing rumor mill to have their fun with? For some reason, the possibility of that felt like a bigger deal than usual. Adding to that, my general apathy confused and frustrated Sam. I was "never psyched," as he put it, the "most talented, least motivated climber." And it was true. I had been fighting my mind since I was sixteen and I was exhausted. Depression weighed me down, making everything feel harder, heavier, bigger—even if internally I felt optimistic.

It wasn't often that I committed to a goal, preferring instead to pretend that I didn't care about anything, but around Sam I started to feel that maybe I could believe in myself. I don't honestly remember where the idea came from, or why, but either way, I decided to attempt to onsight a route on Half Dome.

It was late when we pulled into an empty campsite the night before the climb. Campsites in Yosemite are always reserved, but people don't always show up at the start of their reservation. One tactic climbers use is to wait until late at night to pull into an empty campsite. We assumed that if it was late enough, nobody would get there until the next day. Then we just had to leave before the gate attendant came by in the morning to check reservations and payment. Valley climbers had dubbed this tactic "stealth bivying."

I always fell asleep while Sam slowly drove around before finally pulling into a vacant spot. I wondered if that made me selfish, sleeping while he did the work of finding our spot, or if that was normal. Sometimes it felt like I had spent my whole life trying to decipher what was normal and what was selfish.

We started our day on Half Dome well before dawn, hiking up the slabs below the massive formation in the dark, our headlamps bouncing off rock and trees as we scrambled. The sun was just rising as we reached the base, so we quickly started climbing. We wanted to have as much daylight as possible for the hard pitches higher up the route.

Sam, in full support mode, carried our food, water, and shoes so that I could climb light and free, with only gear and an extra shirt. We simul-climbed the first pitches, moving together and tied in at either end of our 200-foot rope. In this style, one climber goes first, placing gear into the rock as they go, which would arrest a fall if either climber came off the rock—theoretically preventing a catastrophic death fall. But there is always the potential for a massive fall using this efficient yet risky technique.

When we arrived at the first bit of "hard" climbing, it hit me. This was it. I had one try to get this right. Hundreds of climbers ascend this route every year. It's a classic big wall, well known the world over. But nearly all of them resort to aid climbing the cruxes—pulling on gear, standing in slings. Few attempt to free climb it, and fewer still try to onsight. I thought back to the day when, at eight years old, I had one try to go into the gymnastics class late. I hadn't had the nerve then.

The first move was a long, sideways balance move, and I futzed around forever, afraid to commit and fail. "Great, I'm going to fall on the first move," I said.

"No, you're not," Sam admonished. "You've got it. Just get over your head trip and start climbing."

I stepped my foot down to where it needed to go, didn't fall, and continued on.

It was midday when we reached Big Sandy, a giant ledge three-quarters of the way up the wall. We stopped there to sit, our legs dangling over the void below, and ate lunch. The hardest climbing would begin after this. Nervous impatience bubbled up inside me as we ate. I knew I needed to start climbing before I psyched myself out.

This was normal for me. Sometimes when onsighting I would look at a route and feel like I needed to get going before it was too late. Otherwise, I would think about it too hard and start to doubt myself. This impatience could serve me well, but it also got me in trouble. Often, for example, I wouldn't even want to take the time to read the gear recommendation in a guidebook. Then, when I ran out of gear mid-pitch, I'd be forced to either back off or climb, terrified, to the anchor, with a large runout below me.

Once I was back on the wall, I found myself traversing a thin, slopey undercling on one of the crux Zig Zag pitches, my feet pasted to the granite below. Halfway through the pitch I started fumbling with gear, trying to slide a piece into the undercling but unable to see if the placement was good or where it was going.

Seeing me fumble, Sam said, "Just keep going."

Without thinking, I obeyed. I trusted him completely. As I moved farther and farther from my last piece, and my potential fall got longer and more dangerous, I thought, *I should be scared right now, but I'm not. Weird.* Finally, I reached the lip and clipped a fixed piece.

"Well, I'm impressed," Sam yelled up in his usual no bullshit manner. "That was so dicey. I was worried for your safety."

"Thanks a lot!" I yelled down to him, laughing, giddy with success.

Because I understood all too well the concept of "one try or else," onsighting worked well for me. I could completely dissociate and just let my body and intuition take over. I'd start with, "I'll just see how far I get before I fall," but then once I got up there, a fierce, rebellious desire, which I usually kept carefully tucked away, would come bubbling up. But onsighting a single pitch was one thing. Onsighting twenty-three pitches was something else entirely.

By the time we reached the final 5.12 pitch, I was mentally drained. The effort to stay focused and keep control of my nerves and racing thoughts all day had taken its toll. The pitch was not terribly hard, grade-wise, but for me it was the most intimidating. It was a slab, and I was far from confident at slab climbing—it terrified me. I liked to be on steep rock, where I could hold on and engage my muscles. I felt more in control on overhanging climbs. On a slab, where you had to trust your feet on the tiniest of smears, sometimes with no handholds at all, I felt wildly out of control. I imagined falling and sliding down to my last piece, scraping the low-angle rock the whole way down.

As I made my way up the slab, I could hear people at the summit, most of whom had hiked up the back side of Half Dome. Desire, for once, won out over fear. I wanted this. I wanted success and I was going to fight like hell for it. I was not going to give up, afraid of the success, afraid of the desire itself.

There was one final move before the last, big hold. I saw a fixed piece of gear, where Sam had told me he placed a finger once when he'd climbed this route. He had hovered just over the piece without touching it, so that if he fell on the last hard move, he could theoretically catch himself. I stared at that piece of gear, then threw for the final hold in terrible slab climbing style, letting out a yell of effort.

Sam laughed at my poor form from below, but also hooted in congratulations as I latched the final jug.

I had done it. I had onsighted the Northwest Face of Half Dome. That route is probably the accomplishment I am the most proud of in my climbing career. Not only did I do it in a style that felt honorable, but I didn't allow my mental demons to win. I believed in myself and actually *desired* something, then tried hard for it despite my fear. That climb is something I will always hold dear.

One day as we were driving through the Valley, El Cap rising sharply to the right, Sam's phone rang. He answered and put the caller on speaker. The voice on the other end asked who he was climbing with.

"With Katie," he responded.

"Yo, nice send bro!" the caller laughed through the phone, making sexual noises, not realizing that he was on speaker.

"No one is 'sending' anything!" I yelled back, joking and laughing, but breaking inside. I was so worried about what everyone would think, and now here it was—proof that I was a project to be "sent." Well, I'd show them. Regardless of how I felt about Sam, there was no way I was doing anything with him now. I was no one's "send."

The next day Sam told me how he felt about me, but I couldn't do it. I couldn't handle more gossip. I couldn't handle what everyone would say. I felt I had to prove a point. Still though, I didn't want to lose his company, the pull to be near him was too strong.

"I'll still go up the Zodiac with you," I said. I had committed to supporting him on a multiday ascent of a route on El Cap. "But no touching."

He looked at me with confusion. I made no sense, and I knew it. The hot-and-cold me was out in full force.

Halfway up *Zodiac*, a nineteen-pitch route on the right side of El Capitan, I reconsidered my "no touching" proclamation. We were readying our beds on the portaledge dangling more than 1,000 feet off the ground as music played from a nearish climbing party. But every time I thought about what a "slut" I was, what had been said about me over the phone, and what everyone would say about me if I added another notch on the metaphorical bedpost, I just couldn't do it. I didn't want this relationship to be just another of my many fuck-ups.

At one point we got our ropes unbearably tangled while hauling up our heavy bags full of water, food, and camping gear, not uncommon on a wall. I screamed in frustration as I wrestled with them, so loudly that climbers on a neighboring route heard me and hooted back. It was about more than tangled ropes. I was frustrated and angry with myself and my inability to know what my heart was telling me, to understand what intuition even was, let alone how to decipher it with all the other influences, internal and external, yelling at me.

CHAPTER 27

AS FAR AWAY AS I COULD GET

I had stayed in the Valley so long that there wasn't time to get back to San Diego before my next semester was due to start. Luckily, the school I attended had a campus in San Francisco, so I quickly transferred. I had nowhere to live, so I crashed on a couch at a friend's house. I'm sure I overstayed my welcome with Amy and Schuyler, as I had on innumerable other couches, but they welcomed and supported me as I fought to figure out what was next. Eventually, I found my own place to live and plunged into school. I worked at a local climbing gym and went a pretty good stretch of time without any men.

And then one day, seemingly without reason, I decided to take the spring quarter off from school and go to Australia.

When I look back at this time of my life, I'm embarrassed. I made decisions that were illogical, bouncing from one idea to another with shocking speed. It's like watching the emotional decline of someone I don't even recognize. But it was definitely me who, one day while driving to school, realized that the credit card I'd had for many years accrued airline miles that I had never used. I called the number on the back of the card.

"How far can I go with my miles?" I asked.

"Well," they said, clicking away on a keyboard. "You have enough to fly to Australia."

And that's all it took.

I had wanted to go to Australia since I was sixteen, when a climbing trip had been cancelled at the last minute. Years later, I had unceremoniously bailed on another opportunity to visit the country, because I would have been traveling with Liam, officially an ex by then. Now here was my chance. I didn't need someone to go with me. I would go by myself—prove to the world that I was outgoing and confident enough to travel alone, to meet people along the way.

"Perfect," I told the person on the phone. "Let's do that." I randomly picked a departure date after the semester ended.

"Uh, ok," they responded, unsure. "You'll have to pay taxes and fees . . ."

"That's fine," I said, my mind entirely caught up in Australia. It was literally as far away from my life as I could get. The only problem was that I would still be there.

I landed in Melbourne with a deep, intangible fear of seeing people. I emailed the person who had offered to pick me up and told him not to, with no explanation. I had never met him in person, and the thought of being around a stranger felt impossible. Since I was on a trip by myself, this obviously wasn't logical. I would have to meet stranger after stranger to go anywhere. But anxiety doesn't always follow what's logical, and mine had taken hold.

I couldn't afford it, but I decided to rent a car and get a hotel room instead. Unfortunately, it was a holiday in Australia and I couldn't find a rental car or a hotel room. I considered sleeping in the airport but managed to find a nearby hostel and took a bus there.

I wanted so badly to be alone, but the hostel was crowded and I was surrounded by traveling college kids. Exhausted from jet lag and desperate for peace, I climbed into my bunk at the hostel, in a room teeming with people, pulled the covers over my head, and slept for twelve hours.

When I woke, I walked down to the beach and tried to formulate a plan. Not too long before, I had briefly met an Australian living in the States for a stretch, who had mentioned having a car back home. I had his phone number, so I called. I can only imagine his shock when a random American called, from Australia, to ask to borrow his car. Nonetheless, he kindly agreed. The car was at his parents' house, at least a day's travel away, he told me. He warned me that the outside handle didn't work, so I'd have to climb through the other side and open the door from the inside of the car. I gratefully accepted.

Given my mental state, traveling alone was an extremely bad idea. From the outside I probably appeared totally fine, but inside I was desperately clawing about, making random decision after random decision in an attempt to escape my feelings. I literally had no idea what I was doing. The details of the next week are fuzzy, but I know I acted on impulse, without anyone around to say, "Katie, stop—just stop."

Nonetheless, after about a week I finally made it to Mount Arapiles, a remote, world-famous crag packed with thousands of trad routes hours from the nearest city, in my borrowed car. I arrived late and the campground was completely full. Terrified of getting out of the car, experiencing what could only be described as agoraphobic tendencies, I turned around and drove about three hours to the coast.

I woke early, stiff from sleeping in the car, and walked down to the misty beach. At last, there was no one around. No one to "see" me. I took a deep breath of the ocean air. I sat down, slipped off my sandals, and dug my toes into the cool, wet underbelly of the sand. Finally, the panic that had sent me lurching about subsided and I felt my first moment of peace, happiness even. After a long, long time, I stood up and made my way back to the car, ready at last to try and find some people.

I headed back to Mount Arapiles to climb. Somehow, despite my emotional state, I met a group of Americans who invited me to climb with them. After that, I climbed three or four routes a day, even as I struggled to keep my head above water mentally. I avoided the social scene around the campfire in the evenings and would instead dive into a book that would take me to some imaginary place and time to escape reality.

There was, of course, a guy, one from the group I climbed with. Later, back in the States, he bought me a plane ticket to visit him on the East Coast. I didn't go.

After a couple of weeks in Australia, I booked a ticket to New Zealand. I took ten days to travel to see a friend who was spending a few months there with her family. I rented a Wicked Van, a New Zealand brand known for loud color schemes and outlandish sayings.

When I went to pick up my van, I started talking to another American woman, who was also traveling solo. As her van pulled out of the bay, she nudged me.

"Oh god, look at what my van says."

I looked, and sure enough, amid brightly colored jelly beans, were the spray-painted words, "My computer goes down on me better than your girlfriend."

She shrugged and headed off to collect her van.

When my van came out, I smiled. All the characters from *South Park* were painted down the side, and on the back it said, "Screw you guys I'm going home." Back in Moab, Lisa would often say the same thing in her best *South Park* voice. It felt like a sign that everything was going to be ok.

I met up with my friend and her family and followed them up to Flock Hill, a bouldering area set atop a plateau. The approach is about forty-five minutes of hiking up windswept grass tufts. At the top of the hill, the landscape is littered with pock-marked limestone boulders. Sheep roamed the hillsides and we would occasionally see ranchers on horseback, their herding dogs running gleefully alongside. Castle Hill Village looked like it was taken straight out of a moment in the children's novel *Heidi*.

The climbing was unusual, rife with things climbers love, like mantels, stemming up runnels, big moves between bigger pockets, smearing and pressing, and other fun body contortions. The windswept grass meant that we could run barefoot from one boulder problem to the next.

Winter was approaching in the southern hemisphere, so the air was crisp, the rain frequent, and the days short. For much of my time in New Zealand, it was too wet to climb, and I would instead drive my van up the coast, still trying to be ok. It was a weird feeling, being desperate to be alone, then desperate not to be.

———————————

I flew back to the States just as summer loomed, leaving me with months of unstructured time, and no idea how to fill it. My first stop was the annual outdoor retailer trade show, where Ben and I went dancing. It was a welcome reprieve. The dark dance floor—drinks in hand, bass thrumming, music pulsing, anonymous bodies moving—felt like my element. I wished I could stay in that zone forever.

After the trade show, Ben and I headed out on a road trip to Canada. We visited Squamish, where I went to more dance parties, drank more alcohol, and scrambled up moderate routes at the Smoke Bluffs, pretending to be ok, to not care. From there we headed to Canmore, sleeping in our cars parked cozily next to each other outside a local coffee shop. I relished the alpine air. It even snowed one morning, a gentle dusting, despite it being August. We sport climbed at Lake Louise, and spent a beautiful day on a classic multi-pitch line on Mount Yamnuska alongside an ex-boyfriend whose kind and loving nature meant that he accepted where I was at, despite how erratic my behavior had been when we were together.

When summer came to a close, I headed back to Berkeley for my second year of school. Isolation set in, and I began to miss what I had felt with Sam back in Yosemite. I had run from something that felt right, and now I could see that I'd been circling the drain ever since. I sent him a message to see if he wanted to climb that fall, but he was away for several months. I was on my own.

I emailed Robert in desperation. Our friendship had become a life buoy for me, and he had proved over and over that he was someone who understood all too well what I was going through.

This time, I wrote him, "I think we'd actually be perfect for each other."

He saw right through my bullshit and responded quickly but kindly. "No Katie. I will always be your friend, and be there for you as a friend, but I want a relationship with someone who wants all of me."

I knew he was right, especially as my mental health once again plummeted. I was living in a house with some other climbers, but they were frequently out of town. I still could not handle being alone. I needed constant distraction from the pain and ugliness inside. Without it, I felt like a top spinning wildly out of control, running into everything in its path, until its inevitable collapse. There was nobody around to give me a fresh spin.

I couldn't envision a future life where I was a clothing designer working for an outdoor industry company. I was afraid to care about that goal, any goal, and what I might lose in the process of caring. It felt too far out of reach, impossible for someone like me. Even though I had accomplished so much and had experienced amazing, lucky things before, I was convinced that I wasn't deserving of success like that. It would seem that I had learned nothing from my day on Half Dome.

It's difficult to explain, but a real life—one with a career and a permanent address—was for other people, but not for me. For me, all alone in a house in Berkeley, California, there was only chaos and self-destruction.

I stopped doing homework and answering messages. I went to class only sporadically. I slept for hours while my grades dropped. I stopped talking to people. I quit my job. I knew the goal of finishing fashion school was slowly slipping from my grasp. It was at this point that Jack called. He was going to be in the Bay Area and wanted to know if we could get together.

I should have known it was a bad idea. Here was the guy who had called me selfish and an uber bitch—I still had his letter—the same things I had been called my entire upbringing. We'd stayed friends after that, since after all, he was only telling me the same things I thought about myself, but he was the last person I should have reached out to at my lowest point. But I latched onto it as a last-ditch effort to save myself anyway.

"Come visit," I told him.

Jack arrived and we went dancing. I started drinking to numb the unease I felt. I knew it wasn't right. That night, as we lay in my tiny bed, in a room I barely recognized, I suddenly realized I couldn't do this to myself. I could not have sex with the man who had treated me the way he had. I couldn't do this just because I was lonely, just because I needed someone's attention to take away my pain, just because I knew that this guy would come running when I beckoned. It wasn't fair to either of us.

This time, unlike the night with Charlie in the Bugaboos way back when, my body revolted and there was no going back.

"Stop! Stop! Stop!" I choked out, crying maniacally, pulling away. "No, no no."

He pulled back, alarmed, hastily putting distance between us as I curled into the wall sobbing.

That was the moment the bottom dropped out of my life. There was no one left to save me. The only person I had left was myself, and I had shattered into a million pieces.

CHAPTER 28

ONE YEAR

I dropped out of school and made my way to Ben's house in Portland, all while sending messages of bluster and bravado to sponsors and friends. Ben was, as always, a shelter from my storms. He knew everything, often too much, and still welcomed me with the open arms of a friend, never demanding or asking for anything else or anything more. I stayed in Portland for three weeks and considered staying there permanently. But I knew that, ultimately, I needed more sun than the Pacific Northwest provided.

Colorado was where I first started my journey, and it had always felt like home for me. I decided to head back there and start over, yet again. I had just a single goal this time: to stay in one place for one year. A whole year. No running.

I found myself on yet another couch, this one in Boulder, Colorado. Just a few months before, I had been named one of San Francisco's "Hot 20 Under 40," after my climb on Half Dome, but now I barely climbed. I had no degree, no money, and my beloved car was nearing the end of its life. I stopped communicating with all of my sponsors.

I started to try to rebuild my life, from the ground up. I eventually moved off the couch and into a rented room. A friend kindly got me a job at a coffee shop where she worked.

Because Boulder is popular among climbers and other outdoor enthusiasts, people in the coffee shop frequently recognized me. "What are *you* doing working *here?*" they would ask, with confusion in their eyes. It was mortifying at first, but I tried to be proud of myself and take responsibility for the place in life that I now was—almost thirty and without a penny to my name.

I'd laugh. "Cause why not?!" I'd respond. Or, "because it's fun!" Or, "oh, you know, just needed a change!" Then I'd hustle off to serve the next customer so that the questioning eyes couldn't see the tears behind my big-smile response.

I'm not complaining, and I'm not apologizing. I understand that I am one of the lucky ones—that I have had a multitude of opportunities, talents, and advantages afforded to me. I see my privilege. I accept that, rather than creating something out of all the things I had available to me, I squandered many of them, only to end up working at a coffee shop for seven dollars an hour as my twenties drew to a close. It was a bitter pill to swallow. But it was also liberating to realize that I was a strong enough person to take what I'd learned and start over, owning my mistakes, grieving my losses, and moving on from there.

I made it through my one-year goal, and then another. I ended up staying in Boulder for almost ten years. I got married. I had a baby. And during those years, almost subconsciously, I left climbing behind.

It had been happening gradually anyway, but by the time I turned thirty, it was done. I needed to change, to heal, to figure out my patterns and to work to break them, and I knew that I couldn't do that with climbing as a part of my life. My last climbing foray was to film a commercial for a bank, when I was six weeks pregnant. I gave it my all to get the job, knowing that I needed the money to help support the new life growing inside me, and as I stood on top of a tower outside Moab, I said goodbye to the person I used to be.

Whether or not anything had originated with climbing, it had become too tangled up with my mental health issues for me to work on one without abandoning the other. I knew that if I stayed in climbing, I would continue to make poor decisions. I needed to figure out myself, and then maybe I could figure out where climbing fit in, if at all.

It wasn't until I became a mother that I began to truly investigate my life. I hadn't planned to become a mother, but it wasn't something I didn't want. As a teenager I had always imagined a life where I was a parent, but somewhere along the way I had become convinced that I wouldn't be able to have children. After my daughter was born, I often found myself wondering why I had thought that.

But then, "The side effect of the medicine," I heard my mom say in an interview, "was that it made you sterile. So when she got pregnant," she went on, "the one thing he [her husband] asked me, when we met in Boulder, was, 'Is that true?'"

My husband had never met my mom in Boulder. My mind snagged on the story.

I recently looked up Asacol, the only medication I ever took for my intestinal issues, and learned that it does not cause infertility.

I left climbing even further behind when my precious, perfect baby girl was born, falling out of touch with friends and acquaintances without a second thought as I fought to create a new life for my family, and to figure out who I was outside of the only identity I had ever known.

I worried that I would pass down the darkness inside me. I would never wish that on anyone. With my daughter, all I wanted was to do a good job, to not hurt her. To do right by her so that she might grow up without all the pain and worry that I carry around. To break generational trauma.

I went back to school so that I could pursue a career as a makeup artist and hair stylist. There were so many times I felt the tug of my old ways and wanted to quit. So many times. I even took a leave of absence. But my daughter kept me going back. I wanted to set a good example for her, show her that it was important to pursue dreams and follow through. To finish something. I graduated because of her.

Still though, I was plagued at times by stress and anxiety that I would get it wrong somehow, that I would hurt the person I have been given the responsibility to raise.

I am, to this day, terrified of being like my mother.

More than fifteen years after the fight I had with my mom in that kitchen with the torn-out wall, I found myself in her condo in the mountains, staring at a poster of myself.

My brother and I had agreed to come visit for a skiing trip. It was the first time that we were all together: my dad, my mom, someone who I can only assume to be her boyfriend, my brother and his kids, me, my husband, and our daughter. To say it felt awkward is an understatement. I still felt stiff and frozen when I was near my mom, unable to smile or speak with emotion.

While we were there I needed to use the restroom, so I stepped over piles of ski boots, poles, shoes, and other outdoor paraphernalia to get into the guest room bathroom. As I was passing through, I saw a framed poster of a much-younger me on the wall. I was sitting on a rock at the Red River Gorge. My hair was in its ponytail, and I was wearing those dangling Kokopelli earrings I used to love. I had on a lime-green crop top and short shorts—my own private rebellion against an ad campaign I didn't want to do. My arms and legs were skinny, but still sinewy with muscle. I looked about twelve years old.

In the upper left corner, the poster said, "Get a life first. Wait to have sex." I cringed when I saw it. I scanned to the bottom of the poster and saw that it was signed "Eileen Brown" in her loopy cursive.

My mother had signed the poster. Her name. On a poster of me, promoting teen abstinence.

It felt indicative of so many things—the sense of ownership that she had felt over me, my life, and my accomplishments. Did she sign it because she thought it was her? Or did she sign it because she saw what was there as her creation? I'll never know the thought process behind it.

I spent so many years hating and blaming climbing. For so long, I had wanted nothing to do with any of my accomplishments—they weren't mine. Now I understood why—they were hers.

Maybe my struggle wasn't about climbing at all. Maybe all the darkness inside me had originated somewhere else. My confusion morphed into an intense anger, and for the first time I wanted to say, "No, those were my accomplishments! I may have messed up and lost them, squandered my potential, but I want the things that I did back. *I did those things, goddamn it.* That's me on that poster—not you. I worked hard, I stayed silent, I deserve to own those accomplishments."

Maybe it was too late, but hadn't I earned the right to own that part of my life? To tell *my* story? I looked over to the bed, and there were more framed pictures of me. At that moment all I wanted was to rip the poster off the wall and scream. Some pains don't entirely heal with time.

———

Not too long ago, the stress of juggling motherhood and running my own business caused my stomach issues to flare up again. Eventually, it got so bad that my husband urged me to get a colonoscopy.

I fought terror as the appointment approached. Panic attacks left me doubled over, arms curled in as I fought to regulate my breathing. I remembered all of the pain that followed my first colonoscopy. I was certain something horrible was wrong with me.

Lying in the hospital room after the procedure, drugged, I babbled incoherently to the nurses about moms, lies, eating disorders—how it was all so complicated. As I went on and on, the doctor who had done the procedure approached me.

"You don't have Crohn's disease," he told me. "And there is no sign of you ever having had Crohn's disease. You have the colon of an eighteen-year-old!" he joked, jovially.

At this I started crying all over again. I had always known that. It felt as if, twenty years later, my reality had been validated. Deep down, I had known it to be true all along. Finally, it felt like my life was mine—not someone else's—and that I had earned the right to tell my story.

EPILOGUE

It was Mother's Day. After nine years of being a mom, this was the first time that I had an answer to the question, "What do you want for your day?"

I wanted to go climbing.

Climbing, a partnership sport, will perhaps always be fraught with danger for me. I want it, but it is inherently scary to pursue. I still prefer being alone over almost anything. But I do love the movement, the freedom from my mind that I get when I'm climbing, the sense of accomplishment, the familiarity. When I climb, it feels like I'm home. In my mind and in my body.

On that particular day, my daughter did not want to go climbing, which made me doubt my decision. Was I selfish for making her, because it was Mother's Day? It felt complicated, trying to figure out what was normal.

Then, after an hour-and-a-half drive to my favorite sport cliff in the area, a steep and sunny crag, we realized my husband had forgotten his harness. I felt the day slipping away. Old feelings surfaced, feelings that I was wanting something too much. I shouldn't have wanted this. It meant that it would inevitably be taken away. Had something been forgotten for any other activity, I would have been fine. But with climbing, it triggered something deep within me. I thought I needed to turn off the want, to abandon my desire to climb.

I had to remind myself that it was just a forgotten harness. There was nothing hidden behind it. I tried to breathe as my anxiety built. We drove to a nearby outdoor gear store and picked up a harness. By the time we got back, it was two in the afternoon and the predicted afternoon storm had begun to blow in. The crag was cold and windy.

I worried that my daughter, curled up under blankets with her favorite book, was miserable. I worried that wanting something for just me was wrong, that I should let go of it. Just be a mom and wife and stop needing so much.

This time, though, I could hear in those thoughts a reflection of my unhealthy habits. This time, I told myself, it was ok that I wanted to do something. It was ok to climb. I told myself to let go and breathe into the chaos of the day.

Two pitches in, despite cold fingers, the fluttering panic in my chest settled. It was ok. Everything was ok. Climbing is in my blood, I am meant to be a climber, and that is ok. My family was also ok with this. I could trust in their support.

———

The urge, the pull to run, will always be part of me. Sometimes it's so strong it takes my breath away and I find myself doubled over, struggling to breathe, awash in the pain of being present in the moment. But being a mother, and hoping to give the generations to come a better life, keeps me grounded. I hope that the best I have to give is good enough. One day at a time, one foot after another, mistakes and all.

After all, I'm not my mother. The thin scar along my abdomen reminds me of that, sets me apart. And no matter how many times someone else signs their name on a poster of me, I earned my accomplishments, both good and bad. This is my story.

AFTERWORD

Eating disorders are prevalent in climbing, as they are in any sport with a strength-to-weight ratio component. Although I stopped eating in an effort to regain control over something in my life, food and weight, for me, were very tangled up in my relationship with climbing.

I can only imagine how frustrating it is to watch someone you love slowly kill themselves. How that fear and worry might lead to anger. But trust me: anorexia can become a monster so massive that you have no control over it. It is not about willpower. When I was in the throes of anorexia, I did not want to be there. I wanted nothing more than to eat normally. And yet, my fear of eating had grown into a living thing. If I ate too much, if I ate outside of what I had deemed ok, or if I gained weight, I believed something horrible, something catastrophic, would happen. I desperately wanted help, but I probably would have denied it had someone offered. This is a common experience for people struggling with eating disorders, and anger is never the best approach when it is your loved one who is struggling. Only a professional is prepared to help someone with an eating disorder.

A few years ago, I heard an interview with Dr. Jennifer Gaudiani on NPR that helped cement my desire to write about my struggle with food. When I pored through her book, *Sick Enough*, I finally found answers and explanations for so many things that I had experienced. I was lucky enough to sit down with Dr. Gaudiani and examine my symptoms through the lens of a specialist. I'm sharing what I now understand about myself, in the hopes that it may help others. If I can help even one person break free of a disorder that could irrevocably change the course of their life, then my years of struggling will all have been worth it.

Often, one of the earliest symptoms of anorexia is a change in how the person views the world, including depression. I'm not sure what came first for me. If my mom had been less controlling, would I have developed an eating disorder? Or did my mom become controlling because I had developed an eating disorder? Similarly, was my view of the world distorted because I had an eating disorder? Or did I develop an eating disorder because my view of the world was skewed?

When someone is starving, they lose their ability to focus and concentrate. A starving mammal becomes less creative, playful, and optimistic, instead becoming very serious. The brain shrinks and focuses on surviving. Your world becomes very small. You may feel as if you are living with blinders on, or perhaps you experience a sense of unease, a need to be on guard from predators. In the animal kingdom, if you are starving, you are at risk. As humans, we begin to feel that danger lurks everywhere. Historically, if people were hungry, they would migrate to someplace with food. In modern day society, people who are starving may feel agitated and restless, unable to relax despite being physically drained. The body's biological response is saying to get up and move to a place with a more adequate food supply.

I describe a number of my early symptoms in this story, including when my hands, arms, and feet started bothering me. When the body is starving, it takes a number of measures to protect itself and stay alive. One is to divert energy to vital organs by shutting off blood flow to the extremities, literally clamping down the vessels leading to the hands and feet, which manifests as a disorder called acrocyanosis. My blood pressure readings showed a decreased blood oxygen level in my fingertips—a sign of the extreme constriction of blood flow to my extremities. I wrote about these strange symptoms, particularly in my hands, over and over in my journal, but what I didn't know at the time was that it was a sign of severe malnutrition. My body, in a constant state of starvation, had started to radically change how it managed my systems, in an effort to preserve the energy and glucose my heart and brain needed to function.

When my weight was at its most perilous, around the time I was sixteen, I had a whole host of disturbing symptoms, some due to extreme hypoglycemia, and heart complications.

In an interview I conducted with her, Dr. Gaudiani explained it this way:

> In a well-fed state, we eat food, and the carbohydrates consumed provide glucose, because the brain and heart—particularly the heart—can really only run on glucose. Say I develop a GI bug and can't eat for two days. The glycogen that is stored in my muscles and liver gets put into my blood. And I have roughly 2,000 calories of protective glycogen that can emerge and sustain me. Now, say this goes on for more than two days and I can't manage to eat enough to sustain what my body needs glucose-wise. Then it will start tearing apart my muscles and fueling it with my fat in order to synthesize that glucose for me. Your body is literally getting rid of your lean muscle. And that can go on for a while.
>
> But when you have anorexia—and especially anorexia AND an emaciated body—when you've gotten down to your bare minimum of muscle and have no fat left, your body can't synthesize glucose anymore. And you're not eating it. And you have no glycogen in your muscles and liver.

I was on the verge of catastrophe. Those heart symptoms that I described, especially after exercising? That was my body desperately searching for glucose to keep my heart pumping. The most common cause of death among people living with restrictive anorexia nervosa is the heart stopping due to low blood sugar. I stood on that precipice for a long time.

Again, Dr. Gaudiani explained:

> It's not that the heart eventually goes slow enough that it stops—bradycardia, or slow heart rate, is very common—but when the blood sugar goes low enough, the heart muscle will just stop beating. And so you were basically living a Russian roulette in which

90 percent of the chambers had a bullet in them. All the time. It is miraculous to me that your body managed to keep going. And the only reason you did is that you have what is called survivor genetics.

From the outside, it's easy to wonder how a person could have enough willpower to continuously starve themselves. But when you are experiencing an eating disorder, you are powerless to the disease, no matter how badly you want out. I hated every second of every minute of every day I spent thinking about food, but I was also terrified to eat.

Compounding the problem, my body would trick me into thinking I was unbearably full after the tiniest amount of food. Gastroparesis ("paralyzed stomach") is a common complication of eating disorders. Symptoms include feeling nauseous and bloated after eating, feeling stuffed after eating a small amount of food, becoming dehydrated, and experiencing erratic blood sugar. Normally, when we eat, our stomach muscles contract and relax to digest and move food into the small intestine. In anorexia, this movement is impaired because energy is being diverted to other parts of the body. Food stays in your stomach five to six times longer than normal.

Outside of medical supervision, this complication can make treatment difficult. To family or other concerned parties, the amount of food you've eaten seems tiny. It may appear that you are saying you're full just to get out of having to eat, even though you feel excruciatingly full.

In this story, I talk a lot about my struggles with digestion, in particular, the way my gut changed—forever—after taking a course of antibiotics for strep throat that I may or may not have had. I'm going to talk about bodily functions, so if such things make you squeamish, well, you have been warned. For many, a common result of starvation and the resulting gastroparesis is constipation. Others, however, develop a condition called villous atrophy. Imagine sea anemones waving their tentacles back and forth on the ocean floor. Our small intestine is lined with fingerlike projections that resemble anemone tentacles; these villi help our small intestine digest food as it passes through. Blunted villi lose surface area, and food and nutrients skim across the intestines instead of being absorbed. Farther along in the intestines, this unabsorbed food acts like a laxative. This is what was happening to me. Villous atrophy was causing malabsorption. So what little I ate wasn't benefitting me nutritionally. This condition left me chronically dehydrated as well, and lowered my blood pressure and blood sugar.

It is worth noting that gastroparesis can lead to bacterial growth in the gut caused by food fermenting inside you. It can lead to a blockage so severe that it requires surgery. And when food finally passes into the small intestine, it can cause a dramatic spike in blood sugar.

When I took the antibiotic, my already stressed system was overloaded. Antibiotics often affect the natural balance of bacteria in your gut, which is why doctors often advise patients to take probiotics with an antibiotic. Combined with the villous atrophy, however, bacteria were able to easily slip into my small intestine and begin metabolizing food too early, a process that produces an enormous amount of gas, resulting in sudden abdominal girth distention, known as SIBO (small intestinal bacteria overgrowth)—very treatable and common with eating disorders.

Despite all my medical appointments and severely low weight, none of the doctors I visited ever even mentioned the possibility of an eating disorder. The most feedback we got regarding my weight was that I was severely hypoglycemic and should eat more snacks, and that I needed to eat more protein.

When I asked Dr. Gaudiani about that, here's what she told me:

The medical system is complicated and doctors have a profound weight bias. We are taught it, and not much has changed in the past few decades. . . . I suspect that when doctors saw a very thin—frankly, profoundly emaciated—but young, successful athlete, their brains shut off. They didn't have the capacity (to see anything else) because of their own biases and the problems in our society around what women's bodies should be. So, it was their fault. They came in with blinders on. And this is universal for my patients.

248

My doctors failed me. How many others have they failed because of preconceived ideas about success, thinness, and women? In the face of a sixteen-year-old girl whose internal organs were severely underdeveloped, who had never gotten a period—let alone started puberty—how could a doctor assume a quick "she's fine" and "I'm fine" is enough? Is the mother-daughter relationship so sacred in our culture that a doctor will take such a simple explanation from a mother at face value, even when faced with an obviously malnourished patient? Young women need advocates—not doctors willing to look the other way.

This is especially important for someone who might be categorically dismissed. Someone in what our society considers to be a normal-sized body experiencing similar symptoms. Someone in what our society considers to be a larger body, but who is also suffering from gastroparesis from too few calories. Someone who is male, or not white. Someone who is transgender. How do they stand up for themselves?

Back then, eating disorders were rarely discussed. The topic was taboo. And after the incident with the antibiotic, my mom was quick to turn to any explanation for my extreme thinness that wasn't me starving myself. An eating disorder can come dangerously close to implicating the parent, but Crohn's disease didn't suggest some underlying trauma or reflect poorly on her. And I was only too happy to comply. In spite of my desire for a doctor to notice that something was wrong, I was also terrified that they would make me gain weight. Still though, at some point, my pain became more important than being skinny—that was how I began to heal. It's unfortunate that it took so much destruction for me to round a corner, but at least I did, rather than let my heart come to a thudding halt.

I understand how hard it is to break free of an eating disorder. It is so hard to get out. But please, if you have started restricting or dieting so that you can climb harder or perform better in competitions, it will never be worth the shit that you will go through. And if it already feels like something in your life that you are quickly losing control of, please ask for help.

———————

The report from my first colonoscopy stated "possible ileocolitis." From my second colonoscopy, it is clear that I don't have, nor did I ever have, ileocolitis. Here's what was actually happening: When our bodies become malnourished, our tissues become "crabby." Your hair thins, your skin is dry and brittle, you bruise more easily.

The same thing happens in the gut. That fragile tissue becomes even more vulnerable. When food passes through your colon too quickly, it skims along, causing tears and subsequent bleeding. Of course, the scope caused spontaneous bleeding. It was creating micro tears in already damaged tissue.

———————

When someone is recovering from anorexia, bingeing is common and can lead to a lot of shame. I felt so out of control and was ashamed at how rapidly my body changed in size. I would like to normalize bingeing, though, as simply part of recovery.

Imagine you are crossing an immense desert and you run out of food and water. It has been days since you had adequate sustenance. Suddenly, up ahead you spot an oasis with a grove of orange trees. Are you going to pick one, carefully peel it, and calmly and methodically eat one slice at a time? No, you are going to rip the orange from the tree, tear it in half, and suck the juice out as if your life depended on it. Because it does. This is a normal biological response, but our diet-obsessed culture shames people for such behavior. Bingeing can be very dangerous for a recovering anorexic, especially when done in private. Someone going through this process needs support. Reintroducing so much food all at once can lead to disastrous medical complications. The person cannot control themselves.

Binge eating is not a moral failure. It is not about loss of control or gluttony. Once I started eating again, I physically could not stop, and it was incredibly painful, mentally and physically. You are not alone, and you have nothing to be ashamed of. When you are healing, the urge to binge is extremely powerful. Experiencing binge cycles in recovery is completely natural. As Dr. Gaudiani told me, it is a biological urge as strong as delivering a child. If you've ever given birth to a baby, you know what I'm talking about. The only way through binge eating is to tell yourself the following:

> *I eat what I want.*
> *I'm safe in my body.*
> *I eat regularly.*
> *I will not deprive myself.*
> *It is only when I fuel consistently, adequately, and abundantly that my body will settle down.*

Thanks, Dr. G., for the sage advice.

If you or someone you know is struggling emotionally, in crisis, or experiencing thoughts of suicide, reach out for help. In the US, get confidential support by calling the National Suicide Prevention Lifeline, 1-800-273-8255, or call or text 988 to get connected to local resources. Both hotlines are staffed 24/7. Learn more at suicidepreventionlifeline.org.

If you or someone you know is struggling with an eating disorder in the US, call or text the National Eating Disorders Association at 1-800-931-2237. Learn more at www.nationaleatingdisorders.org. Asking for help is the first step on the long road to recovery.

ACKNOWLEDGMENTS

There are so many people I want to thank. A big thank you to the late David Roberts, who was the first to believe in this book, and who encouraged me when I changed my mind a hundred times. An accomplished mountaineer, he wrote dozens of books about adventure and the natural world. He is deeply missed.

Thank you to my husband, who offered me support, as well as metaphorical and literal space to write and process everything in these pages, even though it was hard.

Thank you to Chris Weidner, for believing in this book, and especially for helping fact-check and vet details related to my competitions and accomplishments, which are not always clear in my mind.

A big thank you to everyone at Mountaineers Books, for taking on this project and helping me share my story.

Thank you to my editors, for all the suggestions and kind words.

And of course, my friends—Sascha, Lisa, Julia, Rose, Liz, and others—for being open to listening to me go on and on about my past.

ABOUT THE AUTHOR

Recognized as one of the greatest female rock climbers in history, Katie Brown began climbing at age twelve and soon dominated national and international competitions. She mastered the discipline of climbing hard outdoor sport routes quickly, often on the first try.

Retired from professional climbing, Brown is a writer, makeup artist, and mom. Find out what she's up to on Instagram @katiebrownclimbs.